# Minding My
# Business

# Minding My Business

The Complete, No-Nonsense, Start-to-Finish Guide to Owning and Running Your Own Store

**By Adeena Mignogna**

Skyhorse Publishing

Skyhorse Publishing books may be purchased in bulk at special discounts for sales promotion, corporate gifts, fund-raising, or educational purposes. Special editions can also be created to specifications. For details, contact the Special Sales Department, Skyhorse Publishing, 307 West 36th Street, 11th Floor, New York, NY 10018 or info@skyhorsepublishing.com.

Skyhorse® and Skyhorse Publishing® are registered trademarks of Skyhorse Publishing, Inc.®, a Delaware corporation.

www.skyhorsepublishing.com

10 9 8 7 6 5 4 3 2 1

Library of Congress Cataloging-in-Publication Data

Mignogna, Adeena.
  Minding my business : the complete, no-nonsense, start-to-finish guide to owning and running your own store / by Adeena Mignogna.
      pages cm
  Includes index.
  ISBN 978-1-62636-007-5 (alk. paper)
1.  Retail trade--Ownership--United States. 2.  Stores, Retail--United States--Management. 3.  New business enterprises--United States--Vocational guidance.  I. Title.
  HF5429.3.M534 2013
  658.8'7--dc23
                                        2013028099

Printed in the United States of America

# Contents

*Preface: Why I Wrote This Book*    vii

## Part I: My, What a Cute Little Store!    1

Introduction    3

Chapter 1:  The Pot & Bead: A New Life    11

Chapter 2:  You Want to Do What? Perceptions of Retail    19

Chapter 3:  Leasing, Landlords, and Opening Late    25

Chapter 4:  Safe and Secure    31

Chapter 5:  Employees    39

Chapter 6:  Follow Your Gut (Or How to Lose a Lot of Money Trying to Buy Someone Else's Business)    54

Chapter 7:  Customers . . . Ya Gotta Love Them    60

Chapter 8:  Competition    66

Chapter 9:  They Gotta Know You're There    71

Chapter 10: Putting the Social in Social Media    78

Chapter 11: Hard Work Does Not Equal Money in Your Pocket    87

Chapter 12: Other Things That Keep You Up at Night    96

Chapter 13: How to Survive Those First Two Years    100

## Part II: What Ever Happened to That Cute Little Store?    107

Introduction    109

Chapter 1:  A Double Life    115

Chapter 2:  Money Mistakes We Make    121

Chapter 3:  Money In, Money Out                                131

Chapter 4:  More on Employees                                  148

Chapter 5:  The Internet—It's for Businesses Now!             161

Chapter 6:  Exit Strategy: Getting the Business
            Ready to Be Sold                                   171

Chapter 7:  At Lease's End . . .                               177

Chapter 8:  Take My Business, Please!                          184

Chapter 9:  For Sale, by Owner                                 196

Chapter 10: Closing the Business                              211

Chapter 11: So You Still Want Your Own
            Cute Little Store                                  216

Chapter 12: The Final Word—Why Exactly *Are* You
            in Business?                                       219


Appendix A: Timeline                                          225

Appendix B: Business Plan                                     229

Appendix C: Financial Data                                    251

Appendix D: Lease Clauses                                     257

Appendix E: The Reading List                                  329

Index                                                         335

# Preface

## Why I Wrote This Book

I wrote this book to fill a gap. When I started my retail business in 2002, there were plenty of how-to-start-a-small-business books around and I voraciously read as many as I could. There were also plenty of books out there by successful business folks. For example, *Pour Your Heart Into It* is about the success of Starbucks, written by CEO Howard Schultz. Books like these can serve as a wonderful inspiration. (See Appendix D for a list of great books you should read if you're contemplating starting a small business.)

However, when I was opening my retail store, I was looking for a different kind of book—I was looking to read about businesses *like* mine; I wanted to read about people going through what I was going through. What happens in between the time when you get your business license and when you (hopefully) become wildly successful, I wondered. You don't grow a business like Starbucks overnight.

The content in that first set of books on startups only talked about what happened before the business was up and running; the latter set of books skipped over the really hard parts of the day-to-day life and hardships of the new small business owner. Yes, Howard Schultz wrote about the early days of Starbucks, but he was writing with the knowledge that in the end, it worked. In the end, he wound up with a *huge,* successful corporation. Most people who write these types of books do so from the top of the mountain, not while they're making the climb.

Let's face reality: the majority of small businesses are lucky to be around after the first couple of years. The ones that survive the startup stage can be very successful and bring in a steady income to the owner. Knowledge about what that post-startup-trying-to-keep-head-above-water-and-numbers-in-the-black stage . . . that's what I was looking for. Even though I found Mr. Schultz's story very inspiring (he came from nothing and "Look at me now, Ma!"), most of what he went through with Starbucks didn't feel like it applied to me, so I didn't connect with it.

One of my passions has always been writing, so with not quite two years of retail under my belt, I decided to start writing about my business, The Pot & Bead, while all the problems and joys of new, small business ownership were still fresh. The wounds from my mistakes still stung, and the little joys of a great compliment or an awesome sales day still kept me going. As I finished Part I of the book, my store was approaching its fourth anniversary.

I kept writing because the story kept on going. I continued running the business and gathering more useful tidbits for other would-be small business owners.

A lot was happening in that third, fourth, and fifth year of business. I was living a double life—I had a full-time career working for someone else and continued to be a business owner, while trying to figure out how to balance the two or make a change. I couldn't live the double life forever.

This book is written mostly as a memoir because that's exactly what it is. It covers the start, middle, and end of the life of a business with all the ups and downs that went with it. As you read through it, you'll notice that there was a pretty fundamental shift in my attitude about the business in Part II. For the first few years, the business really was successful; I wasn't taking home a large salary at the time, but I maintained a positive attitude and was hopeful for growth. In the last few years, especially when I started to lose money and I couldn't implement an easy exit strategy, my mood declined with it.

If you're thinking about starting a business, retail or other, then use this book as a supplement to all the "how to start a business" books out there.

What I've written is about what it's like once you've started a business. I talk a lot about the mistakes I made, a lot of which are fairly common, and by reading this book you'll be in a much better position to avoid making the same ones. If you're already in business for yourself, then you might see some similarities between my situation and yours. Either way, I hope you enjoy reading this as much as I've enjoyed writing it.

I hope this book will serve as an inspiration to new small business owners who are also trying to survive their early years in business. I also hope it will fall into the hands of those thinking about going into business for themselves for the first time, particularly those going into a retail business. Retail is *not* easy. It requires *lots* of hard work and dedication and sacrifices in terms of income, family, and time. Many people think of retail as a "build it and they will come" type of business. That's simply not true. This book should serve as an insight into what really happens in that cute little store.

I'd like to thank all the people who were there for me at the start and end of The Pot & Bead. While I worked very hard at the business and at this book, there were so many people around—friends, family, employees, customers, coworkers—who were extremely supportive and without whom things would have been much more difficult. The person I have to thank more than anyone else is my dad, Raymond Mignogna. He was a source of support and advice from day one through the end. He helped edit the book and was always there providing advice. Unfortunately, he passed away before the opportunity to republish this book came up, so I'd like to dedicate it to him.

# PART I

# My, What a Cute Little Store!

# Introduction

"Entrepreneurship is working 80 hours a week so you don't have to work 40 for anyone else."

—Corporate CEO Ramona Arnett

Hi, my name is Adeena and I owned a small business.

You would think that there would be a psychiatric support group for small business owners; the amount of time, effort, and work borders on the masochistic. The sacrifices are great, but at the end of the day, the rewards can be even greater. Yet, you have to wonder about people who start their own business . . . no matter who they are or where they come from, the odds are undoubtedly stacked against them.

That was certainly true in my case. I had a nice, neat little career as an engineer in aerospace, a field I had been interested in since I was a small child. (I'm basically a complete science geek.) That was the only side of me most people ever knew about. I worked on designing and operating satellites, dreamed about being an astronaut, and read science magazines and science books all the time.

When I decided to open my own store, a lot of folks I knew were baffled by my desire to not only work for myself, but to work in a completely different field. However, those who really knew me, my family and close, old friends, knew entrepreneurship was always something on my mind and something I knew I would do. At the end of the day, I needed to be the one calling the shots. I've always known that the only way I would have great rewards in life and be happy would be by taking great risks.

I'm sure those last two sentences ring true for a lot of you reading this book. You're ready to take that risk (or you've already started), you know the odds are stacked against you, and you're looking for some moral support. You want to know how others have dealt with the first difficult years of owning their own business.

There are lots of books you can (and should) read about starting your own business. (See Appendix D: The Reading List.) There are books that cover the how-tos, the legalities, where to get money, and other things. Many books tell you *how* to start a business, but not many deal with what happens right after you've made that leap. This book will tell you about all the little pitfalls that happen along the way and how to not let those pitfalls get in the way of your success.

This book, while focusing on retail businesses, can and does apply to any business in those first couple of years. No matter who you are or what type of business you have, you'll hit some snags along the way. I'm here to tell you to read on and hang in there! You'll make it through! You have a dream, you have a goal, and you can do it!

The purpose of this book is to give you some idea of what to expect (and not to depress you) if you decide to become a small business owner. It might, however, convince some people not to go into business for themselves.

Look at the statistics. In 2008, it was estimated that about 630,000 new small businesses ("new firms" according to the US Small Business Administration) were created. But in that same year, there were approximately 595,600 closures and 43,546 bankruptcies. For each year through most of the past decade, there were also more closures than there were new firms.

The SBA maintains a website (www.sba.gov) that anyone contemplating starting a new business should use as a source of research. If you browse through the "Office of Advocacy" section (that's a good source for small business statistics), its FAQ page states that:

"Two-thirds of new employer establishments survive at least
two years, and 44 percent survive at least four years, according to
a new study. These results were similar for different industries . . .

Earlier research has explored the reasons for a new business's survivability. Major factors in a firm's remaining open include an ample supply of capital, the fact that a firm is large enough to have employees, the owner's education level, and the owner's reason for starting the firm in the first place, such as freedom for family life or wanting to be one's own boss."

It's those first couple of years that can make or break a business. At the time I started my business, many other people started theirs. A year, two years later, I was still in business while others weren't. Five and a half years after I started out, my doors closed, becoming another statistic.

I hope that by writing this, I can give you some insight into what really goes on "behind the scenes." I call it "behind the scenes" because ideally, your customer only sees your best—they should have no idea how much stress and aggravation you're really going through. The downside is that when customers see what I call the "cute little store," it looks like something they can do too, and many times, they do. I don't want you to be one of those who sees the good side and decides to open a business based on that feeling alone—only to have it fail. If it fails, you can potentially lose a lot of money and disrupt the lives and well-being of your spouse and kids as well as the rest of your own future.

When I started writing Part I of this book, the store had been open for about a year and a half and my business wasn't 100 percent out of that early, risky time period. My business had already survived a lot of unexpected occurrences and hardships, but I knew we would make it. As I finished the first part, we'd been open more than three years and we were on track to be in the 44 percent that the SBA says make it to four years!

Why were we surviving while others weren't? I believe it was a combination of a *lot* of upfront preparation work and a good dose of luck. For example, some days I thought how lucky we were to have the location we had. But then I remembered how we got there: all the places we looked at that weren't quite right, examining the demographic numbers of all the possible locations, getting information from other businesses similar to ours across the country, etc. It was luck that the right place existed, but it was also a lot of work to determine that it was the right place, to negotiate and sign the lease, and to keep it going.

I've written some articles and talked to some folks about the perils of business ownership. I've occasionally been criticized for being depressing. I prefer to look at it as inserting a dose of reality. That's because it's not all good stuff—it's not all fun and games.

Around the time I started writing this book, I spoke with a customer who, while she was sitting in my shop, told me about how she was thinking of opening up a store of her own. She and a friend had recently been laid off and were thinking that this might be their opportunity to go out on their own. I'm always willing to talk to people about my experiences in starting up a business, and I'm always willing to refer people to the resources I've used (accountant, lawyer, local Small Business Development Center, etc.). Well, the perception she (and a lot of other people) had is that not only was my business doing well, but that I was personally financially successful. I explained to her that yes, the business was doing well, but that no, I was personally not receiving much financial benefit. That shocked her. She wasn't sure she'd be able to handle the drop in compensation and has since reconsidered her desire to open her own store.

I started writing this book in the middle of 2004. At that time, I expected to take home *maybe* a fifth of what my salary was when I was an engineer. It turned out to be less than that come the end of the year.

I took an informal survey of people I know who were in a similar type of retail business as mine: Only 15 percent were able to say that their salary was $30,000 a year or more, while 12 percent said they were not paying themselves anything. That leaves about 70 percent who were paying themselves less than $30,000 a year!

In Chapter 11 (Hard Work Does Not Equal Money in Your Pocket), I go into a little more detail about how my income went down and up and down (and up and down again) while owning this business.

Basically, I don't want you to wind up in the same situation as these folks:

- One retail business owner I know closed his doors after only a year. He estimates that he is $100,000 in the hole. This money was spent mostly on furnishing the retail space and paying rent.

- Another retail business owner I know decided that this wasn't for her and figured she would try and sell the business after being open for a year and a few months. After about 7–8 months on the market, she sold it for a steal. After everything was said and done, she wound up in about $10,000 of debt. I think what upset her more is the toll this had taken on her two young girls. She told me once while she was in the process of selling her business: "I haven't been able to give either of them a birthday party in two years."

Read this book and think about all the hard questions you'll need to ask yourself while you plan your business. (Why do you want to own your own business? Do you require a certain salary to support yourself and your family?)

This book should either inspire you or have you saying "Oh, wow, I had no idea it was like that." Each of the following chapters should provide some insight into the different aspects of owning and running a retail business.

## Chapter 1: The Pot & Bead: A New Life

What prompts a seemingly normal engineer to up and quit her day job and open a retail business?

This chapter gives the background story to my successful retail store, The Pot & Bead, a contemporary paint-your-own pottery studio located in Ashburn, VA. I'll discuss how the lessons I've learned are applicable to almost any retail business and to new small businesses in general.

## Chapter 2: You Want to Do What? Perceptions of Retail

When you own and run a cute little store, you'll often overhear customers say how they wish they had something like it. As a store owner, there's an amazing mix of emotions resonating through your body all at once that could prompt a meltdown:

1. You're flattered. It's nice to hear that they like your store.
2. You're chuckling inside. If they only knew how much work it took to have that cute little store.
3. Your blood is boiling a little. Are they going to try and open something exactly like it right down the street?

People have their perceptions, often misconceptions, about what retail is and what it takes to run a retail business. This chapter discusses those ideas.

## Chapter 3: Leasing, Landlords, and Opening Late

This chapter tells the tale of obtaining the lease for the location of The Pot & Bead and all the trials and tribulations involved. It's a lesson in research, following your instincts, and negotiating.

## Chapter 4: Safe and Secure

Burglaries can happen. It happened to us. We survived. There were things that could have been done to prevent our burglary that I wish I had known then. I'll tell you all of those things in this chapter so it hopefully won't happen to you, too. Protecting your business, from burglaries and other disasters, is a must for business owners.

## Chapter 5: Employees

When I counsel people about starting a new business, I remind them that one enormous difference between a home-based business and a retail business is the need for employees. A retail business needs and depends on its employees.

As the owner of a *successful* retail business, you *can't* be there during all hours, every single day. (Okay, you can, but you probably will wind up resenting it.) So do you hire someone and hope to hell that when you're not there everything will go just fine? Almost. In this chapter, we'll talk about how to hire, retain, and treat your employees.

## Chapter 6: Follow Your Gut (Or How to Lose a Lot of Money Trying to Buy Someone Else's Business)

This chapter talks about the biggest mistake I made in the first two years of running The Pot & Bead. I attempted to purchase another business similar to my own. It didn't go well and I lost a lot of money. Why? I didn't follow my gut.

## Chapter 7: Customers . . . Ya Gotta Love Them

In this chapter, I will teach you to recite the mantra "I love my customers, I love my customers." I define *customer* as "someone who gives me money." Without them, I wouldn't be in business. I love my customers.

This chapter is the support room for getting past the few customers who are crazy or just plain mean, and will help show you how to appreciate the nice customers who make the business worthwhile.

## Chapter 8: Competition

I define *competition* as "someone who takes *my* money from *my* customers."

Who is "the competition"? Why should you care? How do you deal with it? This chapter answers these questions.

## Chapter 9: They Gotta Know You're There

The bulk of the ongoing work in a retail (or any) business is marketing. Unleash your creative side and have at it, but wait a while to see the results.

## Chapter 10: Putting the Social in Social Media

Social media was in its infancy when I had my store, but it's a key component of business today, so I was compelled to discuss it here.

## Chapter 11: Hard Work Does Not Equal Money in Your Pocket

Admit it—this is one of the top reasons you want to be in business for yourself. You want to make more money than you have right now. Until that happens, you might have to borrow some, will definitely have to spend some, and will hopefully collect large piles of it.

## Chapter 12: Other Things That Keep You Up at Night

This chapter discusses some of the other random things that go wrong in day-to-day business. This will largely involve all the stuff that breaks, the weather, and my own arch-nemesis, Water.

## Chapter 13: How to Survive Those First Two Years

In this chapter, I will give some useful information for getting through the startup phase of any business, but particularly retail. It will include basic information on:

- Business planning
- Organization
- Your team of experts
- Building a support system
- Putting your personal finances in order
- Keeping yourself healthy
- stress-relieving and sanity-keeping techniques

If you do decide to go ahead with your eyes wide open and the advice in this book, you may end up with your own successful cute little store!

# Chapter 1

# The Pot & Bead:
# A New Life

I always knew I wanted to work for myself. I also always knew I wanted to work in the space industry or *in space*. When I was about six years old, I knew that when I grew up, I would own my own company; we would build robots and we'd be doing this on the moon. (At the time, I didn't know that we hadn't been to the moon in a while, I thought we went there every day.)

While in elementary school, I would dream about being called President. I knew about college and believed that I needed to get advanced degrees in a science (computer science and robotics were at the top of my list back then) and in business. I would make pretend business cards for myself. I even started a couple little businesses . . . I had a lemonade stand set up at the end of the driveway, and at one point collected rocks off the beach, polished them, gave them cute names, and attempted to sell them as display pieces.

As I grew older, my goals became a little more in tune with reality. I still wanted a career in the space industry and I still wanted to own my own company. I went to school at the University of Maryland and earned degrees in physics and astronomy. (No-Nonsense Note: A lot of folks have asked why not simply major in aerospace engineering. Well, when I was nearing the end of high school, folks who were graduating with aerospace engineering degrees were still having a tough time finding jobs in their field. I thought that if I got my degree in AE, I would be trapped in something very narrow. I note this because at times in this book I talk about understanding your own strengths and weaknesses, and one of mine is that I'm not very detail-minded. Narrowing myself into one little niche for twenty years, while exciting to some, brings on something akin to a claustrophobia attack when I think about it.)

My physics professor in high school had his undergraduate and graduate degrees in physics and he had done a little of everything during his life: he worked as an engineer, he worked as an astronomer, he worked for different companies doing different things, he taught, and now I believe he's writing, too. I saw physics as something that could lead me to a lot of options afterward. Keeping my options open, not cutting off any opportunities, is something I've always seen as the right thing to do.

During college I worked in a group doing mechanical design and drafting. I was very lucky—at the time, the work I was doing was exactly what I believed I wanted to do during my career. We were designing and building a scientific instrument that would go on to sit on a satellite and study the Sun.

Is this relevant to owning your own business? Yes, most definitely! It relates to knowing yourself. I like to create; I like to do new things and make new things; I like to start with nothing and wind up with something to show for the work I've done. Entrepreneurship also takes quite a bit of creativity and the desire to make something where there was nothing before. This is only one facet of entrepreneurship though and there are several other attributes an entrepreneur needs to possess. I'm convinced that in order to be successful, you don't need to have *all* the traits, but you do need to be able to know which ones you have and which ones you don't. For the ones you don't, you need to be able to find others who do have those skills to supplement yours. (See Chapter 13: How to Survive Those First Two Years.)

After college I worked for several years in various space-related engineering jobs. While working the day job, I tried to be a consultant on the side. I was a computer aided design (CAD) drafter. I had the proper software and computer equipment I needed at home. I had the know-how and I even had some apropos business cards printed up (they looked like a blueprint—quite charming if I do say so myself).

The CAD consulting thing didn't work out too well—the 40+ hour work week interfered with my ability to find consulting work—and consultant-entrepreneurs need to devote a significant portion of their time to selling themselves and marketing their own services. I didn't have the time or money to invest in this part of a business back then, so I wound up doing only one job as a CAD consultant. (A couple years later, I was lucky enough to be in the right place at the right time and did a couple software consulting jobs, but it was pure luck that got me the gig—it wasn't enough to really make it as an independent consultant.)

In the day-job career, I progressed to smaller and smaller companies, moving a little closer to a management position in each company. I learned more and more about financial matters, business, sales, marketing, etc. I knew I wanted my own aerospace company and I *knew* it was only a matter of being prepared when the right idea and right opportunity hit me. I read books, I talked to people, I even thought about going back to school part-time to earn an MBA.

All that time I was keeping my eyes open for that idea that would lead me to break away and start my own company. I amassed a decent collection of "how to start your own business" books.

Well, I was certainly learning a lot. The biggest thing was that commercial aerospace was not making a ton of money. Who wants to buy a small satellite? Anyone? Anyone? It was very hard to keep a small company going.

What really opened my eyes was this: The last company I worked for, in its heyday, had about sixty employees and two main contracts (i.e., customers). Instead of doing some good engineering work, a lot of my job was fighting to keep one of those customers happy so they would continue to pay us. Why? Because if they went away, we would have to cut everyone's pay, or lay people off, or even close our doors!

This didn't make a lot of good business sense to me. Yes, it is very important to keep your customers happy . . . absolutely! But what if focusing on customers' happiness in the moment means you're not focusing on getting the real job done? Giving them the lollipop they asked for now might ruin the special dinner you promised them at the end of the day. (I was starting to have a lot of issues and arguments with my managers . . . no, I didn't have as much experience as they did, but the way they acted and made decisions didn't seem to make common sense to me.)

A lot of independent consultants I know are in a similar boat. They're dedicated to one or two customers at a time—and need to keep those customers to keep themselves in business. That leaves little time to find the next customer. Most consultants in this situation will have on/off work and inconsistent money coming in. That wasn't a life that sat well with me. It was at this point that I truly gave up the idea that I would be a consultant in my spare time or give up my day job to start a consulting business.

For those of you who are comfortable with, and able to lead that kind of life, more power to you! There are some definite advantages to that kind of entrepreneurship. The potential to work out of your house is one of them. Later in this book, I talk about some of the horrors I've endured in renting retail space. After dealing with that, I'd probably give my right leg (maybe not a leg, but at least a pinky toe) to be able to solely work from my home office.

When I finally realized that having a small aerospace company was not likely in the near future, I looked for something else. After I had bought every "how to start a small business" book I could find, I then started collecting and reading all those "how to start a_____" (fill-in-the-blank) kind of business—everything from coffee bar to restaurant to real estate.

It happened one day that I came across the Paint-Your-Own-Pottery (PYOP) concept. One of my sisters had recently painted a small dish for me as a wedding present. It was in the shape of a half moon (she knows how I'm into everything "spacey") and she had painted a light blue background with a face on it. It was my favorite wedding gift and it still hangs on the wall in my living room.

One day, I was sitting in Starbucks with my soon-to-be business partner (more about business partners in Chapter 2) who was going off about how people don't give handmade gifts anymore. I corrected him by mentioning that dish my sister painted for me. I also mentioned that she'd taken my young niece to a paint studio a couple of times. (There's a very colorful figurine in the shape of a snake sitting in my dad's office, a fish on their mantle, and at least one picture frame in the dining room.) My partner then recalled that he had taken his daughters to some places like that back when they lived on the West Coast. That was the light bulb. It was so bright I think it filled the room.

How did I know this was the right idea for me? Well, at this point, I was already very familiar with business plan writing and already knew a little about finding financing. Remember all those books I'd collected? Well each time I started looking into an idea, like the coffee bar or real estate business, I would start writing a business plan. When the plan didn't seem to go anywhere, I'd stop and move on to the next idea. I was waiting for the right idea to come along and fit in. The more I started researching the PYOP concept, the more my gut told me that this was the right thing to do. And about seven months after starting the business plan for The Pot & Bead, we were open for business.

So what was The Pot & Bead? We were a paint-your-own-pottery and bead-your-own-jewelry craft studio. Customers could come in any time we were open, pick out a "blank" piece of pottery, also known as "bisque," paint it, and leave it with us to glaze and fire in a kiln. Customers got the pottery back one week later and it was food, microwave, and dishwasher safe.

Customers could also come in to bead jewelry. They could make necklaces, bracelets, anklets, and more. We did all the "hard" stuff, like attaching the clasps. The customers picked out beads and strung 'em. The best thing was, they got to wear their creations home that day.

Additionally, we hosted parties. Mostly for kids' birthdays, but also adult parties, teambuilding parties, scout troops, and more. Party guests painted or beaded, had some cake, and had a great time!

*No-Nonsense Note: Look at the above three paragraphs that describe The Pot & Bead. I can say those sentences (without talking too fast) in a little less than 60 seconds. EVERY business owner should have a similar 60-second elevator speech memorized that describes their business. I can't tell you how many business owners I've met who really are not able to articulate what they do—at least not before I'm bored and ready to talk with someone else.*

*Another No-Nonsense Note: The paint-your-own-pottery concept isn't original. But opening a pottery studio that is also a beading studio is original. At least it was at the time. Yes, there were one or two others that offered beading, but ours was the first studio to open with both activities as core to our business. The point here is, even if you find an idea that's been done, you can tweak it and make it your own.*

When discussing the early part of this business, I'll sometimes use the word "I" and sometimes use the word "we." That's because I did initially start the business with a partner. When I started writing this book, I was also in the early process of buying him out. It took the better part of a year for that process to end, and when I finished the first draft of this book, it had been over for more than a year. I was extremely lucky—I've heard many buyout horror stories—and even though it took a lot of time, it was relatively painless. To protect his identity, I will call him John for the remainder of the book.

John and I worked together as engineers. We were both fed up with the lifestyle of working for others and had similar ideas about what we wanted to do. They say that you shouldn't go into business with your friends. Well, we were colleagues working together before we were friends, so it seemed okay.

Did I need a partner to start this business? Yes and no. Looking back now, I absolutely, 100 percent believe that I could have done all of this on my own. But I think he was the extra push that got me out the door. (There is also the question of whether I needed him for the business loan process or not . . . more about that in the chapter on money.)

Most entrepreneurs, when they tell friends and family of the risks they're about to take, are met with a lot of negativity:

- "You want to do what?!"
- "Where are you going to get the money for that?!"

- "But you don't know anything about that!"
- "You're making good money now, why would you want to change that?"

I certainly had my share coming from friends and family; I think my ex-husband said each one of those statements to me. (After a year of being in business, however, he apologized for the negative comments and tried to explain that he only knew me as "space geek," so this was a complete shock to him.)

John was that one extra person saying "Yes, we can do it!" and I think I needed that at the time. The partnership did eventually die. Our initial plan was that I would manage the business and he would help out when and where he could. This was done out of necessity—I was able to quit my day job, but with a family of young kids to support, John wasn't. Shortly after the business opened, his job and family situation changed to the point that he could not be a part of the business as we envisioned. It became an unfair situation and necessitated me buying him out.

Here's the thing we did right: when we set up our business entity, we had a lawyer prepare a pretty iron-clad operating agreement between John and myself. This helped make the buyout much more straightforward and amicable. An operating agreement is a document that outlines what each partner is coming to the table with, and discusses what happens if a partner wants to leave, or worse, dies. Many, many businesses that start out as partnerships often end up this way. We had the best intentions going in, and it simply didn't work. If you have a partner, no matter what stage your business is in, make sure you also have an operating agreement drawn up by an attorney or other neutral party.

After many lessons learned, these days I would never recommend doing anything this important without the aid of a good lawyer. (Chapter 6 includes additional mistakes when I didn't use a lawyer and tried to purchase someone else's business.) But if you really, truly feel you can't afford one to do an operating agreement, make sure you have at least *something* written down. Handbooks on legal forms for small businesses can act as a guide, and can be useful if you really can't afford a lawyer. (See the Reading List in Appendix D.)

## No-Nonsense Tips and Tidbits:

- You can learn from and apply any previous experience.
- There's a great feeling of satisfaction that comes from owning your own business and from knowing you can do it.
- Going into business for yourself is a risk!
- If you try something that doesn't fit who you are, you might waste a lot of time and money.
- Know thyself and the business you're getting involved in.

# Chapter 2

# You Want to Do What?
# Perceptions of Retail

One of the first people I told about The Pot & Bead idea was my dad. He wasn't shocked about the idea of going out on my own. He tried the entrepreneurial route more than once and I've had several conversations with him over the years about my frustrations with my career and working for myself. He was, however, surprised that it was a retail business I was interested in.

My family hasn't had big success with entrepreneurship, and retail in particular was looked down upon ever since an uncle of mine went bankrupt in the mid eighties after opening up a card shop. Retail was thought to be too risky—you could be ruined by picking the wrong location, as my uncle did. My dad gave me one piece of very good advice: learn from the mistakes of others. This is a key message I hope that you pick up on, too.

There is one main distinction I want to make here. Yes, I owned a "pottery studio," but the business I was really in was retail. There is a difference. There are artists and other good people who own pottery studios. These are often characterized by:

- being located in an out-of-the-way place
- not having many employees

- an owner who doesn't take or doesn't need to take a salary *or* breaks even but isn't making tons of money
- owners who spend the majority of their time on their art, not on building the business

There is *nothing* wrong with this if this is the lifestyle you choose. This is not the business I was in or what I wanted to do. I was in retail. I characterized this by:

- being located in a highly visible shopping plaza, in the middle of our key customer demographic
- having a store manager (most of the time; more about troubles on keeping a good manager in Chapter 5) and several part-time employees
- my time being spent on marketing and building the business. Increasing sales from quarter to quarter and year to year is a priority. (This is done with customer service.)

This was a *business*—not a hobby or a vocation.

The purpose of pointing this out is to let you know that neither I nor my employees sat around painting pottery all day. Many a customer in my store said something to the effect of: "It must be great to work here! You get to sit around and paint pottery all day!" at which point we politely corrected them. The work we did enabled *customers* to sit around and paint pottery. Just like Starbucks employees don't sit around drinking coffee on their shift . . . they're doing other things so that their customers reap those benefits.

Now, I did want my customers to think of my store as that cute little store that they came to; they should think all was well. When customers were at my store, they should have been able to relax and forget about their problems and not be burdened with mine. The downside was that customers developed a false perception of my business. For the most part, that's okay. Most customers don't need to know anything about the business. What happens behind the scenes is not relevant to their ability to enjoy the service and products we provided.

Occasionally, the cute little store gives a customer false hope. Everything goes so well for them; we made it seem easy and they wound up thinking they could do it too, or even better. That in itself is not so bad. All of us probably see something and dream of having it or doing it. (I'm a big fan of cute little coffee shops, tea rooms, and bookstores and dream of owning them when I visit.) The problem occurs when the customer, based only on their experience in the store, skips a large amount of research, or performs the research with those awful rose-colored glasses on, and thinks it'll be so easy to do. This is exactly the trap I'm trying to warn you about.

Have you been in one of these stores? Maybe it was a cute little store in a vacation spot, maybe it was an independent bookstore—you've thought about having one yourself. If you're a book lover, maybe you've thought about being surrounded by your favorite titles all day, sharing your knowledge with other people about the best authors and your favorite classics. The reality is that in order to keep that store open (and hopefully pay yourself), what you really need to be concerned with is how many books you have to sell every month to make your lease payment. Having gobs of knowledge about the books (a.k.a. your product) is of great value for customer service, but at the end of the day, you have to make the sale to stay in business. I had to sell approximately 250–300 pieces of pottery simply to pay the rent each month. And rent was only about 20 percent of my monthly expenses (more in Chapter 11 about money).

There was this wonderful little coffee shop in Pennsylvania that I frequented. It was in an old historic house on the edge of a touristy little town complete with adorable bed-and-breakfasts, antique shops, and the like. You'd think a coffee shop would fit in perfectly. Each room was very cozy and you could take your time sipping your latte on one of several comfy couches. You could borrow a book to read while having your tea on the side porch. It was relaxing, it was cozy, and they made delicious coffee. It was the kind of shop lots of people like you and I would love to own.

But after a couple visits to this shop, I had a conversation with the managers and was able to find out that they were having huge problems selling enough coffee to keep the doors open. In addition, it turned out they weren't very welcome in the town either. They believed that the local town chamber of commerce was made up of a lot of people who had something against this new coffee shop (even though it wasn't competing with an existing one), which made it difficult to market in the town.

Why did the local people not like the coffee shop? I really don't know—and the information I received from the managers might have been colored by their own exhaustion and despair. This is only one example of an unexpected hardship a business could face. I'm not sure if they're still in business—it wasn't looking good the last time I passed by.

Lots of customers used to walk into my store during a busy time and say something like, "Wow, you're so busy! Things must be going well, eh?" And on more than one occasion, a bolder customer would even say, "You must be doing very well," and I took that to mean they thought I was doing well financially.

To the first customer, I'd always be nice and polite and chipper and say, "Yes, things are good," and smile. To the latter, I was more careful with how I responded. A lot of the time it had to do with my mood, if the customer was a regular whom I knew, or if I thought they had that look in their eye thinking they could make a lot of money with a cute little store, too.

Usually, my response was something simple like, "Well, sales are good." On occasion, I'd get into short discussions about how even though sales were good, that didn't mean I was raking it in hand over fist. I'd sometimes say, "Yes, sales are good, but they need to be because this is an expensive area to keep a business." Usually that's enough for the person to understand.

The county that my business was in was home to LOTS of small businesses and entrepreneurs. Many times I had more frank discussions with someone looking to go into business for themselves. I'm a very positive person so I didn't want to talk them out of it, or be one of those negative people telling them they shouldn't do it. I also didn't want to give away too much information about my own business. But I always told them about some of the resources I used when getting started, like the local Small Business Development Center (SBDC). (See Chapter 13: How to Survive Those First Two Years.) I'd also tell them that I was not making much money at all, that I had no kids (allowing me more time to do what I want to do), and that I worked A LOT.

Before ending this chapter, I want to talk about one other misconception of retail: free time. I've noticed that a lot of people who have yet to own their own business think that doing so gives them more free time, including more time to spend with their kids and family. While this might be true for home-based businesses, it is NOT true for cute little retail shops.

A lot of retail shops are open seven days a week. During the first few months we were open, I was at my shop every day. It was sometime in the second month when I felt I had staff who was well trained enough that I could go home early one evening. I was someone who committed myself to getting staff in place so I could do just that. Other retail owners aren't so fortunate, or simply don't plan for that.

Even after having the staff trained properly to run the place, you can never be completely not there. Your presence is still needed and you need to decide when you should be there: the busiest times, of course. For my store, like a lot of others, the busiest times are the weekends. If I had kids, that would mean I'd be missing soccer games, play time, and, in general, the times when my kids would be home. Now, if you're thinking you want a cute little store so you have more time for your family, please look at other alternatives.

If you've been in a store recently and said to yourself that you want to own a cute little store too, ponder over these questions:

- Do I like what the store sells or would I like providing it to others?
- Can I work seven days a week? (And do the same thing day after day after day?)
- How much do I have to sell to make rent and other expenses?
- What is it about this store that I really like?

## No-Nonsense Tips and Tidbits:

- There is nothing like the feelings of pride in ownership; being your own boss; calling the shots.
- With a lot of time and hard work (and possibly money), owning your own business can be a reality.
- Make sure you are prepared to handle a small (possibly tiny, miniscule) income.
- Make sure you are prepared for time not spent with friends and family.
- Know what kind of person you are. Are you detail oriented or do you only want to focus on the big picture? Do you thrive on routine, or does doing the same thing day after day make you want to pull you hair out? Think about who you are and think about how this fits in with the business you're in (or want to be in).

# Chapter 3

# Leasing, Landlords, and Opening Late

Location, location, location—that's the mantra we've all heard. And yes, it's true. Location is *very* important to a retail business.

When my partner and I were first planning The Pot & Bead, our idea was that it would be in a quaint, historic-y area. After all, lots of pottery studios were located in quaint, historic districts, and the rent would be cheaper there than in a strip mall or shopping plaza. (If you're familiar with Loudoun County, Virginia, we were looking in the historic district of Leesburg.) First, I should point out that we didn't know a thing about leasing space for a business. Books helped a little . . . they explained some of the terminology like CAM or Triple Net and other things to expect in a commercial lease. (See Appendix D for a list of these books.)

We spent a couple of months looking at different spaces available in the historic district. The rents were all reasonable, but none of the spaces were right. They were either too small, or not on the ground floor, or didn't have a bathroom. None of them had good parking. It was frustrating and there were times we were very tempted to settle for something that wasn't quite right.

A new part of an upscale shopping center was in the process of being built at that time in the next town over. At first, while sitting at this center's

Starbucks, we thought it was going to be prohibitively expensive. But on the other hand, we would be getting the right amount of space, good parking, road visibility, a bathroom . . . what more could we want? It was all coming together perfectly.

One of the first major decisions we faced was deciding between a space on the "bottom floor," which faced into the main part of the shopping center, and a space on the "top floor," which faced outside the shopping center, onto the road. The rent on the "top floor" would be slightly less expensive than the bottom. When I say "top floor," though, we're not on the top where you need to take stairs or an elevator to get to us. The "top floor" had its own parking lot, and the entrance was outside.

My partner and I argued quite a bit about this. He wanted to be downstairs facing into the shopping center and I wanted to be upstairs with the cheaper rent and facing the roads. In the end, I won (because of the cheaper rent), and it turned out to be the right decision. Even though the "bottom" floor opened up into the main part of the shopping center, it was far enough away from the "anchor" (usually a big store like a grocery store) that it didn't help much. Up on "the top," almost half of our customers said they found out about us in the first year and a half we were open by driving by on the road we faced. Given that most of our customers were parents with young kids and drove an SUV or minivan, having the parking out front was very important.

The lease negotiations went well. Too well. Looking back, we didn't negotiate hard enough. We were so excited about getting the location that we didn't ask for enough and we took a lot of the things the landlord said for granted. For one, we were supposed to be the last business open on our floor. We turned out to be the first one open. Why is this important? We had to do extra work to let everyone know we were there.

There were a lot of questions we didn't ask during the lease review process, but should have, like:

- "What if the toilet breaks in the first couple months? Who's responsible for that?"
- "Do we get a tenant allowance for buildouts?"

- "What is the landscaping plan?" (Trees were planted at one of the parking lot ends that, when fully grown, made it difficult for people driving by to see us from the road.)

We might not have gotten the answer we wanted to each of these questions, but it would have been better to ask.

After taking possession of the space, the relationship between me and the landlord was pretty adversarial for a long while. My biggest fear at the time was what would happen when it was time to re-negotiate the lease. It was a risk point because the landlord didn't have to renew our lease or make the conditions favorable for us. Yes, the lease had a "five-year option," but that doesn't automatically mean my business would be able to exist in the same space, at close to the same rent, for another five years. Read up on commercial leases so you understand what this means. (See Appendix D for the reading list and Appendix B for my own lease.)

What do they say about hindsight? Knowing what I know now, I wish we had asked for or signed a ten-year lease instead of five. (Note that I'm not necessarily recommending this for others since each situation is unique.) But that would have been a different kind of risk taken at a time when we didn't know if the business was going to succeed at all—breaking a commercial lease is not something you want to have to do. The terms are rarely favorable for the tenant.

We had a variety of problems with the physical space and lease after the store opened. They ranged from "mild headache" to "oh my god this is going to shut us down":

- The windows: We were not allowed to put a sign in our back window (facing into the shopping center) that said we were there. So, many customers in the shopping center had problems finding us. Not a day went by when we didn't get at least one or two calls from customers saying they were lost in the center looking for our store.
- Common Area Maintenance (CAM) increases: In addition to rent, you typically also pay something called CAM or triple-net.

This covers the maintenance costs like landscaping and snow removal in your shopping center. It's typically not fixed—it goes up and down each year based on the real cost of the year before. Also, when the landlord figures out whether or not it goes up or down, they can also charge you a one-time payment to cover the previous year's actual costs (or give you a credit if costs were less than expected). Well, after the first full year, when our assessment came in, we owed almost twice our rent! It was a lot of money at the time and was completely outrageous. It almost put us out of business.

- Snow Removal: Our first winter brought a huge snow storm, and even though we were required to be open, the snow removal in our parking lot was miserable. We got phone calls from several customers saying they tried to get to us but couldn't. In two or three days, I estimate we lost at least $500 worth of business solely from the people who *told* us they couldn't get through. I don't want to think about how many couldn't get through who we don't know about.
- Lights: We had to call several times to get the landlord to turn on the lights in the parking lot after dark. (This problem repeated every time daylight savings ended.)
- Proof of Insurance: For three years, I kept getting letters saying that the landlord needed proof of my insurance. I faxed that proof over several times and still received these letters. (This finally stopped after we had been open for more than three years.)
- Muzak: We had a Muzak sound system installed our first year. This required putting an antenna on the roof and it took two months for the property manager to get back to Muzak with the approval and instructions for doing this.

Am I purely complaining here? No. (Although it does feel good to vent a little—aaaaahhhhhh!) I'm trying to make you aware of all those little and big things that happen while running your business. These are issues that you don't necessarily have any control over and can: 1) give you a headache, 2) cause you to lose business, 3) give you an ulcer, 4) potentially close you down, or 5) all of the above.

Someone recently asked me if I did this all over again, would I want to buy and own my space. The answer is maybe. (It's not easy to give a definitive "yes" or "no" since there are always other factors to consider.) If I was turning back the clock on The Pot & Bead, owning my own space, while giving me a lot more control, would have presented an entirely different risk. We likely would not have been able to be in such a visible area with good parking. We certainly wouldn't have been able to open when we did since construction at our location was already near completion when we signed the lease. But, knowing what I know now, if I ever looked into being in another, different retail business, I would likely want to own my own land and space. Although, if I did this, I would probably want to be the landlord and not actually run a retail business. For anyone considering retail, owning the space is something definitely worth researching. It's a tangible asset that you still own even if the business doesn't succeed.

Once you have your lease (or mortgage, if you've decided to buy your space), it's time to prepare for your cute little store.

Christmas, like it is for a lot of retailers, was supposed to be our busiest time of year, so we were very interested in making sure we were open in time for the season. Originally, we planned on taking possession of the space sometime in early to mid-September (when the building would be finished), and opening at the very beginning of October. (I should point out that during negotiations, the landlord originally planned to have the space ready by August . . . Lesson learned: don't count on someone else's construction schedule. That doesn't mean they are intentionally trying to mislead you, they could really be planning on having stuff ready by a certain date and be held back by the weather or something else beyond their control. Just be ready to hear a new deadline and plan a lot of buffer time for yourself.)

We wound up taking possession of the space a couple days into October, but the real problem was getting our own "buildouts" done. What we received was a "white box," an empty shell. Basic electrical work, plumbing, etc. was all done but we had to put a floor in, paint, and do all the other work to spruce up the place. Luckily, for a retail business, our buildouts were pretty simple. We needed to paint, have a linoleum tile floor put down, and have our back room constructed. (The back room was where we had our kilns: the large ovens we fired pottery in.)

Unfortunately, it would take a couple of weeks before our contractor could do the back room; we needed a wall put up and some mechanical and electrical work done before we could run our kilns. It wasn't until the very end of October and beginning of November that the work was scheduled to be done. This meant we could open, but we weren't going to be able to get anyone's finished pottery back to them.

Now we were *really* going to be cutting into our Christmas season. This wasn't making anyone very happy, so we decided to open up at half-capacity. Opening day was Saturday, October 12, 2002. Without the kilns running, we could have customers bead, look around, and book parties. We even let some lucky first-time customers paint some pottery for free for us to use as samples in the studio.

Then someone (me, my partner . . . I don't remember who . . . it might have even been my mom), had a great idea. Why not let people paint pottery at a discount? We would hang on to it a little longer than usual and when the kilns were up and running, we'd fire it and call them to pick it up. It worked great! Customers painted at a 25 percent discount and we simply had to do a good job of keeping track of all the pottery that was piling up. Some of our best and most frequent, regular customers came at that time and our first couple months turned out to be better than we expected.

## No-Nonsense Tips and Tidbits:
- It's true what they say: location is important!
- The landlord has a lot of control and power over your business. Know what you're signing beforehand. Ask as many questions as possible so you know what you're getting into. If you can afford it, use a lawyer not only to review the lease, but to help negotiate it. Location is supremely important to almost any business—but remember that the best locations typically demand the highest rents!

# Chapter 4

# **Safe and Secure**

It was one small burglary, but I felt this deserved its own chapter because of the mistakes and stress it brought to the surface. When you start your own business, your funds are usually limited—you do your best to cut any corners you can. (We'll talk more about that in the chapter entitled "Money.") You're always asking yourself: Do I *really* need to spend money on that?

I always planned to have a security system, it's a great tool for keeping track of employees coming and going. Each employee had their own code number in addition to their store key. I was able to tell who opened and closed the store and when. (And, if an employee left and "forgot" to bring back the key the next day, I could simply delete him from the security system and not worry about it.)

But it got complicated when they gave me a huge list of options. Do you want this sensor? Do you want the larger box? Do you want an extra button out here? I wanted to keep it simple. I decided to save a hundred bucks and only get a motion detector without a glass break sensor. I mean, if the glass gets broken, the motion will be detected, right? And oh, I could have sworn they told me that things like balloons wouldn't set off the motion detector.

I got my first call from the security company about two hours after closing on a Saturday night, the first day of our Grand Opening party

31

(which actually happened several months after we opened—more on that in Chapter 9). The motion sensor had gone off and they wanted to know if the police should be sent around. I said yes and was supposed to get a call back in a few minutes if the police found anything. Since it was the first time I had been called, I couldn't wait to hear back from them so I wound up calling them myself to make sure nothing was wrong. Nothing was. The next morning, my mom speculated that the balloons from our Grand Opening set off the alarm, but I didn't think so because I thought that wasn't supposed to happen. The next night, after day two of our Grand Opening event, I got another call a few hours after closing time. I was a lot less panicked and this time we were sure it was the balloons.

New store policy: no balloons left overnight in the studio.

About a month later, I woke up in the middle of the night to the sound of my cell phone ringing. (I should note that the security company knew to call my home phone first, and then my cell phone.) I answered it to hear one of my employees say, "Adeena, your store has been burglarized."

In that split second, the picture I had in my head was of all the pottery being smashed beyond recognition. I never thought I could be as awake and alert at 2 a.m. as I was then.

My employee went on to say that the cash drawer had been stolen, the pottery on the shelves was okay, that they had tried calling me a dozen times (I'm a heavy sleeper), and that I should talk to the officer who was there. My employee was really upset and I was the one telling her that it would be okay and that it could have been a lot worse (which is true, by the way).

I'm not sure if I can describe the feeling of being in a hyper-alert semi-daze as the officer explained that a window was smashed, they took my cash drawer, and recounted the story of how they brought out a K-9 team to sniff around. I told the officer I'd be there in a half hour or less and he said he'd stick around until I got there.

So, I hopped into my Jeep and went down to the store. I can't tell you much about what was going through my head during the drive, but it was probably the quickest half-hour I ever drove. I think I was mostly concerned with not being pulled over for speeding on my way and having to explain . . .

When I got to the store, I saw one window pane out of four was smashed. My employee went home and the police officer and my store manager were there waiting for me. The officer took me through all the details.

The "perps" smashed the window with a baseball bat. How did they know a baseball bat was used? They left it. The police confiscated the bat and they would be checking it for prints. The baddies ran off with the cash drawer and the police had to confiscate my receipt printer as evidence. There was a pile of glass on the floor right inside the store, and the computer and monitor were both tipped over but they weren't damaged.

There was a K-9 team involved and the officer explained how the dog tracked a scent down the road and then lost it. He said that was probably where they got into a car. After that, he gave me his contact info and told me that there were 24-hour window fixing places I could call in the phone book to see about getting the window boarded up.

He also suggested that in the future, I should get the glass break sensor. Why? After the alarm goes off, the security company calls the police and tells them which type of sensor was triggered, and the officer said that they can take a little longer to reply to a "motion" sensor as opposed to a "glass break" sensor. He then reminded me about the recent false alarms coming from my store (those balloons from the Grand Opening weekend).

The part I really had never thought about before this occurred was the 24-hour window place. The phone book only listed three or four 24-hour businesses and I called them all. Here's what I learned:

- Just because it says "24-hours" doesn't mean that's current information.
- Just because it says "24-hours" doesn't mean that someone will answer the phone.
- Just because they're listed in my local phone book doesn't mean they'll respond to an emergency in my area. (We were a little too far for one of them to travel to in the middle of the night.)

(As a business owner and consumer, I wonder if this is considered false advertising . . . ?)

I finally was able to contact the right company and they said that they would come in a couple of hours to board up the window. Don't believe that part either—they wound up coming at about 9 o'clock the next morning. In the meantime, my manager and I stayed and painted. Yes, painting pottery relieves stress, I can personally vouch for that.

All in all, it could have been a lot worse. I had to have a new cash drawer and receipt printer overnighted, but I lost less than $200 in cash from the drawer; my insurance covered most of the losses—the exceptions being what was in the cash drawer and my insurance deductible. (No-Nonsense Tidbit: When setting up insurance for a retail business, the money in the cash drawer isn't automatically covered, that's an additional option. Believing that most of my customers would not be paying in cash, I didn't opt for that and still don't. Most of our customers didn't pay cash and after the burglary, we never had more than $70 in the store overnight.)

We did open for business on time the next day. And the funniest thing is that most of the customers didn't even notice anything odd about the boarded up window until it was pointed out. Most of our conversations went like this:

Us to customer: "Hi, how are you today?"

Customer to us: "Oh, I'm fine, how are you?"

Us to customer: "Just fine considering, well, you know (pointing to boarded up window)."

Customer to us: "Huh? What's wrong?"

And then we'd explain what happened.

No, the police never did find out who did it. Yes, I had a glass break sensor installed in my store and will have one in every store from now on. (No-Nonsense Tidbit: Yes, we did have the security company's stickers on our windows. Whoever robbed us either didn't see them, or didn't believe them. I think too many small businesses put the stickers on their windows without really having the system, and most people don't expect a small business to actually have an alarm system.)

About a year later, one of my regular customers asked me if they ever found the person who did it, and if it happened to be a particular individual who was just arrested for a local murder! She had read in the paper that when they caught him and searched his house, his basement was full of stuff that looked like it came from retail stores (my burglary was one in a series of retail burglaries over a couple of months in my county—one not known for an overwhelming number of this type of crime). Who knows, it may have been, but I'm past it now and much wiser.

My thoughts on the burglary: I think something bad was bound to happen eventually. I know another pottery studio owner who had a major flood, and another who had a major fire. In both cases, they were out of business for a while. Remember: I was open for business that day and no one was hurt. I feel very lucky—if this was my bad thing, it wasn't *that* bad.

The weird consequence: I had to change my cell phone ring. Every time I heard it, especially late in the evening, I'd get the *super* uncomfortable feeling that something was wrong. That sound was now associated with something *very bad*. The other thing was that for a while I became a very light sleeper, and if my phone rang while I was in bed, I'd be up and sweating in an instant.

I know that at least one of you, while planning for your new business, has toyed with the idea of attempting to save money by foregoing insurance. Bad idea, drop it right now. Even if you didn't plan on installing a system (like I did because of the employees), I would still recommend it. Imagine: your store is burglarized overnight and is sitting that way when you come in at nine in the morning. Wouldn't that be awful?

The National Federation of Independent Business (NFIB), an advocacy organization for small and independent business, regularly publishes reports based on data collected from samples of small business employers across the country. In 2004, they published a report specifically on "Disaster." From this report, I learned that:

- 30 percent of small businesses were closed for twenty-four hours or longer because of a natural disaster. This includes snowstorms.

(I can relate—my store typically lost one or two days of business each year due to snowstorms.)

- 10 percent experienced a man-made disaster. (Like my break-in.)
- 2–3 percent suffered an extreme impact. (Meaning they were not operational for at least a week and/or had more than $100,000 in damages.)
- Whether or not the business had adequate insurance was most frequently associated with whether or not the business would continue operating.

It's important to note that this survey was published in 2004, before Katrina and the other hurricanes that ravished the Gulf Coast in 2005. It is estimated that there were 900,000 small businesses in the affected area. The survey also pointed out that the percentage of businesses that closed for good due to a natural disaster is unknown because of the difficulty in tracking down owners afterward. Therefore, that first statistic about the 30 percent of businesses that were closed for twenty-four hours or more only counts the businesses that re-opened after a natural disaster, not the ones that didn't. See the NFIB website (www.nfib.com) for more interesting reading material.

Luckily, if you're in a retail location, the landlord will likely require in your lease that you have some form of property and/or business liability insurance. Our insurance company paid for our replacement window and part of the new cash register equipment, and that was really helpful, but there are even some smaller things that most people don't think to insure or secure. Sure, you have your birth certificate, the deed to your house, and other important personal papers locked up somewhere that's fire and waterproof . . . what about your important business papers?

After the Katrina disaster, all the small business magazines were full of stories about owners trying to rebuild their lives and save their business. I was amazed by all the articles about owners keeping their important business papers (like their insurance policy!) in a plain file cabinet, with no backups.

I'll admit that for a while I didn't have some of my important papers backed up, but I corrected that: I bought Adobe Acrobat (www.adobe.com) and used my printer, which also scanned, and converted them into PDF files. These files are easily searched, indexed, and smaller than if I saved them as some kind of image file. I saved all the important files on a CD and made several copies of the CD to keep in different locations. (No-nonsense note: Some scanners let you scan right into a PDF file. Purchasing extra software isn't necessary.)

Here's a list of important business papers you should keep one or more backups of:

- Lease and other property-related papers
- Insurance policies
- Tax returns
- Bank loan documents
- Any other agreements you've signed, or others have signed with you

And don't forget to have backups of any computer files that are important to your business! This goes for any accounting software you use (keep a backup of your data some place safe), point of sale software, and anything else!

Protecting against a personal disaster should also be a priority so that your business doesn't suffer. What would happen if you wound up in the hospital? Or if something happened at your house and you were stuck there for a week? What if the worst happened and your spouse died? Setting up a business that can run without you, having insurance, and even having a will: these are things you should make sure to take care of when starting your own cute little store.

Donna Schreiter, who owns a store similar to mine called The Painted Pot (www.thepaintedpotstl.com) in Chesterfield, MO, had to endure the unexpected loss of her husband of twenty-four years. If the emotional pain of that wasn't enough, she had to take over all of the paperwork (taxes, payroll, accounting), and even install a new computer software system. Apparently, her husband wrote his own accounting software she didn't have experience with, and without him she had to start from scratch. In addition, Donna's husband had another unrelated business with other members of his family and the proper paperwork wasn't in place to pass on his part of the ownership, rights, and compensation to Donna, leaving her to figure out how to support herself and their kids.

It's important for anyone in business to have in place the proper paperwork to transfer ownership and assets if a spouse dies. The law varies from state to state. This is one item that definitely requires the use of a lawyer and shouldn't be put off any longer than necessary.

There's a great book that I recommend over and over again: *The Small Business Owner's Guide to a Good Night's Sleep.* See Appendix D for details.

## No-Nonsense Tips and Tidbits:

- Owning a business means you are constantly at risk for disaster: fire, flood, closing due to weather, accidents, illness. A lot of things can mean you're not open for business. You need to do your best to protect yourself against these happenings.
- Prepare as well as you can. If you know what can happen, you can prepare for it.

# Chapter 5

# Employees

Not all businesses require employees. If you're a retail business, chances are you will want or need to have some—you can't be there seven days a week forever. Or maybe you can. However, business that wants to grow will almost certainly have to take on employees.

Recently, at a party, I spoke with a friend who owns a technology consulting business. He was complaining about not being able to take on some new business clients because he's already putting in sixteen-hour days. I made the obvious suggestion: "Why not hire someone to help you?" His response was something about how they might not do it right, or exactly the same way he would. "Yes, that's true," I said, but I reminded him that it is possible to train an employee about the important parts, and if things aren't exactly the way he'd do it, that would be a trade-off.

I finished the conversation by asking: "How long are you going to keep working sixteen-hour days?" (I wanted to ask other questions like, "Don't you want to grow your business?") He responded with that shrug of the shoulders that says, "Yeah, I know you're right, I can't keep this up forever," and we (okay, maybe it was just me) were promptly distracted by the hors d'oeuvres being carried by.

For a new (or any) retail business, there is an important trade-off: pay yourself or pay others to do work you are capable of doing. If you choose the former option, you're running your store all the time or most of the time. Great! You're possibly saving hundreds to thousands of dollars on payroll. But if you're the one who has to be in your store the whole time, what other things are you missing out on? You might not have the time you'd like to do important things like marketing or attending networking events. You might not even be able to take time to go see a doctor.

Alternately, you might choose to close your store when you're out. There are lots of small retail businesses that put the sign up "Out to Lunch" or close for a week when they're on vacation. That might be fine and dandy, but if you're in a shopping center like the one I was in, you might be required by your landlord to be open a minimum number of hours, and possibly be required to be open seven days a week.

The downside of this "do it all yourself" approach: being open at inconsistent hours can cause you to lose your customers. They think you're supposed to be open—when they show up and you're not, they will be annoyed. That means you've lost out on a sale right then, and possibly lost out in the future as well, since there's a good chance that the customer will find some other way or some other store to meet their needs.

We'd heard complaints about our nearest competitor closing for several days during one of the local county school vacation weeks. Great for us! We picked up the extra business. On the not-so-good side, customers have been VERY quick to call and complain to us when we are supposed to be open at 10 a.m., and it's 10:10 and we're not open yet. This last part also goes under the heading of problem employees, discussed later in this chapter.

So, for these reasons, we're going to assume in the rest of this chapter that a retail business needs employees and that you, as the prudent business owner, will opt to hire some quality folks. When I opened The Pot & Bead, I knew two things: 1) I needed employees, and 2) I had to treat them well. The Pot & Bead was going to be open seven days a week, so unless I planned to be in the store EVERY SINGLE DAY without a break, I undoubtedly needed employees.

Yes, when we first opened, I was in the store every single day, but that only continued for about the first month or so. The first time I left my store in the hands of an employee while it was open, it was very scary, but it was necessary—probably what it must feel like to leave your baby with a babysitter for the first time.

Most of us have been an employee at one time or another and every one of us probably has good and bad stories to tell. We've had bosses we liked, ones we hated; that micromanaging, brow-beating, make-you-work-sixteen-hours-while-your-child-is-being-born boss might be the very reason you want to own your own business.

The last company I worked for before opening The Pot & Bead was marked by daily lessons in "how to *not* treat your employees." It was a pretty small company, and the funny thing is that I initially wanted to work there because I thought a small company would appreciate and reward individual effort. Wow, was I wrong. Size does not matter.

For quite a while before I left, things had not been good. During this time, I was racking my brain to figure out a way to own my own company. The final straw, when I knew it had to be done, was right after returning from a trip to Asia. I had been sent on this trip with a colleague with only two days' notice. The purpose: convince our customer not to back out of their contract. In other words, we were sent to convince them to keep making their payments so we could keep operating. We were successful (at least for the time being), but at a price (of course). My colleague and I both had gotten sick on this trip; I wound up with a nasty urinary tract infection and my colleague had other problems.

When we returned, not one of our managers or the people responsible for giving us this assignment said anything close to "Thank you" or "Good job." Instead, I was personally criticized for the work that wasn't able to be completed while we were gone. My colleague was denied reimbursement for his $60 or so of medical expenses. That would have been okay if the person denying him said something like: "You know that we're having some financial difficulties. We'd appreciate it if you'd cover this." But instead, this person said something a lot more belligerent like: "What!? You think we're going to pay for that!? No way, you're crazy!" (No-Nonsense Note: This isn't an exact quote. And the words weren't the most important thing. It was simply the tone and way it was handled.)

Well, that was the final straw. That was when all my free time went into thinking about how to get out of that kind of situation and into one where I had more control over my professional life. It was only about three weeks later that I had my conversation with John over coffee that led to The Pot & Bead.

The good that comes from having been in those kinds of situations is that I had a very clear idea when I started my business of how I would and would not treat my employees. Knowing that your employees are valuable and need to be shown appreciation is key when you have them.

There are studies that show that the best (and possibly most profitable) retail businesses are ones that have the greatest employee satisfaction or those with the happiest employees. As an example, the grocery store Wegmans has made *Fortune* magazine's list of top 100 companies to work for for the last sixteen years as of 2013. They've made the top ten for eleven consecutive years. When they made #1 in 2005, *Fortune* published an article titled "The Wegmans," praising the company's way of treating employees and tying that atmosphere to the company's increasing market share.

Knowledge is indeed power, but it's not enough. Actually showing the appreciation is much harder than it would seem at first. Three years into my business, I was better at it than in the beginning, but I was still far from perfect.

Employees in a small, customer-service oriented business like mine have *tremendous* power. I don't think they even realize it. A customer's perception of my store is directly tied to their first experience in it, which is directly tied to the experience they have with the staff member they first encounter. Therefore, if the employee provides good service, the customer will most likely come back and will hopefully tell people good things about my business. If the customer doesn't feel like they received good customer service, they might not ever come back. What's worse is that they'll likely tell others never to come to my store.

In order to truly improve and try to expand the business, I also knew early on that I would need a store manager. This is someone who is responsible for the other employees, and is responsible for the day-to-day flow of operations. In the latter case, a lot of the job revolves around making sure customers are happy and have their pottery returned to them on time. I differentiate myself from my manager like this: My manager works "in the busines"; I work "on the business."

In the first three years, I went through four managers. I learned something from each one. Employing a manager is different from employing part-time employees. The manager is often older and more experienced. This means that he/she demands more pay and benefits, like health care. You are competing with other employers to keep this person, and often, a small business doesn't have the resources to compete. (Home Depot or Lowe's can offer health care and a 401(k), I can't.)

So what do I want? Well-trained employees who like to work at The Pot & Bead. Who are these people? Well, in my ideal world they are all-knowing, with Einstein-level intelligence, are constantly beaming a genuine smile, have no other responsibilities besides working for me, are super punctual, can see the minutest of details, can juggle not two, not three, but ten things at once, and love to clean. Did I mention that my ideal world is that same magical fantasy land I dreamed up when I was six and thought I'd be living on the moon?

Back to reality on Earth, anyone who is going to be an employee of mine (or yours, for that matter) is a human being who, although they might be excellent, still isn't perfect and has a life and concerns outside of working in my store. And really . . . what's to stop them from quitting and finding work someplace else?

One time, I asked one of my part-time employees what she liked better about working at my shop versus the job she had prior at a bagel shop. She said she thought my place was more professional and more organized. This was some good feedback. Getting feedback from employees whenever you can is important, whether it's formal or not. The fact that you even bothered to ask, and showed genuine interest in their opinion, is what matters most.

Unfortunately, I don't have a magic recipe for finding and keeping the best employees, but after five plus years, I'd been through my share of them and learned that the process we used to find and hire someone was one of the most important pieces of the puzzle.

First, we had a pretty detailed application and set up a thorough process for hiring someone (even for a part-time position). This involved reviewing the application, having the applicant come in for a thirty-minute interview, and making sure we called their references.

The two times I bypassed my own process and didn't do a good check of references but still hired the person are the only two times where I had to let those individuals go within a few weeks of their start date (and both times I wished I'd let them go a week sooner).

I had potential employees fill out a pretty detailed four-page application. If I was interested in them, they came in for a half hour interview. Once, after an interview with a potential employee, a customer who had overheard the interview commented that he himself had never gone through such a thorough interview for any position. He was in sales and had a six-figure salary.

I look at it this way—it's my business. I'll do what I can to ensure that I'm hiring the best people possible. These people can make or break my business—I want only the best representing my business to my customers.

Here are some things I learned about the application process:

- The potential employee needs to pick up the application, fill it out him/herself, and bring it back. I ignored applications picked up and brought back by parents of high schoolers. It took hiring a couple not-so-great employees to realize that it was the parent who wanted their child to work, not the potential employee him/herself. (I know the parent was trying to be helpful, but next time you're in a store and are receiving less-than-stellar service from the un-motivated youngin' behind the counter, ask yourself if this is this how you want your child to look and act in front of the public.)

- The application needs to be filled out completely! I've had applicants not sign the application, only put down half their address, or put down the name of a reference without any contact information. All this is a sign of someone who really doesn't care. If they don't care about taking the time to fill out their application, why would they care about taking the time to do their job properly? These applications found their way very quickly to the "Do Not Interview" pile.

Then there was the interview. It typically lasted fifteen to thirty minutes. Most of the applicants had worked before, so the questions were phrased in the form of: "What *did* you do in a previous situation?" as opposed to "What *would* you do if a situation happened?" This is called "behavioral interviewing." The theory is that past actions indicate future behavior. The latter form of questioning doesn't give you any real information about the applicant because there is always a right answer to a question like: "If a customer came in upset, what would you do?" The applicant is usually smart enough to figure out the correct response. The question: "In your previous job, tell me about a time that a customer came in to complain. What did you do?" is much more likely to give you insight into how this person would handle a similar situation again.

No-Nonsense Tidbit: Before interviewing anyone for a position, make sure you're aware of the current rules and laws governing this process in your locality. There are federal laws you can find at the USDepartment of Labor's website, www.dol.gov. But also check your local state and county for additional rules and applicable laws. You'd be surprised by the number of things you can't ask on the application or during the interview. Here's a few (this is not meant to be an all-inclusive list):

- Age (unless they are under eighteen)
- Race/ethnicity
- Sexual orientation
- "Family Status" (i.e., Are you pregnant? Are you planning on becoming pregnant?)

You get the idea.

Checking references is an important part of the application process. I did check references, but took them with a grain of salt. After all, the applicant wouldn't write them down if he or she didn't at least believe that the reference would be positive. At least, I've never written one down without knowing that. If it's possible, ask the reference for other people to talk to.

But even after the application, interview, and reference check, there is still no way to know if the person is going to work out. We also try to take into account the "first impression" the applicant made with me and my staff. A person who presents his or her application with a big, genuine smile, speaks clearly, and radiates enthusiasm is much more likely to do that with a customer than someone who drags their feet in, mumbles "herrrffss-muhappcation," makes no eye contact, and leaves. (You can imagine that by now I have accumulated a very large "Do Not Interview" stack.)

As you may have gathered, it's very important that potential employees are friendly, upbeat, have a good attitude, and are responsible. But what about the fact that they'd be working with pottery? Shouldn't they be artistic and artsy and know how to draw as well? Nope, not at all.

You can train someone how to work with pottery, you can even teach them a few things about painting, but you can't teach anyone about responsibility. (Even though we had a long training period, responsibility is learned over a lifetime and, well, I don't have that much time.)

To make sure the employees I hired had a working knowledge of what was going on in the store, we had a staff meeting every month. It allowed for some extra training, made sure everyone was aware of the latest news at The Pot & Bead, and for me to show my appreciation of them with the universal symbol: food.

To train, I usually gave quizzes on topics that I wanted to make sure they really knew. They knew that there would be a quiz, and they knew that it usually involved some kind of prize or incentive.

Employees do have their own lives outside of working for me (or you). You can take the attitude of, "So what?" and "What they do on their own time is their business" and "As long as they're on the clock, they're mine." But none of these approaches are particularly beneficial to the relationship.

Personally, I feel that any time an employee is not on the clock is none of my business and they can do whatever they like. However, I've had several employees take on second jobs and to date, it's never worked out well (for me). I've done my best to try to keep pay competitive and allow for the fact that different employees have different needs for numbers of hours worked. Scheduling each month usually took a considerable amount of my time!

How do you really find and keep the best people? Like I said, I have no magic formula for this, but overall I think we've had more great employees than bad. And a couple of "okay" ones.

Training someone to work at The Pot & Bead usually took several weeks. This cost money; I was paying someone to learn, and usually needed to pay at least a second person to be around to do the training, or I needed to be there. It's a significant cost of doing business and something important to factor in. It should give you some motivation to make your store one that people want to work in and not want to leave. "Turnover" as it's called, is expensive.

I don't care how cool it is to see Donald do it on *The Apprentice* (yes, I'm a fan, too), firing people ain't fun, but it is, unfortunately, necessary at times. I think it does get a little easier the more times you do it because each time you realize that you probably should have done it sooner. Eventually, it sets in that a bad employee can really hurt your business and you can't afford to keep someone like that on your staff. Remember: You're the boss first, friend second.

Here's a list of some of the things a bad employee can do to you and/or your business:

- lie
- steal
- be rude to customers
- not show up on time/not show up at all
- forget to do things
- quit unexpectedly and with no notice
- try to get fired
- call in sick with no notice
- close the store an hour early without permission

I've had employees do all of the above and more. The first two are very difficult to prove, but if you suspect an employee of lying or stealing, you will wind up watching them like a hawk, and they'll wind up doing something else just as bad.

Being rude to customers is also hard to prove unless a third person is around, but at the end of the day, it's the customer's perception that's important. (See the chapter on Customers.)

Not showing up on time, especially when it means the store doesn't open on time, is unforgivable, but being late to any shift is grounds for being "written up."

Forgetting to do things, at first, doesn't sound too bad. Depending on your business, what kinds of things and the frequency are all factors. For me, anything that was forgotten and resulted in a disappointed customer was grounds for being written up. I had an employee forget to lock the store one night—that's grounds for a firing.

I've had at least one employee and one manager quit unexpectedly and with no notice. There's really nothing that can be done to prevent this, I believe. In the long run, it probably winds up hurting them more than me. (Word does get around, you know.)

And yes, I've had at least one employee *try* to get fired. I felt a little bad for her. I think she was under a lot of pressure at home and school at the same time, and felt that if she quit, her parents would yell at her, but if she got fired, then she could tell her parents that I was the bad guy.

After two pages about the bad things employees can do, equal time and space belongs to the good.

The good things employees can do for you and your business:

- keep customers coming back
- have customers telling you how great they are
- give you the freedom to go home
- take care of your business when you're sick and in the hospital
- allow you to go on vacation
- make suggestions for improvement
- allow you to work ON your business and not IN it

Like the previous list, I've had all the above happen and more. Soon after the store's two-year anniversary, I wound up in the hospital unexpectedly for a week and in bed for the following two weeks. The happiest and saddest thing was when I realized that they really didn't need me in the store. And it was that same feeling and concept that allowed me to take a three-week vacation overseas shortly after the store's third anniversary.

On any given day, here's the absolutely best thing that could happen to me: I'm out around town someplace like the grocery store, someone I know (well or not so well) comes up to me and says, "Hey Adeena! I was in your store with my child the other day. The person who was working there was great! He/she was so helpful, yada yada yada."

This nearly exact conversation happened to me more than once, and I looked forward to it happening again. (The second best thing was when I was working in the store and someone came in to pick up their pottery and they said the same thing.)

This is a great place to bring up the concept of having procedures in place for your business. A business needs to have an operations manual. If you're not around, how do employees know what to do? Yes, you trained them, but what if they forget? What if your employee has worked for you for maybe three shifts and you're supposed to be at the store with them for shift number four? Unfortunately, you're stuck in traffic and are going to be late, but the store is still open and this new employee is the only one there. Oh, and let's say you're someplace where your cell phone doesn't get good reception. Luckily, nearly all your procedures are written down, and on the first day, the employee knows that the answers to nearly all of his questions are in the manual.

Then, when a customer comes in and asks for X, the employee should know to check the manual—chances are the answer will be in there. (And if it's not, there's that procedure for handling things the employee doesn't know about—i.e., how to politely tell a customer that a manager or owner will need to get back to them about their question.) I say that, chances are, the answer is in the manual. Your operations manual is a living document. Store policies, products, and services will change over time so your manual needs to change over time, too.

I'm a very process-oriented person (largely due to my engineering background), so it was a very natural thing for me to start writing our operations manual. I did most of it in the few weeks before we opened. I didn't get all of it from the top of my head. A ceramic studio trade association I belonged to provided resources as did other books on retail. After The Pot & Bead opened, there were lots of little tweaks to the manual in the first few months. About a year after opening, I did a major reorganization of it to help with training new employees and every year I looked at it to see what needed updating.

Communication with the employees was another area that always required thought and work. There was always some tidbit or customer service note to pass on to and between employees. What if one of our policies changed? What if a customer had a special request for her upcoming birthday party? We tried several approaches to make sure everyone who worked at The Pot & Bead was on the same page. What started out as a sticky-note system evolved into using an Internet-based web service that allowed us to communicate whether or not we were physically in the store. We used a paid subscription for WebOffice (www.weboffice.com), but that was before Google had Calendar, Docs, and other tools that could have done the same job for free.

Forms, logs, and contracts were also things we used to keep everything straight. (No-Nonsense Tip: Not all commercial printers are created equal. Some specialize in creating forms—printing up a two- or three-part forms where you write on the top page and it's carbon copied to the bottom page(s)—so you can have a copy as well as the customer.)

Keeping good employees around was another challenge. You have a great employee—one who always is there on time, knows what to do, and is great with customers. This person is fantastic and you really want him or her to stay forever and be happy working in your business. But then one day she comes to you; she found another job; it pays more.

Urgh! First, you didn't know that this employee even was having an issue with her pay. Why didn't she at least say something? What do you do? Well, I have to say that unfortunately, I've lost good employees because I couldn't afford to pay them more at the time. The best I could do was re-evaluate what I was paying for their service versus what other local businesses paid. When we first opened, I thought I was paying competitively, but I realized I expected a lot from my employees—they weren't there to simply ring the cash register. They needed to do everything from answering the customers' questions about painting, to taking care of their pottery and running birthday parties. Our base pay was more, but I also wouldn't settle for an employee who wasn't representing The Pot & Bead in the way I wanted.

(No-Nonsense Tip: As a way to improve employee pay, we gave a bonus at the end of the month that was based purely on the store's sales. Each month there was a sales target the store had to meet. How much did each employee get? A percentage based on the number of hours they worked. The idea was, the more they worked, the more they would have contributed to overall sales that month.)

But my learning how to pay people cost me some good employees. The problem, however, wasn't only the pay, it was the fact that I didn't know the particular employees were unhappy with what they were earning. I didn't know that they were already looking for another job—I found out after they had found another job, accepted it, and given me their two weeks' notice.

The real problem was that the employee didn't feel comfortable coming to talk to me about this ahead of time. Unfortunately, this was my problem—I'm not the most approachable person on the planet. In any employment situation, I believe there's a little natural animosity toward "The Boss." The Boss is the bad person who makes you work and controls a big part of your life. Couple that with the perception that The Boss will yell and scream and get mad if you come and ask for a raise, and it makes people think it's easier to quit rather than ask.

(No-Nonsense Note: I have never "yelled" at an employee. Yes, I have been mad and even upset, but yelling doesn't do any good. If an employee is doing something bad enough that would make me want to yell, then this person shouldn't be my employee.)

Tips for folks contemplating owning or who already own their cute little store: Are your employees happy? What are their big issues? It might not even be with you, it might be in their lives at home, but do you know about them? Do your best to get to know these people who help keep your business running. It's hard, and when you ask questions like: "How are you?" you might get the generic "I'm fine" response, but keep at it. Your employees might not tell you everything going on in their lives. That's okay, you're not entitled to that information. But you are entitled to know what's going on in your store when you're not there.

I had an employee who was very nice and pleasant with the customers, but we were starting to have issues because she wasn't getting all the tasks done when she was there by herself. It was strange because she was not the irresponsible type—she wouldn't blow off work simply to blow it off. After working with her some more, we realized that she couldn't multi-task. For example, if she was helping a customer on the phone and another customer walked into the store, she had to finish with the customer on the phone before helping (or even just acknowledging) the customer in the store. Or when a customer was in the store painting, she couldn't do another task once the customer was set up and painting—she had to sort of hover over them. Our normal mode of operation was once a customer was set up, we gave them their space and did other tasks, while checking on them occasionally and being available to answer any questions.

This person's employment came to a quick end when two things happened. First, her *husband* called in sick for her the night before she was supposed to open the store on her own the next morning. Apparently, she had been sick the whole weekend but for some reason they waited until the last minute to call, when it was impossible to get someone to take her shift. Two things wrong here: 1) waiting until the last minute when, if she was sick all weekend, she could have called much sooner, and 2) having her husband call in for her. We only deal with employees—if someone else is calling, then the person should be in the hospital or something really bad like that. I am convinced that this employee wasn't sick but stressed about coming in to the shop the next day, and had her husband call because she didn't want to tell me herself.

The second thing was when I found out that same day that a *customer* had helped take care of other customers because too many things were going on at once. I was floored. Why didn't she (the employee) say something? The day before this happened, I had a discussion with her about the tasks she was supposed to accomplish the next day, it was going to be the first time she would load a kiln full of pottery on her own. Every employee had to do this on their own at some point. I worried that this was a little too soon for her, and we discussed other options: the task could wait or I could come in and do it. She maintained that she could do it, no problem.

Well, apparently, it was too much to get it done and take care of customers at the same time. She was upset that she couldn't get it done *and* take care of customers. She didn't know how to manage both. When I found this all out, I knew I had to let her go. The ability to multitask to some degree is definitely a job requirement in a small business.

The balance of being involved in the day-to-day operations of your business versus empowering employees to deal with things without you is a fine line that constantly needs monitoring and adjusting. Find out what decisions your employees made and validate them or let them know what to do differently in the future. Remember that you can't plan for everything that comes up, but you can plan for a lot and be ready to add a store procedure or policy when something new happens.

The only decisions that employees made on their own that truly made me upset were ones that would make us lose customers or business. I felt a wonderful sense of accomplishment and appreciation when an employee was able to make a decision without me and it turned out to be exactly the same one I would have made.

## No-Nonsense Tips and Tidbits:

- Good employees are one of the best assets you can have as a business owner. Good people are out there—find them!
- Bad employees can really hurt your business. Get rid of them quickly.
- Only you can decide if, when, and how many employees are right for your business. I am a firm believer that in the long run, any business that intends to grow can't only be made up of the owner or founder. Every growing business will need to experience the joy and pain of employees.

# Chapter 6

# Follow Your Gut (Or How to Lose a Lot of Money Trying to Buy Someone Else's Business)

My plan from Day 1: If The Pot & Bead was successful and proves that it had the potential to turn a profit, we'd open more stores like it! This was more than just a thought—a few months after opening, I had my accountant prepare financial projections for multiple stores for the next few years.

At the start of our first summer (The Pot & Bead had been open for less than a year), a store similar to mine went on the market because the owner was terminally ill. They were going to have to sell or close. Quickly. This is all the information I received in an email one day. This other store was also within driving distance of my house.

I looked into it and at first, it looked like a good idea. The store had been open for about four years and was marginally profitable in the previous full calendar year. The current calendar year wasn't going so well. Because the owner had been ill since January, there had been virtually no advertising or marketing done that year. Also, the owner was the store manager . . . he worked both *in* and *on* his business.

Somehow, I saw huge potential. But by the tone I'm using now, you might be able to guess: pursuing this "opportunity" proved to be a huge mistake.

The goal on both sides was to make this a simple, non-costly process. Mistake number one was thinking we could avoid using a lawyer in the process. I mean, there are all these books out there with titles such as *Legal Forms for Small Businesses*, which typically include standard contracts for selling a business. We agreed via email what the terms would be and agreed that these documents would be okay. I snagged one form from such a book, added in our specific arrangements, and it looked like we had a deal.

Some of the details of the deal were that I would be giving the sellers a down payment and the rest of the purchase price would be seller financed. This meant that I'd be making payments to them over a period of time at some interest rate—effectively, they were granting me a loan. As such, they wanted something to act as collateral for that loan. They initially asked to put a lien on my house.

(Important No-Nonsense Note that will come up later: When they asked for the lien on the house, my now ex-husband and I thought to ourselves that that was strange considering we had absolutely no equity in the house. Meaning: we were young (we hadn't had years to build up much equity), we had our first mortgage, our home equity loan, and the business loan that started The Pot & Bead. We assumed that the sellers didn't actually expect us to have any equity in our home and that they were asking simply to show something on paper. In other words: the sellers didn't ask us how much equity was in our home and we didn't tell them. They asked for the lien, we shrugged our shoulders, and said "sure.")

The sale was supposed to be executed on August 1 of that year. The sellers were unable and unwilling to keep the store open past July 31. The value of a retail business plummets when the store is actually closed, so it was in my best interest to make sure it stayed open past then.

The problems started when the sellers were going to be out of town for a few days before and a few days after our execute date. Well, since it seemed like we had an agreement, we agreed that as of August 1, I'd start running the business and we'd sign the agreement when they returned. Sounds simple and reasonable, right?

One thing led to another and the agreement didn't get signed. My husband and I were trying to refinance our house, and that held up some of the paper work getting this other lien for the sellers on our house. It wasn't until the end of August, with the lien paperwork started, that the sellers actually saw that we had three liens already and that was when it dawned on them that we didn't actually have any equity in our home. They didn't like that and called me back and asked me to produce some other form of security for this loan. I think I laughed. I didn't have anything else. We went back and forth on this for a while; they kept asking and I kept saying I didn't have anything. They asked about my parents and whether they could use their homes as a security. Not a bad idea, but my parents had their own financial issues and couldn't afford to get involved in mine.

Eventually, they gave in, probably because they saw the deal falling through if it didn't happen this way. It was a risk they had to take. By then it was September and I was starting to have second thoughts about the whole deal. That was the time that I should have started listening to my gut. I should have cut my losses then. Actually, when we started the whole nonsense about extra security for the loan something in my gut told me then to can the deal, but I didn't. I should have.

But no . . . I let it go on through late October. Right through our Grand Reopening. It was actually at the Grand Reopening when it finally set in that I should get out of this deal. I realized that the type of customer in this area was not the kind of customer that I understood. I had to get out of this deal. Luckily, something happened the next week that made it all the easier. The sellers changed the whole agreement on me. At the start, we agreed on a standard Sales Agreement, which you typically see in many of the legal forms books. They said that they would email back a slightly tweaked version of what we had agreed to, but the day before we were going to execute the deal, they sent a 100 percent completely different agreement! Without giving me a heads-up they had a lawyer draw up another agreement. That was my final straw; we said no.

For a long while afterward, I would tell people that I felt bad about the whole thing and people would tell me, "Don't. It's business." And they were right.

I spent the next several months depressed over the money that the whole ordeal cost me. I was out about $15,000. Operating the business cost more than it was bringing in at the time and I spent money on new marketing materials and advertising.

I have to confess that what made me finally feel better was the following: The sellers did manage to sell the place to someone else. The following January, I got a call from the new buyer who was in a state of panic and despair herself. She bought the business thinking that 1) she'd be able to take a salary, and 2) she'd be able to spend MORE time with her ten-year-old. She said she was nervous about calling me because the sellers had said many bad things about me. I told her I wasn't surprised by that given what had happened and told her my side of it. She wanted to know how sales were when I managed that shop and if I could recommend anything she could do. She told me how surprised she was that she was not able to spend more time with her daughter and the despair she was in over not being able to draw a salary.

(No-Nonsense Note: This is one of the main reasons I wrote this book—it's to help prevent people from making the mistake this woman did. She thought owning her own cute little store would mean more time and money. This is *exactly* the mistake I want to prevent others from making.)

I told her about sales during the time I ran the store and how they weren't covering expenses. I told her how much money I was out. She was upset because she had told the sellers that she expected and needed to draw a salary from the business and was very disconcerted that the sellers knew it wasn't realistic and didn't say anything. Well, it's business. Even though it would have been nice for them to say something, they didn't have to. Their motivation was to sell the business, they didn't care what they were sticking someone with.

The seller didn't conceal any information, they actually didn't do anything wrong. It was the buyer's mistake. This buyer did not practice the concept of due diligence. It's where a potential buyer of a business researches the business in detail by looking through all the financials and any other information. This step typically occurs after the potential buyer enters into some form of agreement, and possibly has even put down some earnest money (it's serious buyers—not just anyone who asks—who can have access to this privileged information). If you're contemplating buying a cute little store, read at least one of the books in Appendix D which discusses buying a business.

In this case, the buyer should have had access to the sales and expense data from the previous owner. Even with a cursory glance at the financials, she would have seen that the previous owner didn't draw much of anything resembling a salary.

The good that came from this was that it probably prevented me from making a more costly mistake later. Businesses go up for sale all the time. Toward the end of that deal, another paint-your-own-pottery business was up for sale. This one *had* been profitable a while ago and was currently on its second owner, who had let the business deteriorate. Even though a part of me wanted that business pretty bad, my gut was definitely saying no; and this time I listened.

Doug Fleener, a retail consultant who I used for a while early on and who authored *The Profitable Retailer*, once asked me: Is it a "nice-to-have" or is it something that can return a profit? That's a question I now ask myself every single time I'm considering opening my checkbook.

I think I get it now. "Nice-to-haves" are the things you want. They might make you feel better about yourself, but if something is a "nice-to-have," hopefully your gut will be telling you "No."

How do you recognize that? If you listen to your inner voice, you'll notice that there is a conflict. In my case, I get some stress symptoms popping up. Yes, your "gut" isn't merely something metaphorical, I believe it really exists and will manifest itself in different ways for different people. Learn to follow it.

## No-Nonsense Tips and Tidbits:

- A risk is a risk. If you don't have the money to lose, don't take the risk. If you lose, you won't have that money for other necessary things or even an emergency that might come up.
- In any situation involving buying another business, you need to use a lawyer!
- You cannot let your emotions affect what you know are sound business decisions—even if that means you'll be perceived as "not nice." Simply put: follow your gut.

# Chapter 7

# Customers . . . Ya Gotta Love Them

I love my customers. They give me money. What's not to love about that? There are, however, challenges to keeping customers happy.

Retail is all about customer service. Yes, my customers like painting pottery, but pottery painting isn't a necessity. If they didn't enjoy the whole experience, they could easily find another way to spend their entertainment dollars.

I was at a business seminar once, and during the introduction, the speaker asked the audience to raise their hand if they were in a customer service business. I thought he was looking to differentiate between businesses that "sell a service," like accounting, but it turned out that I sat there for the next few minutes feeling embarrassed that I didn't raise my hand.

I was, indeed, in the customer service business. I say this now, after trying to convince you only a few chapters ago that I was in the retail business. Those two terms, "retail" and "customer service," should really be interchangeable. Retail is about selling a product to an end user, but customer service is what will make that customer come back, remain loyal, and bring her friends and family.

Did you know that there are businesses out there turning away customers? They do this because there are customers out there who will suck the life out of you. They will browse and ask many questions but in the end, will never buy anything. These retail businesses are implementing the 80/20 rule: 80 percent of their business comes from 20 percent of their customers and they are trying to cut out some of the non-profitable ones by turning away prospective customers who won't spend enough money to make it worth their while.

While I'm not comfortable doing that, I am indeed a believer in the 80/20 rule. In fact, a short time before our two-year anniversary, I analyzed our sales data and found it to be true. Nearly 80 percent of our business came from 20 percent of our customers. First, I want to *super* thank that 20 percent. You are great. You are wonderful. Please keep giving me money. Showing customers you value them is just as important as appreciating your employees. Without them, business would not be good.

Customer appreciation is another one in the long list of ongoing challenges that the cute little store owner must fret over. For our second anniversary, instead of having a generic "Anniversary Sale," we sent some free offers to our regular customers. We divided our top tier of customers into two groups: the best and the *very* best. We sent out invitations to our top customers and their families to come paint special mugs . . . completely free—no strings attached. Most of them did this. It was a pure thank-you.

Are all of our customers wonderful? No. Some can be downright mean. They're not really mean, but a lot of times it can come out that way simply because their expectations aren't being met. I've been told to think of these customers not as "mean," but as "unhappy." The premise is that you can't make a mean customer nice, but you *can* make an unhappy customer happy. (Trying to have some of the younger employees implement that way of thinking is what's really hard.)

Before you can make customers happy, before you can appreciate them, you need to know who they are. Do you know who your customers are? Collecting data and customer feedback is an important activity for the business owner. Okay, it might be my geeky science background, but I'm all about collecting the data. When customers were in the store, we asked them for their home and email addresses. We also asked them how they first heard about us. We used the home address to track where our customers came from, and occasionally mailed them a flyer. We used the email addresses for an email newsletter we sent out periodically. "How they heard about us" was used to keep track of which of our marketing efforts were working better than others.

Our "Point of Sale" software (cash register software) allowed us to keep customer data like phone numbers and addresses with each customer. It also kept a record of the customer's sales history so I could go back and see all of the customers who bought a toothbrush holder in 2003.

To gather feedback, once a year we mailed out a customer survey (this was before services like surveymonkey.com existed, which make it easy to email a survey to customers). Each year the questions on the survey changed based on areas of the business I was looking to most improve. I also gave out mini surveys at the end of programs like our summer camp program that we held each year. I also flat out asked customers specific questions for feedback on specific areas.

What did I do with all this information? I studied it to make it easier to decide where to spend my advertising dollars, who to market to, *what* to market, how to improve customer service, etc. Information from customers is vital.

If you're a business owner, you're still a customer to someone else. Lots of consumer magazines tell us to ask for discounts, lower rates, etc. But then when we're the business owner, we're on the receiving end of everyone else asking for special treatment and discounts. Many customers ask for a special discount because they think they've been to the store a lot. I had a five-year-old boy ask me out of the blue if I could give him something for free.

Most of us grew up with the phrase "the customer is always right" tattooed on our brains. Well, that's not exactly true. Customers are wrong all the time. They get information mixed up, or are simply the victims of miscommunication. It's our job to figure out what they really want, what they're saying, and send them home happy.

Keeping the customer happy is one of the hardest things to do. You have to be prepared to set and meet customers' expectations. Watch

*Seinfeld*—practically every other episode has a significant amount of time devoted to some crappy customer service issue with a retail store or restaurant. Can you picture a retailer really acting like that today? I can't. Service is king, and knowing that is half the battle. If you know and understand the reasons why good customer service rules, you can act on that information. It should be easy but for some reason that's one of the hardest things ever (right up there with employee appreciation).

Doug Fleener believes you should never say "No" to a customer. Nice thought, but is it possible to live up to? Employees need to be trained on when they can say "Yes" if a customer asks for something unusual.

Here's a funny, but true, story: A friend of mine and her husband were out for a special Valentine's Day dinner. They were at a pretty nice steak and seafood restaurant—one where a dinner for two will cost you at least $100. After checking out the menu, my friend realized that they had a special with two lobster tails and other meals with steak, but no "surf & turf" meal. She asked the waiter if she could have one lobster tail and a steak. As she told me the story the day after, I was thinking to myself that the waiter should have instantly said "Yes" to this request, but I knew that was not where this was going. She went on to describe how the waiter had to talk to the head waiter, who came over to verify the request before holding a conference of waiters, cooks, and staff in the back. Who knew that asking to put two pieces of food (that the restaurant already had on the menu) on the same plate would cause such a commotion? Luckily, my friend did get her "surf & turf" meal and has a great sense of humor and can laugh about the whole thing.

Customer service is about training your employees to know when to follow your policies and procedures, but also about training them to know when they can veer from the norm and say "Yes" to make a customer happy.

And then you have to have a thick skin. No matter how hard you try, you can't please everyone. There will be that random customer that isn't happy and you have to let it go. She/he might say something nasty; you have to let that roll off your back and move on. If you've tried your best and couldn't please someone, learn from that experience, keep a positive attitude, and move on to the next customer, whom you *will* make happy!

Keeping customers informed is the other big challenge for a small business. Let's say you have a new product or are offering a new service. How do your customers know about it? In my dream world, we would telepathically send news to customers while they were sleeping. They would wake up each morning thinking of The Pot & Bead and know all about what was happening at the shop that day. Aaaaahhhh . . . I wish.

A little closer to reality . . . we could call each customer and let them know our news. This isn't far-fetched for a lot of businesses and this kind of marketing to existing customers can pay off. But our customer database contains thousands of names, addresses, and phone numbers—we needed something a little more practical to keep our customers informed.

Practical *and* economical. Remember that every time I opened my checkbook, I thought about what the dollars I spent were going to go out and do for me. See the chapter on marketing and advertising for more details on how to spend and not spend those dollars.

If you're in business today, you have it a little easier with the current social media tools, which are very handy for marketing. They're also free. A later chapter on social media discusses applying these tools to your business.

The thought I want to leave you with here is that keeping customers informed is important, but it's a challenge. Remember that you're a customer, too. Every time you walk into some else's store, cute or otherwise, take note of your experience there. Here are some things I look for:

- Am I being acknowledged by an employee? How well?
- If I have a question, how easy is it to get an answer?

Since owning my own store, I try to be more patient in long lines or when I'm in a busy store. I also like to pay attention to other people's problems. Is the woman in line in front of me yelling at the young girl behind the counter? Why? How is the employee handling it? What could have been done to prevent it?

When this happens, I try to be reassuring to that employee. Most times when I witnessed a situation like this, the employee was used as a verbal punching bag by the disappointed customer. Whatever made the customer unhappy probably wasn't this particular employee's fault, but the customer was too angry or disappointed to be polite or to care. The lesson that I took back to my own store is that I didn't want my employees to be used as verbal punching bags. I tried to empower them to handle the situation—to be able to do something to make the customer happy.

Usually it worked, and usually we had happy customers. And when customers told me they were happy . . . well, that simply made my day.

## No-Nonsense Tips and Tidbits:

- The good: Customers give you money—this is why you're here, why you're in business, and what will keep you in business.
- The bad: Some customers demand *a lot* more for that money than you can give them.
- Do your best to take care of your customers and they will take care of you. As a fellow cute store owner, I can tell you that you're not perfect and you never will be and that when you encounter a customer service issue, resolve it quickly, make the customer as happy as you can, and move on. The negativity from the situation can drag you down—don't let it. Think about those wonderful, great customers who are keeping you in business.

# Chapter 8

# Competition

About a month or so before we opened, I found out that a store similar to my own would be opening just five minutes away. Typically, mine is the kind of business you only have one of per town, not two. Someone else was going to try and take away money from my customers.

On an online forum, I commiserated with other paint-your-own-pottery studio owners I knew across the country. They tried to put me at ease by telling me: "Adeena, what's going to happen is that people in your town will go to both locations, and then go back to the one they like best." Translation: We had to be the best. This really meant that we would have to have superior customer service every day.

Soon after we opened, lots of folks would come into my shop and say things like: "Weird, there's another studio like this over in that other shopping center." They would also ask me: "Are you two affiliated? Owned by the same person?" And what still makes me feel good is that they sat there and told me all the differences between the two studios and why they liked mine better. Even after three years, I still had folks saying nicer things about us in comparison.

There was, however, more competition than just the other paint-your-own-pottery shops around. A main source of our business was birthday parties. This meant that everyone else who offered birthday parties was also my competition, like the local bowling alley, skating rink, pool, and even many local restaurants.

Like I said at the beginning of the chapter, anyone who took money from my customers was my competition. I was in competition with all other forms of entertainment to be the activity the customer chose.

Another NFIB survey on competition (www.411sbfacts.com/files/competition.pdf) reported that nearly half of all small business owners' main competitors are located within ten miles of their business. On the other hand, small business owners operate in highly competitive environments and compete against small and large firms, large chain or box stores, and that competition can be located anywhere on the globe.

This means that in your cute little store, you need to be thinking about the *quality of customer service you offer* and *the quality of your product.* These are the two major ways in which small businesses are able to compete.

One thing I made sure never to do was bad-mouth the competition. If a customer started putting the competition down, I listened politely, but didn't chime in. When I was asked if we were affiliated, I politely said no, it was a coincidence that we opened at similar times, in close proximity. If people asked me if we were alike (when they've heard of the other place, but haven't been there), I politely pointed out our differences, but of course, I didn't say anything bad about the competition. We stayed positive and focused on who we were, and I trained my employees to follow my lead in this area.

Occasionally, a customer might say something good about the competition and that's very hard to hear. (It's like hearing your boyfriend or spouse tell you that his ex was great at something.) But you must resist the temptation to instantly point out one of their flaws in retribution. That's simply too negative. Just smile and nod politely. I mean, the customer is telling you what they think or feel from their own perspective—you don't want to be the person to invalidate that. It might be appropriate to point out what you do that's positive and similar. You might even wind up learning something about improving your business.

How do you compete? What makes you different? What makes you better? These are all questions you have to ask yourself and be prepared to answer. Then, every year or every few months you need to go back and ask these questions again. (There are lots of books on business that cover what is called a S.W.O.T. analysis: looking at your Strengths, Weaknesses, Opportunities, and Threats. See Appendix D.)

What are your differentiators? In a retail business, they can be anything from location to the products you offer. In a retail business like mine, the thing that makes the biggest difference is customer service. Customers want service. They don't want to be ignored or treated badly; they want to be acknowledged, they want their questions answered and their expectations met.

Another thing that set us apart was pricing. Our prices were generally lower than our competition, but we didn't compete on price alone. Although it should be obvious—lower price is (almost) always a better differentiator for a customer—beware of lowering prices *solely* to beat the competition because you might be labeled as a "you get what you pay for" type of business.

Product is another differentiator. Do you offer products your customer wants? We frequently responded to customers who said "I wish you had . . ." by expanding our offerings if and when it was possible. We wanted customers to know that we had the products they wanted.

Other things that might differentiate your business: hours, policies, truly unique products and services, etc. At the end of the day, you need to be able to clearly and concisely say and know what sets you apart from your competition. In order to do that, one of the things you need to be aware of is what the competition is doing and how it may affect your business.

First, understand who your competition is. (Remember from above that it's not only the obvious competitor.) In the county where my store was located, there were three other paint-your-own-pottery stores in operation. Then there were all the other places that did birthday parties. Make a list. Better yet, make a spreadsheet that you can update regularly.

In order to understand what your competition is doing, you have to do some research. The easiest way to begin this process is to look at their websites. I looked for the following information and added it to my spreadsheet:

1. Address and phone number
2. Hours
3. Main products and/or services
4. Pricing (pick a sample product or two)
5. Years in business

This is only the start. Next, if it's at all possible to visit the business, then that's what ya gotta do. If you're like me and feel a little weird walking right into the enemy's territory, then send a proxy.

I frequently sent family, friends, and employees to "spy" on the other paint-your-own-pottery stores and gave them very specific instructions about what to look for. They didn't simply go in, look around a little, and leave. They had to go in, pick a piece, paint it, store some information in their head, and then leave.

(Important No-Nonsense Tip: If you're not in business yet, researching your potential competition is very important and should be included in your business plan. This is especially true if you're seeking financing. One of the things a potential lender wants to see is if you know and understand your competition—only by understanding them can you compete.)

Competition gives me a weird feeling in the gut. I have to admit a little secret here: I really don't like confrontation. So every time I come face to face with competition or something similar, I get a little shaky and am looking for the nearest rock to hide under.

That's one of the many stressful things we all have to deal with. We deal and then move on.

## No-Nonsense Tips and Tidbits:
- The Good: Competition forces you to be better.

- The Bad: There will always be other businesses and people out there competing for your customers' dollars, no matter what you do.
- Know what your competition is up to. Find them on Facebook, Twitter, and send in people to see what they're selling.
- Put on your thick skin, get in there, and compete. Be ready to offer higher quality and better service than your competition.

# Chapter 9

# They Gotta Know You're There

Marketing is getting people to know about your business and convincing them to come in and give you money. I consider advertising to be a subset of marketing; it's the marketing you pay for.

Marketing was one of my largest sources of stress, yet it was also one of the most personally rewarding parts of owning my retail business. It was stressful because you ALWAYS need to think about it. It's great that this month might be a good month, and sales are high, but good sales this month don't necessarily have anything to do with sales next month or the month after. We need to think now about how to get customers through the door in the future. But I say this was rewarding because 1) it allowed me to show my creative side, 2) some marketing events and activities can be directly tied to sales, which was rewarding, and 3) some marketing events generate immediate praise from the people who see them. (Praise is good.) It's important to track marketing events to results—you want to know what worked and what didn't.

Here is a list of specific things we did to market The Pot & Bead. (No-Nonsense Note: WWFMMNWFY—What Works For Me May Not Work For You!)

- Grand Opening

  - What: A few months after we opened, we held the official event where we invited our existing customers to come paint a tile that we would use to decorate one of the walls in our studio. It was completely free, no obligation to buy anything, but we did have a sale for those who wanted to.
  - How well it worked: Really well! We wound up with more than three hundred tiles for our wall and had decent gross sales that weekend, too. Most people who painted a tile decided to paint something else as well.
  - Amount of effort: Ahead of time, we created and mailed out invitations, arranged to have a helium tank for balloons, and ordered food. The two days of the event were a lot of work since we had nearly a full store all day, both days. Afterward, we had the task of glazing and firing all three hundred tiles, then putting them up on our wall.
  - Variations: There's not much I would have changed about this event. It went really well. Years later, people still came into the store to see their tile on the wall. It had the additional effect of making us part of the community.

- Survey (Mailing)

  - What: We sent out a double-sided survey to existing customers in the mail. If they filled out the survey and brought it back in, they would get one dollar off at the store. Each year we did this, the questions focused on a different aspect of our business (i.e., one year we were interested mostly in birthday parties).
  - How well it worked: The first year, it worked well in the sense that I expected to get 1 percent of them back and the return was slightly higher. I figured out that if 1 percent brought it back and used the coupon to paint in the store, the survey would have paid for itself. The second year we did this,

although we got a lot of them back, the mailing was larger (more customers in our database after two years), and it didn't pay for itself.

- ○ Amount of effort: I had to design the survey and the mailing, then have it printed and mailed. The effort was worth it, the cost was not. Several hours would be spent afterward tallying the results.
- ○ Variations: We continued to do surveys, but not through the mail. We transitioned to using an online survey that was emailed to our customers. It's much more cost effective and the results are tallied for you.

- Email Newsletter

  - ○ What: We sent out a newsletter via email approximately twice a month.
  - ○ How well it worked: I think this is one of the best, most cost-effective marketing efforts to employ. We collected customers' email addresses when they came in to the store and added them to the mailing list. They always had the option of removing themselves and I received lots of positive feedback from customers who said they enjoyed receiving and reading our newsletter.
  - ○ Amount of effort: It took quite a bit of creativity to keep this fresh and interesting. It's a good thing that I like to write.

- Attending Local Marketing Events

  - ○ What: In the county where my business was located, we had a very active chamber of commerce that hosted several events throughout the year to let small businesses market themselves.
  - ○ How well it worked: These events gave me the opportunity to make one-on-one contact with other people who could become customers in my store, and several have.

- ○ Amount of effort: That depended on our involvement in the event itself. Some events I only attended and handed out my business card and flyer. At another event, we were the "key sponsor" and took that opportunity to get the other 150 attendees to do some paint-your-own-pottery right there. (Typically the key sponsor gives a 15- to 20-minute speech.) This event required a lot of preparation on our part ahead of time, but we gained several new customers and stood out in the chamber of commerce in a different, positive, and certainly memorable way.

One of the misconceptions of retail that I want to debunk right here: the "build it and they will come" theory. This theory doesn't work in retail, and when it occasionally seems like it does work, it's usually a temporary effect. Marketing is constant. Marketing doesn't go away. You always need to be thinking of how to bring customers to the door. Bringing customers inside is one of the hardest things a retailer has to do.

The Pot & Bead opened right at the beginning of the holiday season: mid-October 2002. We had an *amazing* holiday season, it surpassed all my projections. We did some marketing, but some of the best marketing was done for us before we opened. We were in a brand new building, in the center of our community. In the first year, there was a lot of natural curiosity from people who had driven by the shopping center for months wondering what was coming. There was a lot of anticipation and buildup that we benefited from; but that was just the first year.

A year later, two years later, and beyond, new shopping centers continued to pop up within a few miles of my shop and the anticipation and excitement always seemed to go where something new was happening. Not only did I hear people talk about it, I felt it too.

Let's get back to that major misconception of retail, that "build it and they will come" mentality. It is probably one of biggest myths in retail, and the one that gets the most people into trouble. They don't realize the amount of time and effort they will need to devote to marketing after they've built it. Marketing is a constant activity—whether you've recently opened or are several years into your business.

What happens when you let up? At the start of our third Christmas season, I found myself in the hospital for a week and confined to the bed and couch for almost two weeks after, and it took a while to really get my strength and energy back.

The day-to-day business went on just fine (thanks to the great employees I had!), but since I was the person responsible for marketing, that wasn't getting done. Specifically, email newsletters weren't going out, new flyers weren't made, and special activities that I wanted to plan for winter break didn't get planned. The result: a very unspectacular Christmas season in terms of gross sales.

After that, I tried to plan marketing activities further in advance and gave more marketing-related tasks to my employees. For example, I came up with a flyer or mailing and turned it over to them to have printed and mailed.

## YOUR BUSINESS WEBSITE

I don't care who you are, where you're located, what kind of business you're in: YOU MUST HAVE A WEBSITE (or some permanent place on the Internet like a Facebook page). Period. Don't let anyone convince you otherwise. Also, don't let anyone convince you that you *must* spend a fortune to have one, or to have a decent one. Yes, to a large degree, you get what you pay for, but this is definitely one area where a startup business can scrimp and do something very cheap at the beginning just to have something there.

When you're choosing a name for your business, consider choosing your website address at the same time. Ideally, you want them to be one and the same—it makes it easier for people to look you up and tell others about you.

Many, many, many good books have been written about how to set up a website, so I won't go into all the details of how to do it here but I will tell you that once you have your website up, make sure it has the following:

- Your address and phone number prominently displayed! This is not information that someone should have to hunt for.

- If your business is one with regular hours (as opposed to, say, a consultant), again, make those super easy to find.
- Put your website address on everything else! Business cards, flyers, advertisements—anything that will get into the hands of potential customers.

Once your website is set up, there are other ways to advertise it online, like the cost-per-click advertising systems that Google, Yahoo, and Facebook offer. When you set up this kind of advertising account, you essentially say, "I want people who search for X to see my ad," where "X" is your product or service. So, your ad pops up when people search for "X" and you pay if and when the person actually clicks on your ad, taking them to your website. Managing your ads is actually a little more complicated and takes some effort on your part to set up the correct search words and ad text, but you get the idea.

Did you read Chapter 7 on Customers? Here's where keeping track of all that customer data becomes really important: targeted marketing. We want to bring customers in with the least amount of money and effort, right? One of the best ways to do that is to target customers you already have and try to let them know about new products or services that are similar to ones they've purchased from you before. For example, all those customers who purchased a toothbrush holder in 2003 might be interested in the new soap dish on the shelves. Or all those customers who attended one of our special events might want to know that we're holding another similar special event. In that case, we might send out an invitation to only those customers instead of our whole database, or a random selection of people in the town. We target a hundred customers who've purchased the product or service before, who we believe would purchase again, instead of sending out 10,000 mailings to people we don't know.

Remember, marketing is important to *any* and *every* business venture. Writing this book is another excellent example. My time and money went into this project, the book got published, and is available for sale.

I need to tell people about it, I need to get the word out. (How did you find out about this book? Who put it in your hand?) If you're reading this, then however you found out about it, you did, therefore some form of marketing worked. That's wonderful!

I hope that you're enjoying it and I hope you will tell someone else about it. You can find me talking about this book and ask me questions at: twitter.com/adeena

## No-Nonsense Tips and Tidbits:

- Marketing is where you can unleash your creative side.
- If you're doing it right, you can boost your sales—always a good thing!
- You can never stop marketing. You can never take a break. It's nearly impossible to sit back and relax.
- Marketing is an ongoing effort for the small business owner. You can't rely on the "build it and they will come" theory. They won't come if they don't know about you, think about you, remember you, or have a good reason to.

# Chapter 10

# Putting the Social in Social Media

When I opened the doors to The Pot & Bead, there was no Twitter, no Groupon or Pinterest, not even Facebook. The term "social media" didn't even exist. I was left with what are now considered to be "traditional" or even antiquated (depending on who you talk to) means to advertise. Oh, we had a website, of course, but at the time I opened the doors, our core users had not yet become the super savvy online shoppers that they are now.

I'm jealous, because in 2007 when I signed up for my personal Facebook and Twitter accounts, I could see how fantastic it would be for business if only my customers were also using these sites. I even created a Twitter account for The Pot & Bead in late 2007 and gave my employees access to it. I told them to Tweet interesting things. Now this was also in the time before one could Tweet pictures—which would have been very useful to our business.

The account still exists. There were a grand total of fourteen tweets, mostly posted by my employees. The last one was posted on June 26, 2007:

"unpacking some new pottery, now we have penguins and Spiderman banks!!!"

Unfortunately, at the time we only had maybe ten followers, and half of those might have been my newly converted tweeting employees.

We closed our doors in early 2008, before the social media boom. Today, there are more than a billion people who use Facebook every month, half a billion Twitter accounts, and Pinterest, a fairly new site and one of my favorites, is already up to over twenty-five million users and growing. I've connected with former customers and former employees (the same ones who gave me weird looks when I gave them our Twitter account password) on Facebook and LinkedIn. Oh, I am so jealous of businesses today that they get to connect with their customers in this way!

Before going any further into this chapter, I have to make a few assumptions that you're one of the following:

- You've heard of Facebook and Twitter, and maybe some other sites
- You want to do as much free stuff as possible in your business
- Your time is limited, or you're worried about wasting too much time
- You're worried that you're going to open up a way for people to take unfair pot-shots at your business
- You either already embrace social media or you don't
- If you embrace it, maybe you're not making the most of it?
- You embrace it, you love it, you see how it already helps your business (in this case, you might want to skip to the next chapter).

Susan VonAchen, a social media strategist and expert in social media marketing, acknowledges that today more people understand what social media is "and they're able to figure out at least a little bit of it. Enough to get them started." What you shouldn't do is ignore social media. Your competition probably doesn't. Your customers probably don't. (Now is when you might want to take a break from reading and search for your competition on Facebook or Twitter.)

My purpose is to convince you to embrace it without letting it take over your life. Social media is free. It doesn't have to be—there are social media experts who you can pay to help set up your social media campaign. Personally, I would prefer to do everything that you can for free first, then if you get stuck, call in some expert help. I have nothing against the experts. They are business owners, too! But it's the same reason I haven't yet hired anyone to clean my house. I can do it myself. When there comes a point I think I need that time more than I need that money, I'll hire someone else to clean it. Until then, I'll clean my own house, thank you!

Have you heard the term "word of mouth advertising"? Probably, and you probably understand the basic concept: a happy or unhappy customer tells his friends about his good or bad experiences with a business. Ideally, you want that customer to have had a happy experience and to tell his friends about how awesome your business is and how they should become customers, too.

When I had The Pot & Bead—remember it was pre-social media—word of mouth was *truly* word of mouth. The idea was (and still is) to make it easy for a happy customer to spread the word. We tried a few tricks in that regard. We handed out "bring a friend" coupons and gave existing customers cards to give to their friends for a discount when they came in for the first time.

Online, there wasn't a lot to do at the time except put a "share" button on our website. The share button would bring up a form that people could email to others with a link to our site. We also sent out a regular email newsletter with similar opportunities to forward on to others. But that was mostly it. Our options were limited.

Today, a few short years later, your options as a business owner have expanded greatly. It is so easy to "like" a business page on Facebook, and when you like it, your friends can see that you've liked it, and, based on your endorsement (since you wouldn't like it if you *hated* it), they might like it to. I've done that once or twice. I liked my local farmer's market and even a couple of restaurants.

When I started to write this chapter, I realized I was going to need to get in touch with other business owners to get some of their stories. Where did I go looking for them? The Internet. I tapped into my own social media network—I posted on my Facebook, Twitter, and LinkedIn accounts asking people to share their stories. (See, I'm not really the novice at social media that I pretend to be.) It worked, although not all the stories I received really fit what I was looking for—many friends were eager to share stories about how they reconnected with long-lost high school buddies, others had Groupon horror stories to share. I don't consider Groupon and similar sites like Living Social to be "social media." They are more properly characterized as "social coupon" sites. If you've heard of them and are considering them, please Google the topic and find some other business owners who've used them before diving in.

People responded because what I was trying to do was socialize. That's putting the "social" in social media right there. Indirectly, I'm still promoting myself and my books, because that's the undertone of the reason why I'm posting anything, but my goal was to interact with customers. You see, social media is all about promoting yourself, but it's also about being available to interact with current or potential customers.

David Troy, owner of the startup 410labs (410labs.com) was an early social media adopter and promotes the mantra of authenticity: "I think the key is in using tools appropriately. Social media is not a silver bullet and it always has to be authentic. You can't use it to sell garbage, and you can't fake your message. If you can be really authentic then it tends to have solid rewards."

Susan VonAchen agrees, adding: "Buyers are expecting transparency. They want to know who they're buying from, who they're partnering with. Buyers are shopping where their friends shop. That's how social media comes into play."

Sound familiar? You're a consumer, too. If you need a product or service, would you rather open the phone book and pick a business at random, or ask your friends who they used? Social media simply makes it easier for consumers to have these conversations, directly or indirectly, with each other. As a business, you want to make sure it's easy for them to have that conversation about your business!

I also had the pleasure of speaking with Laura Talbert, owner of two businesses, including a tattoo parlor, and a social media coordinator for a third. I asked her about the conversations she has on social media sites and if she directly correlates them to sales. It's not always easy, but Laura knows that her customers are listening when they come in to one of her shops and reference something that was posted on Facebook a month prior. Sales might not be an immediate return on investment via a click-through, but if you have something interesting to say, someone will be listening.

And people really are listening and reading, which means you never, ever, ever want to turn a negative review or comment into a shouting match. You also don't necessarily want to delete it from public view. Laura had, what I think was, the perfect solution to this problem. Someone had posted a negative comment about her modeling business. She didn't respond right away—she slept on it. That's something we should all do for *any* negative situation.

She thought about deleting the comment but knew that wouldn't really help anyone. Anyone and everyone in business is going to run into something negative at some point—people know that—but Laura felt that addressing it publically wasn't appropriate. Instead, she wrote a response similar to the following: "I hear your concerns and will respond via a private message." It tells anyone watching that she's willing to address a situation. So anyone else might feel more comfortable doing business with Laura knowing that she's not going to run and hide when things get difficult.

While The Pot & Bead didn't have tons of social media experience, I do have some myself. My books on the business are a mini-business itself. I have a product I'm trying to sell: the books. A simple business, yes, but business nonetheless. There are expenses and income involved, and I continue to use social media to promote them. I have accounts on Twitter and LinkedIn. I try to be the most interactive on LinkedIn and answer questions that other business owners have. I often don't directly tell them to buy my book—but the concept is that if they respect what I have to say, it's obvious that I'm also an author and they might become interested in the book that way.

When I am in "book promote" mode, I log on and scroll through the new questions users post on message boards. I look for not just anything, but things I know I can answer primarily about starting a business from scratch. Questions like: "How do I write a business plan?" or "How do I handle this employee?"

The worst response I could imagine providing would start out like this: "The first thing to do is to buy and read my book . . ." Instead, the best responses, and the ones I try to provide, simply answer the question asked: "Here are the steps to writing a business plan . . ." or "Sit down with your employee and have a face-to-face discussion . . ."

Often, I wouldn't even mention my book in the text of the response. I think there was one occasion where the question was explicitly asking about small business books—in that case, it was appropriate to respond with mine, so I would end my response like this:

"Hope this helps! Feel free to email me if you have any other questions on this topic.

—Adeena Mignogna

Author of . . ."

How much time does this marketing take? Certainly more than five minutes a day, but my time spent goes up and down to match the available time I have. It's true that you'll get out of it what you put into it. During the months I consistently spend 2–3 hours or more per week on this method of promotion, my book sales go up.

Social media is worth the time because it's free. Mostly. Yes, you can pay for ads that show up on Facebook. Yes, you can pay an expert to help you with your campaign. But you don't have to, and with a little planning, it doesn't have to suck up too much of your other precious resource: time.

As I said earlier in the chapter, I assume that you are familiar with sites like Facebook and Twitter and maybe some others. You might not have your own account, but most people you come in contact with will. More important, chances are your customers and potential customers will. So while you might not engage in sharing the latest pictures of your kids, or passing around snarky images, or telling everyone what you had for dinner, well, these aren't the kinds of things you'd likely post in relation to your business anyway (unless you're a photographer, graphic designer, or chef). Therefore, spend a little time, don't spend any money, and set up an account on one or more of these sites.

Which sites? How do you choose?

First, consider polling existing customers. What social media sites are they on? Second, which sites are your competitors using? Consider setting up accounts on the same sites because your competition might have already figured out that customers are there.

After that, here is my two cents on what sites you should use. (Note that the Internet is an ever-changing medium, and a year or two years from now, some of these sites might not exist—but more likely, there will be something even newer and better.)

For any business, at a minimum, I would set up a Twitter account. If your business has a visual component to your products, I'd set up a Pinterest account. Maybe an Instagram account as well. If your business is a product or service to other businesses, I'd set up a LinkedIn account. If your business has a physical location, make sure you're on Yelp. And I can't think of any reason why any business wouldn't want or couldn't use a Facebook page.

Finally, think like a consumer. When you want a new product or service, where and who do you turn to? Where do you read reviews? What are your competitors doing? If I search for "paint your own pottery stores" online, I see several on Pinterest, and that would have been one of my target social media sites too because of the visual components.

What if you're a service business? You're an accountant or consultant and you don't make a physical product? My own accountant regularly posts on Facebook to let people know that there have been changes to the tax code, that he's teaching an upcoming seminar, etc.

No matter what type of business you have, you could also create your own infographic, which is an image representation of information, like a subway map. It should be one page or less and a size someone could view on his computer screen all at once. Choose a pleasing, bold color for the background and a bold font that's easy to read—or choose two. Write down the key components to your business on the graphic related to something your customers want to learn. For example, I would title my infographic for The Pot & Bead: "How to Paint." Then, I would list four to five steps of painting: 1. Choose your piece of pottery, a brush, a paint color. 2. Take a pencil and draw a design. 3. Use light colors first. 4. Paint three coats. Then I would post it to all of my social media sites. Even if you're a service business, this is a great way to create some content and circulate it. Remember to put your business name, website, Twitter feed, etc. somewhere visible at the bottom. This method promotes your service but also shows that you have something useful to say.

I'll finish by saying that in researching this chapter, I read several other books on using social media to promote and grow your business. Most of them, since they are site specific, might be out of date in a few months from now. But there were two that I firmly believe will stand the test of time a little more because they relate to how you, as a business owner, promote yourself online regardless of the specific site in question. These two books are *Likeable Social Media* and *Likeable Business*, both by Dave Kerpen. The first book is very Facebook focused, but I think the messages he conveys are important:

- Have a conversation
- Listen to your customers
- Provide content, don't simply forward other people's content (although do forward if relevant)
- Be professional in your postings—remember that these are public forums

If you really and truly are a newbie, there are and will continue to be lots of books and websites to help get you started. *Facebook for Dummies*, *Twitter for Dummies*, and even *Social Media Marketing for Dummies* are all really good starting points and will likely still be available since the series does get updated periodically. Kindle also has a host of free books available at any given time, including books on this topic.

Because I attempt to practice what I preach, I'm on social media, too, and I agree with Dave Kerpen that even a book can be social. Ask me any questions you'd like over on: twitter.com/adeena

## No-Nonsense Tips and Tidbits:

- Set up accounts on places like Twitter, Facebook, and LinkedIn
- Take some time to learn how the sites work
- Listen to what others are saying
- Be professional at all times, even if a customer posts something negative about your business
- Take any unpleasantness out of public view, but let the public know you addressed it
- Take a survey of existing customers: What do they use?
- Find your competition online
- Ask customers who've had a good experience to post positively about it

# Chapter 11

# Hard Work Does Not Equal Money in Your Pocket

George I., who recently sold his successful small medical practice and was on his way to a secure and active retirement, asked me this question regarding starting my own business: "For love or money?"

I replied, chuckling a little, "For love *of* money."

The reality is, if there wasn't at least the potential to make more money than we are currently making we wouldn't be in business for ourselves. It might not be on the very top of the priority list, but it's going to be at least in the top three, right? You can admit it, there's no shame in that. However, if money turns out to be your *only* motivation, then there might be a problem.

"It takes money to make money" is probably one of the truest statements I've ever heard. Be wary of a business that requires little money up front, like micro-franchises that proclaim "Spend $500 for this kit on how to sell X and make millions!" Why? One reason is that it makes for easy competition.

The Pot & Bead was initially financed mostly with a Small Business Administration (SBA) guaranteed loan. Many people, including myself, get this confused with an "SBA loan." There really is no such thing as an "SBA loan." In general, the SBA isn't in the business of loaning out money themselves, although they do have some special programs like microloans. You can find all the information about the loans they offer on their website, www.sba.gov, and more specific information at www.sba. gov/category/navigation-structure/loans-grants/small-business-loans/ sba-loan-programs.

What the SBA actually does is guarantee loans. What does this mean? This means that if my business goes under and I am unable to repay the loan, the SBA guarantees 85 percent of it to the bank. Meaning, the bank will be able to get 85 percent of its money back from the SBA. The catch that most people don't realize at the beginning is that you're still required to pay the SBA back.

One thing that took me a while to understand was the issue of collateral. When you have an SBA guaranteed loan, if you have collateral, you need to put it up to secure the loan. At the time, I was recently married and my husband and I had just bought a house. We had very little equity in it. This was also the time when interest rates were declining to (near) record lows. We were under the impression that you didn't need to put your house up as collateral for this kind of loan. We had that impression because we knew other people who did not own a house and had no significant collateral but had still gotten an SBA-guaranteed loan. We learned that the SBA does not require you to put up equity in a home or significant collateral if you don't have any, but if you have it, you do need to put it up.

My now ex-husband was not the most supportive person in this venture. We mistakenly thought that since he wasn't 100 percent on board with my opening a store, that he wouldn't need to be involved at all. I thought my business affairs were mine alone and he wouldn't need to sign things. Wrong again. The fact that we were married made the business a joint asset—he was just as legally and personally responsible as I was. This meant that he had to sign the loan and the lease. My business partner's spouse had to as well.

The biggest mistake we made was in not really shopping around for a bank. One of the first things you'll read about in most books on starting a business is that you shouldn't necessarily go with the first bank that says yes—you should shop around for rates and terms. That's not so easy in practice when you're anxious to get your business started!

We put in applications with two banks at the same time and were in the process of going around collecting the paperwork to apply at more banks. The first bank said no. Now chances are, you're going to hear that a couple of times. It happens all the time in life—college applications, job interviews, etc. It is, however, a bit of a blow to the ego. Once this starts to happen, you get worried. Is *anyone* going to give us a loan? Will it happen on our timescale? We wanted to be in business by the start of the Christmas shopping season—would it happen? We couldn't sign a lease without a loan commitment. So, when the second bank said "Yes!" (and their terms were reasonable) we abandoned all plans to pursue working with any other bank.

Obviously, because I'm telling you this, there were problems. The first problem was what most people go through when they are doing something new: we didn't know the right questions to ask. Therefore, we didn't get all the information we needed at the beginning. This really only affected our (specifically, my) stress level during the loan process.

The one big question I recommend asking is: What should we expect during this process? (Meaning: How long should it take?) Other related questions to ask are: Will I (and possibly my spouse) need to take time off work to sign papers? Are there papers we need to gather ahead of time to make the process go much faster?

Knowing what to expect would have taken away a lot of the stress and saved a couple of "Oh, I didn't know you needed that piece of paper," which dragged the process out to be longer than was really necessary.

One of the questions we did ask was whether or not my business partner and I would be able to refinance our homes. After all, this was during a period of time when interest rates kept dropping. We were told by the bank that it wouldn't be a problem. When it's time to refinance, apparently the bank temporarily "lifts" the loan off the house for a day so the refinance can happen, then puts the loan back on.

Well, it turned out it was a problem. My husband and I were not able to refinance our home. Now that's stress. To this day, I'm still not

100 percent sure why it didn't happen. The mortgage company had all the papers and were ready to go to closing, but then no one (not me, my husband, nor the mortgage company) could get a hold of anyone at the bank that held our business loan. No one at the bank would call us back!

A little more than a year later, I wound up refinancing the business loan with another bank. This time I shopped around. Actually, I had met several bankers through the local chamber of commerce I belonged to. One in particular, and his family, had been one of my first customers at the store. I felt that because of this, he knew and understood my business and my business concerns a little better so I wound up using his bank. (The terms and rates were slightly better, too.) Relationships in business are very important. From day one, anyone looking to go into business for themselves should be cultivating helpful and productive relationships with others in their community.

One major thing we did *right* with the first business loan was to get a loan that included enough working capital (cash available for day-to-day operations of a business) to get through the first several months. Another thing we did right was hire an accountant from the beginning. We initially wanted to only apply for the startup expenses, but my accountant pointed out that this was not a good idea. Lots of businesses fail because they don't have enough working capital, meaning, they don't have enough money to pay expenses for some period of time while they are building the business and trying to increase sales. Therefore, we made sure that our loan included not only our startup expenses, but enough capital to cover us for approximately the first six months of business. I'm not sure we would have survived without that. My accountant also helped put together the financial section of the business plan and has been with me ever since.

But, of course, there were a bunch of mistakes that were made with money after the store opened. Some of these involved personal finances— remember that I had recently given up my engineering job and salary so my personal finances and habits went through a drastic change. This took a while to get used to. During that time, I made one major mistake: I bought a new car. I paid off my old car a few months before the store opened, but for some reason, about two months after we opened, I was convinced that I had to buy a new one. It was a completely emotional decision; I was tired and working so much, I hadn't done a single fun thing for myself in months. Somehow, buying a new car made sense to me at the time. About six months later, I realized it was a horrible mistake since it added a burden on me financially.

Years later, though I still acknowledged it was a mistake, it was one that I finally came to terms with. If I could go back in time, I wouldn't have done it, but eventually I didn't feel the pressure of the monthly payment anymore.

For a small business owner, money is always on your mind in some form or another. (No-Nonsense Tip: Purchasing good accounting software, like QuickBooks, is a must and absolutely should be included in your startup budget.)

Here are some items you need to consider as a business or cute little store owner:

**Paying yourself**: How much can I pay myself? I put this one first since it's probably the first question one who is contemplating a new business wants answered. It's going to vary, business by business, but going into something new, you shouldn't expect to pay yourself for a year or more. Yep—I said a *year* or *more*. So start saving now . . . before you quit that day job, make sure you have enough in the bank to pay your own living expenses for that period of time. (This includes paying off personal debt like credit cards and car loans.)

**Paying employees:** How much depends on a lot of things like experience level and local going rate. Make sure you're aware of the current local, state, and federal minimum wages. Make sure you're aware of the regulations governing employees and things like how and when you can, or are in some cases, required to pay overtime. See The US Department of Labor's website (www.dol.gov/dol/topic/wages/) for a good introduction to things you need to know about paying employees. For my own business, payroll was my highest expense after rent.

**Accountants:** If you're not one yourself, then you're probably not an expert on taxes. If for no other reason, this is why you should hire an accountant. Mistakes can be costly! The best way to find a good accountant is to ask other local small business owners who they use. A good accountant can also help you understand the entire financial picture of your business. The going rate for an accountant varies by location, so ask around to get an idea of the rate. Over the years, I paid approximately between $100–250 per hour.

**Taxes:** There's a colorful array of federal, state, and local taxes that businesses are subject to, which vary from state to state and county to county. For this reason, I highly recommend seeking out a good accountant to help. No matter where you're located, it's likely that there will be at least one type of tax that's due monthly (like sales tax) and there are several federal taxes due quarterly. If you estimate how much your sales are per month, then you can estimate your sales tax. Other taxes can come out to be as much as a few thousand dollars, quarterly! (They depend on your sales, payroll, etc.)

When I first opened the shop, I thought I would do it myself, but it was way too confusing. (Did I mention I'm an engineer with a degree in physics? I'm not stupid, but I couldn't figure this tax thing out.) My accountant visited me once a month to prepare all the tax returns. I only needed to write the checks and get them in the mail.

Your personal taxes also become more complicated now. Before owning The Pot & Bead, I did my personal tax returns on my own, but the accountant does them now as well.

**Insurance:** You need insurance. What kind and how much will depend on the kind of business you have, your location, your financing, your landlord, etc. At a minimum, expect to have a business policy that covers your business property, and if you're working anywhere outside your house, expect to have some kind of accident liability policy. If you have financing from a bank loan, you will likely be required to have a life insurance policy. If you have employees, you'll be required to provide worker's compensation insurance and the rules governing worker's compensation vary from state to state. Your insurance agent should know the rules in your state. Don't be afraid to shop around for better rates.

**Lawyers:** Do you need to pay a lawyer? Sigh. There are a lot of books on starting your own small business that make it seem like you can do a lot of things on your own. There are books on "Legal Forms for Small Business" that many people recommend new entrepreneurs buy as a way to save money in the beginning.

I recommend that you read these books because they will help you understand some standard contracts like leases and sales agreements. But then when it comes down to it, you still want a lawyer to review any legal document that you might sign.

Just like looking for an accountant, ask around to see who other small business owners use. When you're working with the lawyer, don't be afraid to ask ahead of time how much time they expect to spend reviewing something like your lease. If you think it's too long, say so. Find someone who you can really work with.

**Credit Cards:** You will likely need one for your business. Luckily, as in your personal life, there are a lot of credit card offers out there that come with rewards like cash back on purchases or airline miles. But just as in your personal life, credit card debt is not good to carry around with you. Hopefully, before you start your business, you're free from any personal credit card debt.

**Advertising Costs:** We touched on this in the chapter on marketing. I'll repeat the important points here: 1) any marketing you can do for free should be done, 2) keep good records of what you paid and what business you believe was generated from a particular advertisement, 3) keep records of other advertising offers (i.e., today you might not be interested in the package that was sent to you about advertising on your local cable network, but tomorrow when you're planning, you might want to know how much it would have cost).

**Profit/Loss:** . . . or as it's usually called: P&L. This is one of several financial statements you'll want to review on a monthly basis for a financial picture of your business. Software like QuickBooks can output this report on request. There are several good books on small business finance that can help you understand this statement. (Some are listed in Appendix D.)

**Budgeting:** I found that this gets easier with time. The first year of business was an educated guess. After three years, I had much more solid data to base my budget on (i.e., I looked at how much I spent on inventory in a certain month one year to have a gauge for how much I'd spend the following year in that same month on inventory). There are several books out there that can help you figure out how a startup budget and business plan should look. However, they don't give the prospective new business owner an idea of the numbers that go in there—that will take research on your part.

**Personal vs. Business Finance**: These are unfortunately not always as separate as one might like them to be. I have my personal bank account, and I have a business bank account (with the business name and address and myself listed as the signatory). I have credit cards that once were personal, but are now used only for the business. Any credit extended to me for the business (this can be anything from a bank loan to setting up a utility, like the phone) goes on my personal credit report.

The good news is that many things that I used to pay for personally can be paid for by the business, like gas for the car and my cell phone. They're used for the business, so they're business expenses.

**Borrowing from Relatives/Friends:** There's good and bad here. Many books on financing a small business recommend seeking out relatives and friends that will help finance your business with a personal loan. While there are many benefits, like the fact that this loan won't show up on your credit report and your family probably won't repossess your house if your business fails and you can't pay them back, there's an emotional side to consider too. What happens to your relationship with this person if you can't pay the loan back right away, or ever? Will it be forever damaged?

If you're going to borrow money from a family member or friend, there are two things you should do:

1. Get a loan agreement in writing. Agree on the amount and repayment terms and write it all down.
2. Make sure that this person can handle the risk. They are taking a risk. Make sure that if the worst happens—the business fails

and the money is lost—the person who loaned it to you can live without it.

## No-Nonsense Tips and Tidbits:

- Accountants are helpful, especially if you're not an accountant or financial wizard yourself. An accountant is very useful in helping to sort out taxes and all other business expenses.
- It's true that you need to build relationships in business, especially with your accountant and lawyer.
- Decisions based on emotion will bite back every time (i.e., settling for the first bank that says "Yes" to your loan application or making a major unnecessary purchase).
- Not having the capital to get you through the crucial startup phase of your business can kill your business in the first year!
- Keep your debt load as small as possible. Learn all you can about money and finances. Hire a good accountant and ask lots of questions.

# Chapter 12

# Other Things that Keep You Up at Night

We all handle stress in different ways. Stress affects me by keeping me from getting a good night's sleep. And it's not always the big things that will do this to you, sometimes it's the little things.

The point of this chapter is to make you aware of all the other little things that happen once you're the owner of that cute little store. These are all the behind-the-scenes things that the customer who comes in and says, "You've got such a cute little store here!" will never know about. These are the things that give you headaches and cause never-ending amounts of stress.

Water has been my arch-nemesis ever since my first apartment was flooded in college. Now, no matter where I go, it seems determined to break my spirit.

Within the first couple of months at The Pot & Bead, we had to call a plumber in to fix the toilet and back room sink. The sink still didn't work well for a long while after. The hot water refused to turn off all the way so we would use the off valve under the sink to control it. (I finally realized that instead of paying a plumber hundreds of dollars, I could buy a book on plumbing from Home Depot and fix it myself.)

The hot water was also too hot, but on busy Saturdays during the winter months, we would run out of hot water long before the day was over.

**Mini-Lessons Learned:** 1) In the lease, be clear what the landlord will and will not be responsible for after you take possession of your space, 2) If you yourself are not handy with minor plumbing and electrical things, find a friend who is before running off to spend tons of money on a contractor. I've learned that many things that seem to be a big deal can be fixed on my own, or with the help of a friend.

Things will break when you least expect it. Make sure you or someone else are prepared to deal with that. This includes:

- Keeping all the manuals in one place where anyone can access them.
- Empowering employees to take action when something breaks.

**Mini-Lessons Learned:** Similar to above—keep things written down, know who can fix what, and teach employees to fix things.

Our computer, which we used as our cash register, needed rebooting a lot. Our kilns, which were our main production equipment, would break often. It seemed like every other week it was something. One time, an employee told me that the heat didn't seem to be working in the middle of winter. "Oh poo," I thought. (Okay, I'll admit . . . I said a word to myself that was much less polite than "poo.") Since our first winter, we knew that there was a flaw in the heating unit's circuit board, which required occasionally going into the circuit breaker box and flipping a switch. At least a month earlier, I had told this employee about that over the phone. Now, with the heat not working again, she told me she had flipped the switch, but it didn't work.

I figured that before I go call an expensive contractor (No-nonsense tidbit: I'm not implying that all contractors are really expensive, but when you planned on spending zero dollars, spending anything more can sometimes be too much to handle emotionally and break the budget), I would try it for myself. I flipped the switch and viola! We had heat! (Turns out my employee hadn't flipped the right switch—apparently I wasn't that clear over the phone.) I was stressed out for an entire day for what thankfully turned out to be nothing.

**Mini-Lessons Learned:** Troubleshooting skills are important. Have backup plans available; have backup equipment, if possible. Stay calm and remember to laugh after the fact.

My cell phone—it was always on. I wished I could turn it off, but I couldn't. It's my business, it's my store, and at any point in time, something really bad can happen and I need to be reached.

Even when the store was closed for the day, I couldn't turn it off. What if there was another burglary? What if I'm going somewhere and my cell phone doesn't get service? I thought I had to prepare a backup plan so there would be different ways of reaching me if needed.

This was a constant source of stress that wouldn't go away as long as I was the business owner. It was something that I eventually got used to, I think. It eventually stopped keeping me up at night, but I would cringe every time my phone rang with the feeling of "What now?" To get rid of that feeling, I always reminded my employees that they were allowed to call me when something really good happened (like a customer just spent a lot of money, or they got wonderful compliments about the store, etc.), and they did.

**Mini-Lessons Learned:** Your business is part of your life and if certain aspects are a constant source of stress, you need to find a way to deal with that, or else it will burn you out. Find ways to turn negatives into positives.

There is an excellent book out there called *The Small Business Owner's Guide to Getting a Good Night's Sleep*. The point of that book is that lots of bad things can happen, yet you can be prepared for many of them.

It took me a long time to get through reading that book. Planning for the worst is a hard emotional thing to do. I could barely get through a chapter without becoming incredibly tense and stressed out. Finally,

I convinced myself that several of the issues the book raised were ones I needed to deal with. Most were not too difficult, they only required some thought and writing those thoughts down.

Having procedures for worst case scenarios was the best way to handle this stress (if you don't even have procedures for basic day-to-day stuff, go back to Chapter 5 on Employees and read about why you need them).

## No-Nonsense Tips and Tidbits:

- All the little things that can happen and keep you up at night can be dealt with.
- All the little things that can happen DO happen, often when you least expect it (or five minutes after you thought you could go home for the day).
- The more prepared you are, the better you will sleep at night. You can practice laughing at my mishaps in the hope that when it actually happens to you, you'll be able to laugh afterward, too.

# Chapter 13

# How to Survive Those First Two Years

With all the bad stuff that can happen, is it even *possible* to survive? Yes, absolutely. Read on for how to get a good start on your new business. Already in business? That's okay, you can still catch up and regain your sanity.

## BUSINESS PLANNING

. . . is exactly what it sounds like: planning and research. The first step is creating a business plan. I don't care what business you're in, you need a business plan. Let me say it again: YOU NEED A BUSINESS PLAN. Find a small business that failed in the first two years and I'm willing to put money on it they didn't have a business plan.

If you go to a bank or other institution for a loan, they'll ask you to include a business plan with your loan application. If you rent retail space, lots of landlords will ask to see your business plan as part of their decision making process. If you don't need either of the above, you still need a business plan, but it probably doesn't have to be as elaborate. In this case, you are the reader and you can get away with a minimalistic plan. In this case, you need it for YOU. Your business plan will clearly define your business. It will outline your goals. Yes, you might have all that in your head. That's not good enough. Get it on paper. The act of putting things on paper solidifies your business concept and can help you identify flaws before they sink your dreams.

A friend of mine, who's now on his third business, learned the hard way the first time around. He had a great idea for a consulting/seminar business, and was so eager to get going, that he simply got going. He had no business plan, no financial plan, no plan to bring money in, but he was paying a lot of money out in advertising and other costs. He couldn't keep it up for too long before he realized it wasn't working out the way it was going. Luckily, he didn't lose too much money. But, he learned that he needed a business plan before starting his next venture. (Also, luckily, this experience didn't kill his entrepreneurial spirit.)

If you don't have a business plan, go grab a couple sheets of paper. Yes, right now. Get a pen, too. On the top, write the name of your new business. If you don't have a name, write something like "Adeena's Bookstore" (substitute "Adeena" with your name and "Bookstore" with whatever business you're planning). Underneath, write one or two sentences about what the business actually is: "Adeena's Bookstore is/will be a specialty retail bookstore focusing on the science fiction and fantasy genres."

If you need further help writing and developing your business plan, see Appendix D for a good reference. Your local small business development center is also a great resource.

## ORGANIZATION

This is one major area where WWFMMNWFY (What works for me may not work for you), but at the end of the day, you need to be organized. I truly believe that at least 70 percent of running an operating business is keeping up with all the paperwork. Mail, bills, vendor catalogs, solicitations, applications, tax forms, advertising rate sheets, etc. build up VERY quickly.

Early on, ideally on day one, you'll want to establish a system for keeping yourself organized. Many papers in business can't be thrown away.

A lot of papers you won't want to throw away—what if that customer comes back? What if you want to compare this guy's advertising rates with someone else's? What did you buy last summer?

I started out with a small hanging file folder box that I quickly outgrew. I upgraded to heavy duty plastic stackable cabinets with hanging file folders; they're easier to move around than the old-fashioned metal file cabinets (as I found out recently when I rearranged my office at home).

What worked for me was hiring a professional organizer. This is someone who I routinely ran into at my local chamber's networking events. After being in business less than a year, I had so many things to do that I was nearly paralyzed and felt like I couldn't get anything done. I hired her to help me with organization and time management.

That was one of the best things I did for myself during that first year. (No-nonsense tidbit: A retail consultant I've worked with has a hard time believing that most small business owners don't devote any time or resources to continuing personal development.) She helped me consolidate and reorganize my to-do list and helped me realize that there isn't enough time to get EVERYTHING done, therefore everything can't be a number one priority.

The next spring, through my local chamber of commerce, she was offering a three-part course on organization. The course covered some of the time management topics we worked on the previous summer as well as other physical organization skills. It was offered at a significant discount through the chamber, so I went. (No-Nonsense Tip: A good chamber is a good resource for the small business owner.) I'm glad I did. I was able to finally get my home office together. The previous month, my office had been such a disaster that it was preventing me from getting anything useful done. I couldn't even look in that room without feeling the stress bubbling up. It's much better now.

I liken organization to something like Weight Watchers. You don't go once and get fixed automatically. It's a constant process that involves some commitment and self-discipline, and you occasionally need external reminders.

## YOUR TEAM OF EXPERTS

Having a good accountant and a good lawyer are definitely the first places to start. You can't be an expert on everything—there are areas of your business where you will need help. Developing good relationships with some key experts will definitely help to preserve some of your sanity and avoid mistakes.

During the early business planning stages, I read an article in a local newspaper about an accountant who recently went out on his own and specialized in helping small business startups. It was perfect. He was intimately involved in the earliest financial models for my business and is still my accountant today.

Finding a good lawyer was harder. That's mostly because of my own biases against lawyers—I always had this feeling that too many of them are simply milking you.

So, initially, we didn't want a lawyer to do anything but the absolute minimum—help us set up an operating agreement and file the proper paperwork to form the Limited Liability Company (LLC).

However, as business developed and new things happened (like when I wanted to buy someone else's store), I realized that lawyers do perform a valuable service in today's society and economy. Later, I realized that I wanted a lawyer who understood my business a little better, who would be a little more involved, and who would be there as the business grew.

## BUILDING A SUPPORT SYSTEM

Your support system is made up of the people and things that will keep you sane. They might be your spouse, family, or best friend. They might be the hobbies and things you like to do.

Make sure there's at least one person in your life who you can openly talk to about your business. Many times this will be your spouse. This should be someone not super involved in your business, but someone who's supportive nonetheless. I had my significant other, my ex-husband, my father, and the rest of my family and friends. (I'm very lucky.)

It is lonely at the top, even if it's the top of a small business. I didn't think I was going to miss not having colleagues anymore—not having those people to discuss my work with. I also didn't think I was going to miss one positive aspect of working for someone else: my own performance reviews. With a couple of the individuals I worked for, I found performance reviews very helpful. For me, they provided some useful feedback and it was always good to hear that I was doing well.

There's no one around to tell you if you're doing a good job at your small business. The only way you ever know is if sales are good. Occasionally my ex-husband or dad would say something nice, but that was rare. Overhearing customers saying nice things is usually good. Overhearing one of my regular customers say "This is my daughter's favorite place to come to" was like a positive performance review.

## PUTTING YOUR PERSONAL FINANCES IN ORDER

It's funny, I'm telling you this and it's still something I have yet to master. It's one of those "if I could do it all again" things. Getting your finances in order will definitely have a humongous impact on surviving those early years.

If I could do it all again, I would have done my best to get rid of all my credit card debt before I opened the business. I also would not have bought a new car that I really didn't need during the first couple of months of business operation.

Something that we did do right in the personal finance department: my ex-husband and I bought a cheap home. I don't mean "cheap" as in quality. I mean we bought a house that cost less than half of what we were approved for. This was all before the business started and the business wasn't our motivation for doing that. But I'm glad we did . . . if we hadn't, I wouldn't have been able to quit my decent-salaried engineering job to make next to nothing.

One thing to realize is that reducing your income will take some getting used to, but you can do it. You might opt to sell your home for a less expensive one. Make sure you realize that in starting a business, you're taking a risk. Assume the worst, and decide what happens if you're forced to close and liquidate your business. What would this mean for your personal life? Will you be able to keep the roof over your head?

## KEEPING YOURSELF HEALTHY

Eat well. Exercise. Sleep. Everywhere you turn, you hear these things. Well, it's even more crucial when you're in business for yourself. If you're sick, who's taking care of your business?

The first winter we were open, I was pretty paranoid about getting sick. I took very large vitamin C pills several times a day. I was really worried because for the first time in my adult life, I was being exposed to TONS of kids who carry every kind of germ. I did get a bit of the sniffles that winter, but nothing terribly bad.

My second year in business, I got a little lax in this area and wound up getting some bad colds that rendered me useless for several days.

## STRESS-RELIEVING AND SANITY-KEEPING TECHNIQUES

As I said earlier in this chapter, WWFMMNWFY. What is true is that when you start your own small business, you'll have a lot of stress and you'll need to deal with it or seriously risk your health and/or business.

Some ideas and some things that work for me:

- Remind yourself why you're doing this. Think of the alternatives.
- Find an excuse to pamper yourself—maybe a visit to a local day spa for a massage after your busy season.
- Drink tea. Green and other herbal teas are supposed to be healthy and stress-relieving.
- Go to the gym. Exercise is a proven stress reliever.
- Remember what makes you smile or laugh.

- Take some time for yourself. Your business is your priority and a major responsibility, but you can't obsess over it twenty-four hours a day, 365 days a year. Allow yourself some time to be "off."

## No-Nonsense Tips and Tidbits:

- You can give your new business venture the best chance of survival by planning well up front.
- Lack of upfront planning can mean your business collapses before it really ever had a chance.
- Starting a business takes a lot of planning to ensure that you'll survive the first couple of risky years. The more you are able to do ahead of time, the better off you'll be.

# PART II

# What Ever Happened to That Cute Little Store?

# Introduction

"Business is always personal. It's the most personal thing in the world."

—Michael Scott, *The Office*

It's January 22, 2008. I just left two voice mails for a potential buyer of my business. Actually, he's more than a potential buyer—we currently have a signed contract, complete with a non-refundable deposit. He should be *the* buyer. But last week he told me that the sixth bank he applied to for a loan turned him down. I offered to lower my price if he still wanted to go with his backup plan of using funds from his retirement account. Unfortunately, he's in the same boat everyone is in now—his retirement funds are worth about 20 percent less than they were three months ago when he came up with that backup plan. It's a Tuesday and I'm waiting for a call or email back from him. I was supposed to hear by the end of this past weekend. This does not look good. If this sale doesn't go through (and I'm not optimistic), I'm going to need to close my business.

Now picture the time in which this is happening. We all woke up this morning to the top headline on the news: "Global Stocks Plunge on Recession Fears." The economy is not in fantastic shape right now. This is largely what is preventing him from getting a loan and is responsible for all our 401(k)s losing a ton of value.

The economy hasn't been helping sales at the store recently, either. Add to that, today I received three letters in the mail from random companies I'd never heard of that want to "help you solve your financial problems." All of them begin with the sentence: "As you are probably aware, a Federal

109

tax lien was filed against The Pot & Bead LLC on December 26, 2007 in the amount of $7,932." Actually I wasn't aware of that at all!

How did it get to be this bad? We'll go through the ups and downs in this part.

I'm not a negative person. While I've had a very bad day and a not so fantastic month so far, things really aren't that bad. As a business owner, you're going to have ups and downs. And they could be major ups (from being a finalist for a small business award) to major downs, like today. Through all my downs I've constantly reminded myself that I'm healthy, I have a roof over my head, plenty to eat, and I could work my way out of this bad situation one way or another.

The purpose of Part II of this book, like Part I, is not to depress you. It is written with the intent that you, as the owner or soon-to-be owner of a small business, have the ability to benefit from my mistakes. My hindsight is your foresight. In 2008, The Pot & Bead became one of the half a million businesses that close each year. Yours doesn't have to.

I started writing, and wrote most of, Part I in early 2004. At that time, The Pot & Bead had been open for a year and a half. I wrote that part after trying to buy a second business (which failed miserably), after a burglary, and after I'd started the process of buying my absentee partner out—a lot had happened in that first year and a half. It was also after I tried very hard to seek financing for additional Pot & Bead stores, with zero success. I was very depressed and decided to do something productive with my energy—to write about the experience so I could hopefully help others.

In the two years since I'd started writing that part, a lot had changed in my life and with the store, and my focus was on maintaining or exiting the business. This second part is about maintenance and exit strategies; it's about controlling cash flow; it completes the story of the business.

The changes for me and The Pot & Bead started in late 2004. I spent most of that year depressed and deflated. I didn't have the chain of paint-your-own-pottery stores that I'd planned, my marriage was effectively over (but because I was taking no income from the store, I was unable to separate and support myself), and I was missing some aspects of my engineering career. As much as I loved my store, it wasn't providing anything to satisfy my geeky, techy nature. Although I didn't realize it at the time, I was also missing the office environment. As the owner of a small retail business, you're by yourself a lot. The personal interaction is minimal, other than interacting with individuals for the sole purpose of trading goods and services for money, and you have no colleagues. Employees don't provide the same kind of interaction as colleagues do. It's surprisingly lonely.

I knew I had to change things in October when Burt Rutan's company, Scaled Composites LLC, won something called the X Prize. This was a competition that I'd followed since it began ten years earlier when I was in college. It challenged individuals and companies to push the limits in aerospace. Around that time, I also saw a therapist/social worker who was able to figure out very quickly that I was unhappy. She immediately picked up on the reason, too—I was unhappy mostly due to dissatisfaction with my career.

After thinking about it, I decided I wanted to go back and work for someone else, forty-plus hours a week.

Was I crazy? Was I going to wind up the same burnt-out engineer I was when I left? I made two lists. One was the pros and cons of taking on a full-time job. The second was the pros and cons of sticking it out as a retail business owner. In the end, the pros of taking a full-time job far outweighed the cons, and outweighed the pros of not taking the job. So that's what I did. In December, I became a "work for someone else" person again. But I went back with a completely different attitude toward work and what was important in life.

I thought about still keeping the business. Could this be done? Have a full-time career and manage a retail shop that's open seven days a week? I had to try. At that time, I had a full-time store manager and it was working out well. She was there during the weekdays so I could be off someplace else.

I could also sell the business. When I took that engineering job at the end of 2004, it was with the belief and intent that by the following summer, I would have sold The Pot & Bead. Unfortunately, by early 2006—when Part I of this book was sent to the publisher and I started writing the material for Part II—I still had a day job, still had The Pot & Bead—without a manager—and had no end in sight to my double life. Here I talk a little about managing two completely different careers at the same time—engineer by day, business owner by night. I talk about trying to sell the business, close the business, managing cash flow, controlling spending, and all the little things I know now that I wish I knew then.

Like Part I, this part is also written for the person who is thinking about starting their own business. Exit strategies might not seem important when you're starting out—I certainly shrugged them off—but they need to be an integral part of your plan from the beginning. You never know how and in what direction your life will go.

There were changes in my personal life that had a major impact on my career and business. The biggest change was my divorce. This affected my business because when I was married, my then-husband had to cosign papers like leases and loans. When we divorced, it took some effort to remove him from the documents. Afterward, a man named Dave came into my life, and while we weren't married, the fact that we lived together meant that he became involved in my business. There was no way to prevent that from happening. He did everything from taking out the trash and being my Mr. Fix-It, to acting as a sounding board and source of advice.

Whether you're just starting out, planning your new venture, or already in the middle of it, this part of the book includes a complete picture of a business from start to end, with a timeline and financial data.

## Chapter 1: A Double Life

As if quitting one's career to start a business wasn't a big enough change, in 2004, while continuing to run my business, I went back to that career.

## Chapter 2: Money Mistakes We Make

I thought that I was done making significant mistakes with money when I wrote about my attempt to purchase a second store that went awry in Part I. If only!

## Chapter 3: Money In, Money Out

Yes—it is all about managing your money.

When you're starting a business, what's the one thing you can never get? Real financial data from a real business. Well, here is our financial data to use as a source or guide.

## Chapter 4: More on Employees

Next to money, your employees are your most valuable resource. This chapter contains more information about hiring and managing them.

## Chapter 5: The Internet—It's for Businesses Now!

It's more complicated than ever to navigate the increasing number of options for marketing and sales that the Internet provides.

## Chapter 6: Getting the Business Ready to Be Sold

In this chapter, I write about making the decision to sell and get the business on the market.

## Chapter 7: At a Lease's End . . .

Selling isn't the only exit strategy. With a lease expiring soon, I had to consider alternatives!

## Chapter 8: Take My Business, Please!

This chapter tells the story of the first buyer I thought I had for the business.

## Chapter 9: For Sale, by Owner

With a new lease on life, I wanted to try selling the place again. This time, no broker.

## Chapter 10: Closing the Business

Yep—closing did become the answer. This is how we managed the process and got through it.

## Chapter 11: So You Still Want to Do This

You're still convinced that a retail business is your next professional career move. This chapter is a checklist to help make sure you don't repeat others' past, deadly mistakes.

## Chapter 12: The Final Word—Why Exactly *Are* You in Business?

Remember why you're here: it's about making a profit. I look back at the good and the bad of owning The Pot & Bead and attempt to relay some final advice regarding goals and profit.

## Appendix A: Timeline

Here I provide a timeline of all the events discussed in this book that are relevant to the business.

## Appendix B: Business Plan

This appendix contains the complete text of the business plan that was used to obtain the business loan and lease for The Pot & Bead, LLC. Only names have been changed or removed.

## Appendix C: Financial Data

I provide tables detailing operating costs, projected revenue, financial statements, and comment on my business plan.

## Appendix D: Lease Clauses

This is the entire lease that I held for five years, with my notes sprinkled in. The purpose is to show you a real, fairly common commercial lease.

## Appendix E: The Reading List

A pile of books that I highly recommend reading.

# Chapter 1

# A Double Life

An amazing thing happened on October 4, 2004. Burt Rutan, known for being the first person to fly an airplane non-stop around the world back in 1986, and the company he founded called Scaled Composites, LLC won the "X Prize." The X Prize was a competition that offered a ten million-dollar prize to the first non-government individual or organization that launched a manned, reusable vehicle into sub-orbital space twice within two weeks. Burt Rutan and Scaled Composites' SpaceShipOne achieved that feat.

The X Prize first began when I was in college. The idea was to spur people into advancing technology. It was modeled after similar prizes that were designed to encourage innovation in the aviation industry less than a hundred years ago. The concept worked. Because of this, a new industry is on the verge of being born—space tourism. The X Prize and similar concepts are not only good for technology, they're good for business. These kinds of contests are responsible for a lot of useful technical and business innovation. For example, a lot of modern aviation can be traced back to advances made by Charles Lindbergh and others of his era who entered and won similar contests.

A few days after SpaceShipOne became the confirmed X Prize winner, I was in the store telling my store manager, Diane (not her real name), and my employees all about it. Diane remarked that that was the first time she had seen me so excited about *anything* in a long while.

It was also about that time that I had seen a social worker/therapist. I was very depressed over the lack of income in 2004. I also had no luck with starting an additional store. I was very far away from the plan of a small chain that I thought I wanted back when I started the business in 2002.

In order to generate some personal income, I had a wild idea early on in the summer—I'd be an egg donor. I was accepted into the donation program and part of what I had to do was see a social worker a couple of times. She was there to ensure that donors understood the ramifications of their decision and to make sure donors were emotionally stable and could handle the fact that donating eggs was a big deal.

I told the social worker the reason I was doing this was for the money. She didn't buy that answer for a minute—it was too easy. We kept talking and she managed to get to the root of my issues: I wasn't satisfied with my career and the direction it was going.

It was soon after that last breakthrough appointment that the X Prize was awarded and I realized that I wanted to be in engineering again, at least for a while. I was very worried that leaving the field for a couple of years would make it challenging to get back into it, but I prepared my resume and sent it to Burt Rutan's company (they are located in the Mojave desert in California . . . I really had no plans to move out there but I felt that sending it in got me over an "I can do this" hump). While that resume was out, I got a little lucky.

About five years earlier, I had worked for a company that was building a satellite and the computers to control it from the ground for one of their subsidiaries. I had left that company before the project was 100 percent complete. A lot had happened in the meantime to both companies and I never thought I'd ever be involved with either again. Then one day, a guy came into my store to paint pottery with his daughter. He worked for the subsidiary company and I remembered him from those days. When he remembered who I was, he asked me to come back to work for his company. "Adeena—we just won this big contract and we're hiring. We need engineers! Come back!" is pretty much what he said to me. That was in early 2004 and I said no. At that time, the thought of working for an engineering company again wasn't on my mind.

He returned to the store a couple more times that year, and I think the third or fourth time he asked the same question happened to coincide with my desire to be an engineer again, so I said, "Sure, I'll send in my resume."

I did, and I was hired, and I began that job right before Christmas 2004.

What was happening at the shop? How did I know I could be away from it forty hours or more a week? The store manager I had at the time, Diane, did nearly everything except pay the bills and organize the marketing and advertising activities. In Part I of this book, I stressed the importance of making sure all your employees know how to do everything in the day-to-day running of the business. This involves training and having a good set of written procedures. I'm glad I had those procedures in place because on November 16, before I even interviewed for the engineering job, I found myself unexpectedly in the hospital.

Did I mention that I was donating eggs? Well, the morning of the 16th was the egg extraction procedure. I was supposed to be home by that afternoon. Instead, while they were extracting my eggs, a blood vessel was inadvertently poked and I lost a lot of blood. A lot. Enough to warrant a blood transfusion and keep me in the hospital for most of the week and in bed for the next two weeks.

There were two really good things that came out of that experience. One was that while I was sitting in the hospital, I had nothing but time to think about a lot of things, the least of which was how lucky I was to be going home. You see, they had me stuck in the cancer ward. I was in extreme amounts of pain, but I knew that the pain would go away, I would heal, and I'd be going home soon. I also knew that many of the other people I saw there wouldn't be. That has a way of making you feel kinda lucky and thankful.

The other good thing I discovered during that experience was that the store really could run without me. That was kind of sad in a way—they didn't need me—but it was a good realization that it was okay for me to be unavailable for forty-plus hours out of the week. My employees got along fine without me. I decided then that I could definitely take on a "day job."

I discussed it with Diane. At the time, she already knew that at the end of the school year (the following May), she'd be moving out of the area. I wished it wasn't happening, but was thankful to have six months' notice (most people don't have that). I considered this to be my initial deadline for selling the place. Training a new manager wasn't something I wanted to do.

I took the day job and decided that right after the New Year, I would put The Pot & Bead up for sale. You'll read more about my attempts to sell the business in later chapters, but I'm going to give you part of the punch line right now: It didn't sell before my manager left. In fact, it didn't sell before early 2006. Or even early 2007.

In the middle of the spring of 2005, I realized I was going to have to find (and train!) a new manager. I wasn't looking forward to this. Aside from Diane, I hadn't had great success with managers.

Luckily, one of my existing employees—young, but very responsible—expressed interest in becoming our new store manager. Hallelujah! I thought my troubles were over. She became the manager but lasted in that position only a few months. She decided that she really didn't want all the responsibility that came with the job and had a problem being the "boss" of her peers. She left the position but not the store—she stayed on as an employee.

I never took on a new manager after that. When she gave up the position, I looked at my payroll numbers and decided that the best thing to do at the time was to have extra part-timers instead of a manager. I could have more employees and we could be more competitive in pay.

I would act as manager.

And keep the day job.

I didn't believe I had a better option.

Following that, I was engineer-by-day, Pot & Bead owner and manager by night, weekend, and any other free moment I found.

After returning to the day job, it became obvious to me that I wasn't going to be wildly successful with The Pot & Bead. It needed more attention from me than I could give it. How could I have been so gung ho about it for only a year or two and no longer?

The entrepreneur, the person who starts a business, isn't always the best person to make a business successful. Some of these people are fantastic at getting something off the ground and are called "serial entrepreneurs." Other types of entrepreneurs are well suited to working with the same company through all stages. Look at Steve Jobs and Steve Wozniak, the co-founders of Apple. Steve Jobs was the CEO, while Steve Wozniak left Apple in 1987 and went on to start other ventures.

It's not that a business doesn't necessarily work. The hard thing is to determine whether or not it's the business or you. In my case, the business worked when it had my full attention, and sales fell off a bit when I devoted even a little of my energies elsewhere. That told me that it wasn't the business, it was me—I wasn't the best person to keep this business going. Having realized that, there were only two options left for my cute little store: I could sell it or I could close it.

Selling it of course would be ideal. I was off to a fantastic start and would have loved to see someone pick up where I left off and make the business wildly successful. But I had to remember that closing would always remain an option.

When you start your business, you're not thinking about the end, about the exit. You're so excited about getting things up and running and building the business that the thought of what happens later on takes a back seat. However, a good business plan includes an exit plan from the start. The exit plan isn't necessarily required to be part of the formal business plan (although a section on "Contingency Plans" is usually good to include), but there should be some ideas captured in writing. This is even more important if there is a business partnership from the beginning. What if one partner wants out of the business and the other doesn't?

If you read Part I of this book, you'll remember that I did start out with a business partner and wound up buying him out in 2004. Luckily, the operating agreement we had from day one allowed that to occur with minimum hassle. We had considered the exit for one of the partners from the beginning, but not for the remaining partner.

If you haven't given any thought to planning your exit from the business, do that now. It doesn't matter that you might be saying to yourself "But I'm sure I want to do this for the rest of my life!" Sometimes you need to exit a business not because you want to but because you have to, like due to an illness. Doing a little advance planning will make the actual exit easier.

List in your exit plan:

- Some reasons why you might want or need to exit (need to move, illness, want a change, etc.)
- A time frame for the exit (this may vary depending on the reason why you are exiting)
- Possible ways to exit (pass the business on to an heir, sell the business to another individual or another business, close the business)
- What things you need to do to make the exit possible

I didn't know it at the time, but my overly simple "sell or close" plan was not detailed enough to make it happen in the time frame that I wanted to get out.

## No-Nonsense Tips and Tidbits:

- An exit plan is as important a document as any other when you're starting your business, and like a business plan, should be revisited and updated periodically.
- It's okay to decide you want to do something else with your life. You are not a failure if you do so!

# Chapter 2

# Money Mistakes We Make

In Part I of this book, I wrote about how not following my gut led me to spend a pile of money trying to buy a second store, which didn't pan out. I thought that was the largest and only serious money mistake I had or would make. Hardly. Looking back now as I compile the data, I realize that I made a lot of mistakes, especially in the first six to twelve months, and that affected my business for years after.

Simply put: I spent too much money the first year in business. Even after that, I was slow to adjust my spending habits. It wasn't until the fifth and last summer that I really figured out how to be cheap and bootstrap, but by then it was a little too late—in the last year, I got behind on my taxes.

I was not trying to *not* pay my taxes, it was just incredibly easy to make them last on the list. Rent, payroll, and inventory were the things that I had to pay to keep the business in business—no two ways about this. But everything else seemed like it could be a little late: the electric company complained only after three months; some companies and vendors could go even longer.

Any piece of mail from the tax man—county, state, or federal—went into a pile. My accountant came by once a month to put all my papers in order and leave me with a homework list: things to pay and file. But if I didn't have any money, I ignored the pile.

When business picked up during the last summer, I was able to start getting these paid off. My accountant has always told me that the most important tax to pay is the federal payroll tax (also known as the "941" tax). But simply filing, even if you can't pay, is just as important. Unfortunately, as a "bill," this is the most expensive tax to pay. It's hard to write a check once a month for $900 or $1,000 or more (when your monthly income might only be $10,000 to $15,000).

Since the beginning of my last full year in business, which was 2007, I knew that I would use any tax refund I received from 2006 on my personal return to pay off taxes my business owed. It was only fair. Unfortunately, and randomly, my return was late in coming. Apparently, my ex-husband and I somehow forgot to file our 2001 tax return. (Forgot? Yes. When a couple is involved in buying a house, moving, starting a business, etc., all within the space of a couple months, it happens. We actually filed an extension from April to August that year, but had completely forgotten about it by August.) I got a letter about filing for 2001, took care of it, and got my refund. As soon as I did, I used it to start paying off my old payroll taxes.

But I didn't do it soon enough. A week after I made almost $4,000 in payments on my federal payroll taxes, a tax officer came by the store and dropped some papers off about the past due taxes. I called him and explained that his papers were out of date—I had just made that large payment. It was a long and confusing conversation where he contradicted several things I thought I knew; like I thought I was supposed to pay off the oldest taxes first. He said that any money I paid was automatically applied to the most recent tax period.

In that conversation, he talked about putting a lien on my business—which didn't seem to mean much for a business with no property or collateral that very well may be closing in a few months. But he said that since I had made those payments, I was under the lien threshold and as long as I submitted some papers (tax returns), then I wouldn't have a lien.

The day after I spoke with him, I received an official letter in the mail requesting the tax returns (and requesting a whole pile of paperwork that he didn't mention on the phone). I had a little less than a month to get all the paperwork back to him. If I did, and got "current" on my payroll taxes, meaning that I needed to make the next payment on time, they would keep the lien off my business and keep me from getting deeper into trouble. He said once he had all the paperwork, we could talk about working out a payment plan for the past balance owed.

I did exactly as he requested. The next month when my federal payroll taxes were due, I was able to make the current payment. I also made sure to send in all the papers he asked for—copies of my bank statements for that year, copies of my payroll tax returns for that year, and a copy of the receipt for the payment I had recently made. (The request also asked for a copy of a 1065 form from 2005. I looked through my stuff . . . no 1065 . . . what was that again? It's the "partnership" tax return. Ah! I had no business partner in 2005, hence no 1065—I included a note to that effect.)

When I mailed in all this paperwork, I made sure to do so with a postal return receipt. I've decided that as a general rule, whenever I'm mailing anything to the IRS, I need to have proof I did it (to prove that I did send it in by the deadline). When it comes to the IRS, the burden of proof lies with the tax payer. Meaning, if the IRS claims they did not receive something, it's up to the tax payer to prove that they did.

In the meantime, I watched one of those commercials on TV about getting tax relief—granted, it specified that it was for people who owed at least $10,000, which wasn't me, but I was curious if this made any sense. I asked my accountant about these tax relief companies one day. Was tax relief really possible? He said no. He said that a good number of these companies are scams and suggested that I perform an Internet search on complaints against tax relief companies. He was right. A Google search yielded more than 200,000 results, and nothing on the first few pages was good.

My accountant said that as long as an individual has an ability to earn a living, the IRS won't give you "relief." They might be willing to work out a payment plan, but you will need to pay the tax owed. I also checked out the IRS website and the only "relief" discussed was for those who've been victims of natural disasters such as floods or hurricanes.

Have you also noticed all these commercials on TV offering tax relief? There's a reason why these companies exist, and there are lots of them. Many Americans owe back taxes and a good number of them are small business owners or the self-employed, just like me. In a single week, I'd been contacted via phone or letter by four such tax relief companies. They knew about the lien placed on my LLC (that I wrote about in the Introduction) because these things are public record. These companies monitor court records looking for new filings to pop up, at which point they send you a letter telling you they can help! One even called my business. They said it was *urgent* and that I *must* call that day about my 941 (aka payroll) taxes. The way my employee gave me the message made it sound like it was the IRS and not a company calling so I called back. As soon as I got the receptionist, I knew my mistake (it wasn't the IRS). Two individuals got on the phone with me to talk about how they could help with my tax problems and how much it would cost. They were a business that essentially gave out loans to pay off taxes. No thanks.

The Government Accountability Office (www.gao.gov) released a report in July 2008 that claimed that as of September 30, 2007, more than 1.6 million businesses owed over $58 billion in unpaid federal payroll taxes (including interest and penalties). Yep, I was one of those 1.6 million, and apparently, I had a lot of companions. You, the reader, either are in business for yourself or are contemplating it. If you're already in business for yourself, hopefully you aren't part of this sad situation. If you are, *do everything you can to get caught up!*

If you are behind, my accountant has recommended that taxes get paid off in the following order:

1. Federal taxes, both the 941 and 940. Payroll taxes are always the first priority
2. State withholding taxes
3. Sales tax. Miss too many of these and you're inviting a sales tax audit. No one wants to go through that!
4. State unemployment
5. County taxes

The thing that makes paying taxes off in the order above so difficult is that the 941 tax is typically the largest bill. I would so rather be working from smallest to largest, it feels much more satisfying to be able to pay things off, and usually the smaller county taxes that are possibly well under $100 are easiest and doable. Unfortunately, the federal payroll tax is the one that is going to get you in the most trouble if you get behind.

If you're behind, at a minimum, file your returns, even if you can't pay. Interest and penalties accrue for simply not filing. Every day that passes and you're late on a return, you're accruing extra debt. Just file.

How does one prevent getting behind in the first place? Well, if you are a master of budgeting, you are well prepared ahead of time. You can probably skip the rest of this chapter. Or if you are like me, you set a budget, say $4,000 for a particular month for payroll. That's the "before tax" budget. You schedule employees within that budget. Good. That's the easy part and you're able to stick with it.

Next comes payday during that month. The Pot & Bead's payroll was done every two weeks, so let's say you have two paydays a month, and $2,000 per payroll. Happily, you're not actually writing checks for the entire $2,000. You're only writing checks for the employee's after-tax pay, which is only $1,200 (depending on their withholding status, state, and local taxes, etc.). Woohoo! The remaining $800 in taxes isn't due right now. It's not due till the middle of next month, or right after the end of the quarter, so it seems like you're not spending the money you budgeted. What you need to remember is that when it comes to payroll taxes, what you are doing is not paying taxes *you* owe, but paying taxes *your employees* owe. You're giving that money to the government on behalf of your employees.

If you're a saint at money management, then you're putting that extra $800 somewhere safe for when it needs to get paid to the respective government agencies. Or better yet, you go ahead and file and pay early. There is nothing wrong with filing and paying taxes before they're due.

But if you're a business owner caught in a recent economic downturn, or simply had fewer than expected sales that month, you need that $800 now for inventory or the electric bill. It falsely feels like you have that

125

money to pay your rent, or purchase much needed inventory. The taxes aren't due now, and you honestly believe that you'll be able to pay them with sales coming in when they are due next month or quarter.

Well, next month comes around and you need the money you have then for more inventory, current payroll, and to pay the plumber to replace the water heater that went out unexpectedly! To top it off, sales haven't rebounded yet, either.

What happens? The repairman must get paid the day he's there; you need to pay your employees—they've already performed a service for you and you can't have them quitting; the electricity will get turned off if that doesn't get paid; and you need more inventory so you have something to sell so you can go through this all over again. Taxes? It seems so easy to honestly put them off till later. Yes, there will be a late fee, yes, there may be some notices in the mail, but your employees are still there and happy, customers can shop, and the lights are on.

With the experience that comes with five years of business and many troubles, what would I do differently? I would take a lesson from all the personal financial advice out there: "Pay yourself first."

In the personal financial world, experts seem to agree that you need to have a cushion of three to six months (or more) of living expenses to fall back on in case of an emergency. This applies to your business, too, although here we typically call it "working capital." But I have a slightly different twist that I wish I had thought of long ago: open a business savings account. Every week or every other week or every month, transfer some fixed amount of money into that savings account. Do this first; do it before you pay your bills, before you pay your employees. This becomes your cushion. This is "paying your business first." This becomes the business emergency fund.

If we were back in 2002, the day I got my business loan, I would have opened up a savings account right then and immediately transferred $15,000 or $20,000 of the working capital portion there. Why is having a savings account important? Why don't I simply say "don't spend it"? Well, it's very hard when it's sitting in your "working" checking account—it's too easy to spend.

I'd had a similar problem with my personal finances, but I got into the "pay yourself first" habit several years ago. I put money into my personal savings account and I have trained myself that this is a "do not touch" account until it's *truly* needed. *Truly* means anything from the washing machine broke to "I need new windows," not "I need a new iPod."

I've trained myself to love to see what's in my savings account—a high number makes me feel good. Now I am loath to spend whatever I put in my savings account. My checking account is different, I need to use it all the time—to buy groceries, gas for the car, to pay the mortgage, etc. Had I trained myself to think about my business finances in the same way, I might not have had such a tough time of it financially.

It's still early in Part II, but if I had to choose the most important thing from this book that I'm passing on as advice to you, it's this: Have both a business checking *and* savings account. Train yourself to love to put money into the savings account. Pay this account before anything else. Train yourself to hate to take money out of it. Do this only when the alternatives are fines, late fees, levies, and liens.

## The Financial Aftermath . . .

In the last operating month of my business, February 2008, I had to start to worry about the financial aftermath of my venture, my decisions, my mistakes, and what to do about it.

I had a business loan that was going to need to be repaid. I had back taxes that I owed, some credit card debt, and I even owed one of my vendors a few bucks. I had a lot of stuff to sell, but it was clear not everything was going to go before I had to be out of my space, so I already knew that my new part-time job would involve selling stuff on eBay.

I contacted my bank to talk about wrapping up all of my debt into one loan. While I was going to carry a large amount of debt for many years to come, wrapping it into one loan with one financial institution was the least stressful way to take care of things. I would have one payment from now to eternity.

The bank I used to love had changed hands a couple times and the original banker who was fantastic and who was responsible for me being a customer with them no longer worked there. Luckily, someone else I knew was still there and turned out to be a business loan specialist. When I spoke with him, he asked me to provide a personal financial statement and information on the total loan I was interested in.

A few days later he called me after having reviewed my finances and told me he wasn't going to be able to help, but he was referring me to a "troubled loan specialist" at the bank. He was talking to this guy and I was going to hear from the specialist soon.

Alan, the troubled loan specialist, called me a few days later. He was nice and cheerful—but I was a stressed-out loon. He said he wanted to wait a month or so until after I completed the liquidation to see what I had left regarding debt. While that probably sounded okay to him, it left me as stressed as ever. With the back taxes, I didn't know if I'd be hit with another levy to my bank account wiping it out before I made my next loan payment. I didn't want to wait if I didn't have to. The least stressful thing for me was to wrap it up as soon as possible.

He suggested I detail my total tax liability (yes, this was something I was dreading and putting off and as of that day, wasn't sure what my total liability was). He said I needed to break it out into the principle, interest, and penalties and that I could try a settlement with the IRS offering to pay a lump sum of the principle.

I wasn't sure about that because I hadn't had good dealings with any personnel at the IRS office to date. I also wasn't sure about making a lump payment. If I used what savings I had, I wouldn't be able to make next month's credit card payment or loan payment, but I was determined to get this all under control. I emailed my accountant to ask for help— how do I figure out my taxes, and did offering a lump payment make sense to him? Could I do that?

My accountant said that I needed to call the various tax agencies. Before I called, I took all my current papers and organized them and forced myself to open every envelope from every agency I had received in the mail. I also made a spreadsheet to help keep track of what I owed and what I thought I had already paid.

Then I called the agencies, in order—first the feds, then the state. Here's the interesting thing: none of these agencies could easily look up and give me a complete balance of what I owed. This was the most frustrating part of the process. The first thing they asked me (before they would even tell me anything) was whether or not I'd be sending in a check that day. My witty retort: "That depends on how much I owe: I may be able to, I may not."

It turns out that I was square with the Feds. My 940 tax (which is the federal unemployment tax also known as the FUTA tax) was all up to date, and with the most recent levy against my bank account, I was good on my 941 (payroll tax), too. *Phew.*

As for the state, I was mostly delinquent in sales tax. Luckily, that one was reasonably easy to deal with in terms of paperwork. I had all the sales tax "coupons" filled out, I simply needed to send them in—with payment. Some of the payments were coming from my personal accounts at this point. It was a liability and it needed to get paid.

What about tax relief? As discussed before, there is no such thing. At least not if you have an income over a certain government decreed minimum. The government doesn't forgive taxes owed.

During that final month, I also had questions regarding my liquidation. Did I still charge and collect sales tax on furniture and other used non-inventory goods? Quick answer: yes. My business license was expiring at the same time I needed to be out of my space. Did I really need to renew it? Yes.

In the end, through liquidation and my personal savings, I was able to pay off the back taxes. Unfortunately, I wound up not being able to wrap anything (like my credit cards) into a new or refinanced business loan. Instead, the bank changed the terms of my repayment to a monthly payment that I could manage on my own after the business closed. This changed the monthly repayment amount, term, and interest. My credit cards and anything else were something I was going to have to repay separately on my own!

I'm not proud of the money mistakes I made while running this business. I'm not proud of how I've had to push off paying some bills till the very last minute and how I've had to stress out myself and some suppliers by waiting till their fifth phone call or email or letter before I would write out a check.

Hopefully you either see yourself in this story and it's not too late to dig out, or you see how some better planning and management can prevent some common business financial pitfalls in the first place.

## No-Nonsense Tips and Tidbits:

- Be a cheap bastard. Be frugal. Bootstrap.
- Open a savings account and regularly siphon money to it. Treat it as an emergency savings account and build up a six- to eight-month emergency fund.
- Always, always, always *file* your taxes, even if you can't pay them.

# Chapter 3

# Money In, Money Out

I happened to be working at The Pot & Bead one evening and there were some women painting. When one found out I was the owner, she started telling me about how she and some friends wanted to open a bookstore. Their only worry was that "people don't read anymore." (As an avid reader and writer I disagree, but that's another discussion.) I reminded her that it's not about whether or not people read, it's about how many books they buy.

Unless you are independently wealthy and own the space you operate your business in, you're going to need to sell some minimum amount of your product to remain in business. We'll use books as an example.

Let's say you're in the early planning stage of your business, so you're not open yet. Fantastic. It's time to create your financial plan. My financial plan is included as an example in Appendix B. If you've been putting this off, now is the time to take out a sheet of paper and make it happen. Don't worry about getting the numbers perfect in this round. You can always go back and adjust those numbers later.

1. Make a list of your estimated expenses. Include your rent or mortgage, utilities (electricity, water, gas, phone, Internet, even website hosting), insurance, and payroll if you're planning on having employees.

2. Include a line item for each type of tax.

3. Include some amount for "renewable supplies"—cleaning products, office supplies, etc.

4. Include some amount for advertising/marketing.

5. Include some amount for your product (if your business includes purchasing some product wholesale). In the case of the books, estimate how many books you need to buy to replenish your supply each month. This is different than the amount you need to purchase at the start of your business; that gets included in startup expenses, not here.

6. Don't forget credit card fees—that's an expense, too. When you accept credit cards, you pay the credit card merchant a percentage of each sale (and possibly a monthly fee, and a per transaction fee). The only alternative is to not accept credit cards, but nearly one-third of all consumer purchases in the US are made with credit cards. You don't want to lose those sales! There are an increasing number of people who don't carry much cash around and will not walk into a store if they don't see a credit card logo on the window. Seventy-two percent of the sales at The Pot & Bead were done by credit card (14 percent by check and only 12 percent by cash). Note that I don't differentiate between credit cards and debit cards. To us (and a lot of businesses), a debit card is just another Visa.

I can't fill in the numbers for you—that's your job. You also will likely need some more lines for other items; there are probably things that are unique to your business. Guesstimate numbers are okay for now. Sometime between now and finalizing your business plan, you'll need to do your homework and get more accurate estimates.

To figure out the right numbers for The Pot & Bead, I did a lot of research, including talking to owners of studios located in other states (since they wouldn't be considered competition). I went to several stores and looked online to figure out how much supplies would cost. I talked to inventory suppliers, got their catalogs, and put together sample orders.

Some of these expenses vary from month to month: payroll, taxes, renewable supplies, etc. Be reasonable but conservative in your estimate. For your business plan, create a table that lists expenses per month over the year and account for these variations.

Do you have a start to your list? Did you estimate some numbers? Then congratulations! You now have a reasonable estimate of the amount of money your business will need to take in every month without digging into your working capital (or your personal savings).

What if you're a service business (i.e., consultant or some other business that doesn't have a physical product)? If so, leave out what doesn't apply to you. If you're working out of your house, that's fine. Likely your only monthly expenses are going to be related to the phone and Internet. You might not have the rent, payroll, or lots of other expenses that apply to a retail business. Not yet. I say "not yet" because as your business grows, you might move into a professional office space and take on employees.

Now what if you have an online business or consulting business out of your house: You need to live, right? Are you expecting your new business to pay you enough to cover your living expenses? Maybe you have a spouse that will take care of everything household related or maybe you have a full-time or other job that pays all the bills and you're planning on starting your business part-time. If either of these is true, then you don't need to consider adding yourself as an expense. But if you're planning on quitting your job and you don't have anyone to support you, then you need to add up all those expenses, too (or you'll have to dig into capital or savings in the bank). In this case, add to that list your mortgage or rent, your utilities, your food; everything you need to maintain your current standard of living. (And before you quit that job, make sure you have a savings cushion to fall back on in case the business doesn't work out as planned.)

If you're operating your own business right now, I really hope you already have a handle on your expenses and your sales. If you don't, now is a great time to go through the exercise above. The only difference is that you won't be making estimates—insert the real numbers for your utilities, taxes, payroll, inventory, etc.

The next part of your financial plan deals with income. Let's talk about sales. Take out another sheet of paper and make a separate estimate of the amount of product you hope to sell in a day, week, and month. Extend this over twelve months and account for seasonal variations. A lot of businesses have slow times of the year (as The Pot & Bead and other pottery studios did in September and October) and busy times (the end-of-year holiday season). For example, how many books, at an average of some amount per book, do you expect to sell? Where does an aspiring business owner get that information since existing businesses typically don't tell other people what their sales are?

It's all about research. Time-consuming research. Take a look at my financial plan in Appendix B to see an example. Putting this together when I was starting out took research, which included talking to another studio owner located in another part of the country, *but* with a similar demographic as my area; similar in that the number of people within five miles of the store were comparable and the income in that area was comparable to where I expected to be located.

That's an important point. You can't talk to a store owner in New York City and expect their sales numbers to be a reasonable estimate for a new business a hundred miles outside of Cheyenne, Wyoming. Also recognize that the sales numbers from a business that's been operating for five years aren't going to be applicable to a new business. It takes time to build the business up to those numbers.

Search the Internet for "book industry sales" or "book industry trends" or "book industry statistics" substituting your product for the word "book." You never know what you'll stumble across—a small business blogger posting the details of her business or an industry trade association that shares this information with its members.

Camping out in front of a competitor's store, literally counting the people coming in and out, and trying to guess at their purchase amount is also a valid way to get some data. It's fairly easy to do this in a cafe or coffee shop, but not so easy if your competition is the little corner bookstore. They might notice and get a little perturbed.

One thing—no cheating. Don't look at your expenses when you estimate your sales. It's tempting to fudge your expected sales numbers to match or exceed expenses, but that is cheating. You don't want to dream that your sales will be sufficient to cover expenses if that's not really the case.

When you're done with the sales portion, look at your estimated expenses and income side by side. Do your estimated sales exceed your estimated expenses by some reasonable amount (like say, at least 10 percent)? If so, you have the beginnings of a good business and business plan. If not, you need to alter your plan. Or you might not have a business that will work. Go back and look.

Can you cut back on your expenses? Maybe find or negotiate a less expensive location? Fewer employees for the first year? Can you offer additional products and services? Can you advertise less and market more? If you can't get those expenses under the sales (without fudging the sales numbers), this might not be a good business to consider. Show it to someone else for an objective opinion. When you're done, you have a financial plan to include in your business plan.

Once you're in business, keeping track of your sales is important to have real data to use when you plan the next year. I kept a very simple spreadsheet that had a column for the date and a column for the total sales that day. With that alone, I plotted graphs of sales over the month and year. After I was in business for more than a year, I was able to plot month vs. the same month for two years in a row. It became very easy to see whether sales were rising or falling. Most accounting software packages, like QuickBooks, have the ability to graph numbers for you, too. I prefer the simplicity of a spreadsheet that lets me easily change what I want to graph.

With my business, the trend was a peak during the holiday shopping season leading up to Christmas and another peak in the spring time (holidays like Mother's Day and Father's Day were big), and lulls in September and early October. This was consistent year after year, so we planned for this ahead of time.

If you research thoroughly before starting your business, you will have a good idea of when the peaks and lulls will occur and your data should only confirm it when the business is up and running. Yes, it's that pesky research that will tell you about the peaks and lulls. You need to know this ahead of time so you can prepare, plan, and budget appropriately.

Once you are tracking your sales data, you'll be able to answer these questions easily: What month was your best sales month? July 2004. What month was your worst? September 2007. What was your best day? $2,152 on January 29, 2005. Your worst day? The Pot & Bead had a couple days with no sales. You will see more of our sales data later in this chapter.

You should take time to examine your data. *Why* was your best month your best? What did you do right? It might have been part of a market- ing effort that started the month before. What did you do wrong in the worst month? Do these months correspond to the seasonal nature of your business? In my case, my marketing efforts started to drop off after I returned to a full-time day job, and the effects on sales from that started to become evident in late 2005, a year after returning to the job. In 2006, the general economy started to deteriorate; housing prices began to drop in late 2006.

When you're in business, go through a similar exercise to answer ques- tions about your expenses and spending. When do you spend more? When do you spend less? Are you spending money on extraneous expenses? Do you need to spend more money in other areas like advertising or beefing up inventory selection or adding more employees?

When you have a handle on your real expenses, you can play some "what if" games to see what your business can accommodate and what it can't. The following is an example:

The Pot & Bead was a 1250-square-foot retail store. We were always short on space, but for the most part, we made do. For a while, I rented space in a storage facility to keep some of our extra supplies. The one thing I always felt we lacked in the little store was a separate room to host birthday parties. Parties were held in the main studio, with any extra seat- ing reserved for walk-in painters. This was acceptable but the one thing I think we could have used as a point of distinction between us and our nearest competitor was having that separate party room. The store next to mine was empty for a long time, so I got the idea that maybe we'd be able to take on that space to expand the business.

I performed the exercise outlined at the beginning of the chapter to determine whether or not I could handle this new expense. What were the monthly expenses involved in the additional space? Additional rent, utilities, payroll (not to mention the capital expenses involved in construction). Next, I conservatively estimated the additional sales that the separate party room might bring in.

It didn't add up. I was looking at probably an additional $6,000 per month in expenses (about half of that in rent). The average party brought in about $150 and the average regular sale was about $35. We already hosted five to twelve parties a weekend. Moving the parties to a party room would probably only bring us a few additional parties a weekend and a few customers (with that average $35 ticket) wouldn't need to be turned away. I figured the most *additional* business we would be able to bring in was maybe $3,000 or $4,000 a month. Maybe. Based on this analysis, I couldn't justify the addition at that time. As much as I really wanted it, the numbers didn't add up.

One of the messages here is to set a financial threshold for yourself (it could be $1,000 or $10,000 or even only $500) and whenever you are contemplating a purchase over that amount, go through this exercise or somehow vet the idea by some impartial method. It can help to separate what is a useful improvement to your business from an expensive "want" that won't help increase sales. You should have pretty high and well-researched confidence that an investment of this magnitude would bring in enough additional sales to cover the expense.

Just because it doesn't work out one year, doesn't mean you can't revisit a purchase or an idea later. Had business grown to the point that we were turning even more people away because our studio was full, or we were losing more birthday party business because people wanted the party room and we didn't have it, we could have revisited this idea again. What is useful in a situation like this is to keep track of the lost business— people who you have to turn away and who don't come back, people who didn't book their party when they found out we didn't have the private room. Maybe a year later we would have estimated higher sales and found ways to cut expenses (like negotiating a better rent deal with the landlord if the space continued to sit empty for a long time).

Let's get even more specific and look at what really was the "money in" and the "money out" for The Pot & Bead. In this next part of the chapter, I'm opening my books. I'm laying out all of our finances for the time that The Pot & Bead was open and operating from October 12, 2002 through February 27, 2008. That's almost five and a half years that we were open— 1,919 days (not counting holidays and other days we were closed).

# SALES

TOTAL SALES: From 12 Oct 2002 through 27 Feb 2008:
   $988,169.52 or roughly $185,000 per year.

Total number of pieces of pottery sold: 39,174
Total number of birthday and other parties: 1,544 ("Other parties"
         includes "Mom's night out," end of season sports teams, scout
         groups, etc.)
Percent of sales using cash vs. credit cards vs. check: 14% vs. 74% vs. 12%
Total number of receipts: 24,428
Average amount/receipt: $40.45
Total number of customers in database: 10,009
   Note that the customer database was far from perfect. It relied on employees ensuring that they entered in a unique customer if it was the customer's first time at the store; and relied on employees *not* entering a duplicate customer. The first version of the software we used also didn't have a setting that forced a customer entry—so a lot of customers from the first several months were never captured in our database. (There are actually about 1,500 of those 24,000 receipts that don't have a customer's name attached to them.)

However, if we round this number to an even 10,000 we can derive the following interesting information:

Average number of visits per customer in five years: 2.5

The average number is not as interesting as the "median." The median number of customer visits was actually 1. This means that half of the customers in the database only ever made one visit to the store. The other half came more than once.

The maximum number of visits by a single customer was 69. Yep, I had a customer who came in 69 times. It turned out this customer was an artist and routinely bought pottery and paints to take home—but she was a customer all the same. The next highest number of visits was 58. And the next was 53. Yes, we had some pretty regular customers who were simply fantastic.

Average sales per day: $510
　　Min: $0 (yes, we had a couple of days with absolutely no sales)
　　Max: $2,152
(I did not include February 2008 in these average, minimum, and maximum sales since our numbers were a little skewed that month because we were liquidating. We had one sales day in February that was more than $5,000, but that was the day we sold one of our kilns—not a normal thing for this business.)

Why are we looking at all these statistics? Because we want to see how we compare to the business plan. Ideally, a business owner is reviewing and updating the business plan once a year—maybe more, maybe less depending on the business. The original business plan is included in Appendix B. Our numbers, at least initially, far exceeded the business plan projections. I had updated the plan once, when The Pot & Bead had been open for less than a year and I was looking to expand.

This next table lists our sales, i.e., our income for each month that The Pot & Bead was open for business.

Sales by month in dollars:

|       | 2002   | 2003   | 2004   | 2005   | 2006   | 2007   | 2008   |
|-------|--------|--------|--------|--------|--------|--------|--------|
| Jan   |        | 17,350 | 18,139 | 15,153 | 11,961 | 10,435 | 8,655  |
| Feb   |        | 14,864 | 16,087 | 13,298 | 10,270 | 10,484 | 19,055 |
| Mar   |        | 16,597 | 18,446 | 15,165 | 12,560 | 10,570 |        |
| Apr   |        | 17,260 | 20,610 | 16,901 | 15,626 | 12,853 |        |
| May   |        | 20,460 | 17,599 | 13,371 | 15,369 | 11,942 |        |
| Jun   |        | 20,554 | 18,322 | 14,869 | 15,714 | 15,219 |        |
| Jul   |        | 21,054 | 22,359 | 17,932 | 15,317 | 17,833 |        |
| Aug   |        | 18,063 | 17,736 | 16,846 | 16,038 | 17,502 |        |
| Sep   |        | 14,239 | 11,562 | 8,525  | 9,643  | 7,192  |        |
| Oct   | 3,954  | 14,430 | 15,925 | 13,936 | 8,230  | 7,729  |        |
| Nov   | 20,551 | 20,462 | 15,559 | 15,312 | 14,035 | 14,301 |        |
| Dec   | 20,403 | 21,136 | 17,804 | 18,425 | 14,299 | 14,078 |        |

- Note that sales numbers are rounded and include sales tax collected.
- The best month was July 2004, almost two years after opening.
- The business was seasonal with a peak near the holiday shopping season and in the spring (shortly before Mother's Day), and a lull in September and October.

The average sales per month (average amount of money flowing into my checking account) was $15,320.

Here's the average monthly sales per year:

    2003: $18,039
    2004: $17,512
    2005: $14,977
    2006: $13,256
    2007: $12,511

The important questions to ask about the sales numbers: Is the income enough to cover expenses? Is the business making money or losing money?

To find some answers, let's take a look at the money that was flowing out of the business.

## CASH OUT

This next table is the amount of money that was debited from the business checking account each month. This includes **all** the money that was spent on the business—both necessary and unnecessary expenses.

| | 2002 | 2003 | 2004 | 2005 | 2006 | 2007 | 2008 |
|---|---|---|---|---|---|---|---|
| Jan | | 28,287 | 20,069 | 16,141 | 18,422 | 12,018 | 10,729 |
| Feb | | 22,181 | 18,729 | 13,806 | 13,319 | 13,053 | 13,359 |
| Mar | | 16,814 | 16,363 | 17,837 | 10,824 | 10,869 | |
| Apr | | 30,700 | 22,833 | 22,025 | 17,171 | 10,688 | |
| May | | 17,004 | 18,776 | 15,866 | 12,552 | 11,554 | |
| June | | 25,180 | 16,310 | 13,209 | 18,168 | 14,312 | |
| July | | 21,252 | 20,364 | 11,600 | 14,607 | 22,137 | |
| Aug | 7,548 | 26,591 | 20,999 | 26,315 | 16,340 | 18,071 | |
| Sep | 10,376 | 20,555 | 16,217 | 11,016 | 13,027 | 10,447 | |
| Oct | 35,411 | 14,601 | 13,802 | 27,064 | 9,368 | 9,323 | |
| Nov | 9,263 | 18,390 | 15,745 | 18,916 | 16,546 | 13,418 | |
| Dec | 26,819 | 31,348 | 18,179 | 16,940 | 13,009 | 15,104 | |

The average amount of money out of my checking account each month was $17,275. Included in that were all the months listed above, even the ones before opening and the month we closed. In the previous section, we determined that the average sales were only $15,320. See a problem?

The average cash out per year was:

    2003: –$23,370
    2004: –$18,199
    2005: –$17,561
    2006: –$14,448
    2007: –$13,416

Over the first two to three years, I learned to control spending, but I didn't learn quickly enough. The last two years, spending was proportional to sales due to what was spent on inventory. It's expected that the first year be a little high—we spent money on buildouts and one-time things necessary to get the business started. That should have been only in 2002. The year 2003 should have been the year of cheap boot-strapping. It wasn't. According to the business plan, I was supposed to lose money the first year, but not after.

On average, I was always spending more than I was taking in. The interesting part is that my first year, I was spending on average $5,000 a month more than I was taking in. In later years, I was only spending $1,000 to $2,000 a month more. That extra $3,000 in the beginning was on things I didn't really need but justified because I thought I was preparing to have multiple stores. Instead, I should have nixed those expenses and focused on getting that single store to make money.

Every month my accountant came in and reconciled my bank account and gave me a report. I always looked at it, but never with the big picture in mind. My big picture was: "I have to spend some money to grow the business, to put us in the position of having a repeatable business so we will be a chain." This was the wrong way to look at it.

The months when the reconciliation showed that more money went out than came in, I should have been concerned, especially when it was happening month after month.

If you are already in business for yourself, make sure you have these numbers handy so you see the big picture. If you are not yet in business for yourself, be ready to examine this aspect of your business and question it. Control those expenses from the beginning. Then stay in control. If your expenses seem to be getting away from you, question them, even if they are expenses you had already planned and budgeted for.

There was a moment I thought I ought to get out of one of my advertising contracts to save money. I had signed the contract a year before I knew I was going to close. The contract was in the middle of its term when I became certain of closing. I had already fallen behind on my payments to this particular vendor. I spoke with the accounts receivable person and asked her if there was any way I could get out of the contract. She said she didn't think so, but that maybe I needed to talk to the sales representative I originally worked with. Well, that "didn't think so" discouraged me from pursuing it further. The contract played out over the next four months, which totaled around $1,400. It was the only paid advertising we did in our last year of operations, and it's one I should have avoided. I shouldn't have let that "didn't think so" dissuade me from doing something I knew was best for me and my business. I should have pursued it further and at least spoken with the ad rep and possibly even a higher-up manager.

I didn't stay in control of my expenses and wound up digging the financial hole a bit deeper.

## EXPENSES

So what was all that money spent on? Certainly, there were several expected expenses: payroll, rent, inventory, utilities, advertising, taxes, insurance.

I've now come to think of expenses in terms of "essential" and "non-essential." Many of the big essential items have their own row in the table below. The row for "all else" is a combination of some essential (like renewable supplies, insurance, and taxes) and a pile of "non-essential" items (like extra books, trade convention, the time I hired a consultant to help understand and train employees, etc.) in dollar amounts.

| | 2003 | 2004 | 2005 | 2006 | 2007 |
|---|---|---|---|---|---|
| **Rent** | 36,455 | 42,395 | 37,252 | 35,714 | 39,060 |
| **Payroll** | 95,352 | 59,286 | 56,476 | 54,328 | 49,100 |
| **Inventory** | 51,595 | 62,631 | 36,088 | 52,312 | 38,217 |
| **Marketing & Advertising Printing** | 19,039 | 12,911 | 8,960 | 6,043 | 2,281 |
| **Utilities** | 6,497 | 5,333 | 5,300 | 4,097 | 4,585 |
| **All Else** | 71,502 | 35,832 | 66,656 | 20,882 | 27,749 |

Answers to some questions:

Q. Why did rent seem to go up then down? It's fixed according to the lease.

A. That's true, but real estate taxes and CAM (Common Area Maintenance) are not fixed, vary wildly, and are part of rent.

Q. Wow, payroll was huge and then almost got cut in half! Why?

A. 2003 included my owner's salary, which was originally supposed to be $45,000. When sales started to drop, I cut my salary in half around the end of 2003, and then in early 2004, stopped taking it altogether.

Q. What's in that "All Else" category?

A. That includes: loan payments, legal and accounting fees, any other consultants that I hired (which I did in 2002), dues to organizations we belonged to such as the chamber of commerce, taxes, the annual convention (which I only went to in 2003), miscellaneous supplies, monthly staff meeting dinner, repairs, and literally everything else. Half of this was necessary (loan payments, accounting and legal fees, taxes), but the other half probably was unnecessary and is why there was a large difference from the first full year to the last full year.

## PAYROLL

I'm giving payroll special treatment with its own section because it's 20 percent of all the money that went out of the business over five years.

That's a significant chunk of coin and well worth looking at in more detail because it's one of the few expenses you have control over (who you pay, what you pay them, for how long, etc).

Here are some general statistics on employees at The Pot & Bead:

- Day first employee started: 24 Oct 2002 (12 days after opening)
- Total number of employees over 5 years: 41
- Total payroll: $244,803
- Hourly rate range: $6.00/hr—$12.50/hr
- Average Hourly Rate: $7.57/hr
- Most hours worked by one part-time employee: 3,519
- Fewest number of hours worked: 2.5
- Average number of hours worked by employees: 685
- Average length of employment: 11.5 months (I didn't count the 5 employees who lasted less than a month. If they lasted past this, they survived the training period.)
- Average number of employees per month: 6.5
- Maximum number of employees at a given time: 10 (This occurred over the period of May through August 2006.)

What I can't account for here is the number of "free hours" I got from people that I would have had to pay for otherwise. That includes friends and family members pitching in to help out when I needed it. Looking back on five years and forty-one employees, there isn't much I would have done differently. Sure, a couple folks I hired were not gems, but overall, I had really fantastic people who worked hard and deserved their pay.

Each employee received considerable training, which was a significant upfront cost. We had a sixty-day probationary period, but it was the first two weeks, roughly six or seven shifts, with at least four hours a shift, that was pretty much solid training. Using the average hourly rate above, that works out to over $200 per employee for initial training. It's a lot because of the risk that a new employee might not last past this training period. I spent over $8,000 over five years solely on initially training employees. For a small business, that's quite a bit and was the reason I was so careful and attentive when hiring people.

Almost all of the employees I ever had were part-time students (high school and college). This was due to the financials of the situation. While I paid above minimum wage, I certainly wasn't able to pay a livable wage for our area or provide benefits. I was, however, able to provide some intangible benefits like flexible work schedules and discounts on our products (almost all the employees I ever had enjoyed painting pottery themselves).

## REALITY VS. THE BUSINESS PLAN

After months of planning and five years of operation, how did the business plan compare to reality? A few months after opening, I went back and tried to reconcile the real numbers with what was in the business plan. What I saw was 1) our sales were way off and 2) our expenses were way off.

Our sales were way off in a good way; they were much, much larger than expected. The business plan anticipated a slow ramp up in sales over the first year. Instead, we were hit—boom!—with the higher end of sales right away.

But our expenses were off, too. The biggest one was rent. We wound up in a completely different type of location and paid about three times the rent that the business plan called for. However, there's a correlation between rent and sales. If we weren't in the location we had, our sales might not have been as high. The trade association we belonged to did a financial survey one year and compared rent to gross sales and found a definite relationship. Studios with higher rent had proportionally higher sales.

Five years later, I'm still very proud of this business plan. It ensured that we thought through things from the beginning and enabled us to get the lease and business loan necessary to start the business. A business plan is a living document and while I made an updated version in early 2003, a few months after we opened, I didn't keep it up much beyond that. I didn't continue to operate with a good plan and certainly didn't have an exit strategy. The two things missing from this plan: the exit strategy and explicit goals of profitability.

The financial plan shows profit after the first year, but the rest of the plan doesn't explicitly support that. The rest of the plan justifies the existence of the business and shows that we did as much homework as possible ahead of time, but it didn't show a commitment to profit, a return on the investment of time and money. Hence, I didn't make money at the business. I lost money.

## No-Nonsense Tips and Tidbits:

- When you have an idea for a business, think about it in terms of the kind of income you need to cover basic expenses before going anywhere with the idea.
- A simple financial plan isn't a daunting task, and it will demonstrate whether or not your business idea is viable.
- In nearly all businesses, including mine, sales will fluctuate throughout the year. That's okay as long as you're prepared.
- Don't worry about growing your business, i.e., expanding beyond one location, until your core business is healthy.

# Chapter 4

# More on Employees

My first two employees started work on October 24, 2002, two weeks after The Pot & Bead opened for business. Since that day, forty-one people have been employed at various times, for various durations, over the following five and a half years. Good ones, bad ones, ones whom I didn't fire soon enough, and ones whom customers continued to ask about and request long after they were gone. Employees are the face of your business to the customer—they had better be good.

How do you find good employees? Unfortunately, you will never truly know if you've got a good one till after they've worked for you for at least a few shifts. The trick is to make sure you identify and keep the good ones and get rid of the bad ones (as quickly as possible!).

Some use the method of going to other retail stores and looking for employees who give excellent customer service, and then hiring them. I've never been bold enough to say something like: "Hey, when you get tired of this place, give me a call . . ." or "How much do you make here?"

I know another pottery studio owner who did use this technique. Michelle Booth of Glazed Over Ceramic Studio in Houston, Texas, went to her local mall and walked into thirty different retail shops. She reported that only three employees said hello, two did "okay," and the other twenty-five either completely ignored her or didn't approach her at all. The two who did okay were managers and were already paid more than Michelle could offer. She also noticed that most of the employees who ignored her were very focused on getting their "chores" done.

What can we learn from this? If you are the owner of a cute little store, is this how your employees are reacting to customers walking in? To provide excellent customer service, employees need to be trained to understand that getting their "chores" done is important, but when a customer walks in, that customer is more important than anything else. (This relates to the multitasking I talked about in Part I; employees need to be able to juggle whatever they are working on and handle the customers who walk in. Usually, this simply means pausing the task, saying "Welcome," making sure the customer's needs are met, and then returning to the original task. It seems simple, but clearly isn't.)

It also helps if the employees are recognizable in a crowd. I hired a retail consultant during my first year of business who did a walk-through of The Pot & Bead and one of the first things he noticed was that, of the people he saw in the store (especially when we were a bit busy), he couldn't immediately pick out who the employees were. I required them to wear aprons with our logo after that. I thought about this before we opened, but resisted buying aprons or shirts or any other kind of uniform due to the cost. It seemed that aprons were too expensive, but I understood why this was important and I required new employees to pay for the cost of their apron from then on.

Unfortunately, it's not only customer-employee relations that the business owner needs to worry about. Employee-employee interactions are just as important, and even more so because if two employees aren't getting along, that negative attitude could impact customers in the store. In a small business, employees must work together, trust each other, and be comfortable around one another. Otherwise, the human resources department (uh, that's you—the business owner) is going to hear about it!

Sexual harassment is not something you expect to have to deal with in a cute little store—I never thought it would ever be an issue, but then one day we hired someone who met all my hiring criteria. He worked two short shifts with me and several other employees during a busy weekend.

Then he worked a shift alone with my most senior employee at that time, who had trained a lot of the newer employees.

At the end of the day, I called the senior employee and asked her what she thought of the new guy. "He's creepy," was the response. Of course I had to ask her to elaborate, and she went into how he started talking about porn movies. I can't go into the details of the conversation here since the rest wasn't PG! It made her extremely uncomfortable and she was worried about him being left alone with any of my younger (under eighteen) employees (as was I at this point). I've handled a lot of weird issues with employees, but this was a new one and I didn't know what to do. Was it sexual harassment? I'm not qualified to say that for certain. My employee certainly felt as though she was being harassed. If this had happened to her at a larger company with a full-time human resources staff, it might have been easier to deal with. She could have filed a complaint with the HR department, and someone would have had a talk with the offending employee, possibly resulting in some action. Not so easy to deal with in the cute little store. As the owner and manager, you are the HR department. But even though it's a small business, having a policy in place from the beginning helps to handle situations like this. Small businesses are not immune to issues and need rules and procedures, too.

I didn't have a policy to handle this yet so I wasn't sure what to do. I reached out to other pottery store owners for advice. Overwhelmingly, they all said I needed to let him go as soon as possible. Several of them had run into situations so similar, they were convinced I had hired the exact same person, and in each case when they attempted to give the guy another chance, it didn't get any better.

I let him go that night, before his next shift which was scheduled for the next morning. His comments were sufficiently inappropriate that I didn't want to risk continuing to employ him.

What were the risks?

1. He might do something similar to other employees.
2. This was a sign of something worse.

3. This would upset my current, wonderful employees to the point where they would be stressed out and not looking forward to coming in and working their shifts.

People have been known to quit jobs over these issues rather than face unpleasant coworkers or continue to work in an unfriendly environment. I absolutely favor supporting existing employees whom I know, trust, and who have performed good work for me, over a new employee whom I don't really know and is already exhibiting questionable behavior.

When I told the original employee about my decision, she was relieved and then went on to say that on his third day of work he was already complaining about not liking the kid's birthday parties—a major part of our job! He clearly wasn't the right employee for my business.

When you must do the unpleasant, here's my advice on how to fire someone. First, solidify in your mind and on paper why you are taking this action. Second, if no warnings have been given, decide if it makes sense to give a warning or not. If you are giving a warning, write it down. When you discuss it with the employee, they sign it and it goes into their file. I had a form called an Unsatisfactory Performance Notice handy for these occasions. After the title, it had a lot of blank space to write down whatever was necessary to describe the issue and space for my (or a manager's) signature and the employee's signature at the bottom. Third, pick up the phone and do it. It helps to have a script or some bullet points. Something along the lines of: "Jane, thank you very much for trying, but it's not working out here." Or "Jane, you seem to like working with children, but overall this doesn't seem to be a good fit." Even though this individual didn't work out in your business, it doesn't mean that he or she is a horrible person. Offer as much positive feedback as possible. "Jane, while you weren't working as hard on the daily tasks as is required, you were fantastic with the young children."

Some employees respond with "Oh, okay. Thanks," and then it's done. Others don't let go so easily. The question you'll usually be asked is "Why?" Be prepared with a couple short items. Answer the "why" question, but try not to let the conversation drag on too long and try to not be too accusatory. I like using the words "I need someone who can . . ." rather than the words "You can't . . ." "You can't seem to be able to . . ." or "You were . . ." Any of the "You" statements invite the offending employee to offer a defense. This is not a debate.

Some examples:

"I need someone who I can depend on to show up for their shift on time, every time," as opposed to "You were late three times." The first statement is not arguable. The second statement invites the employee to say "but my car broke down," or try to offer another excuse.

"I need employees to greet every customer when they walk in," as opposed to "You seemed to ignore all the customers when we were in the store together on Saturday." Again, they can't argue with the first (except to maybe say "I did do that," to which you can simply respond, "No, not in the way we trained you to do it"), and the second begs for an excuse: "I thought you or one of the other employees were doing it" or "I was told to put out some inventory" (or some other task that they knew to put down the second a customer walked in).

I've had to fire seven people in three and a half years (there were no firings in the last year and a half). There were others that I should have, but they quit before I had the chance.

Firing by phone versus in person: which is the better option? Most articles I've read recommend doing it face to face, but I think those are geared for the professional office environment and not retail shift workers. I decided that firing on the phone was okay; if I didn't want this person showing up for their next shift, then by phone was fine. I've fired employees in person, too, when I wasn't able to get a hold of the employee before his or her shift.

What's not okay is delegating this chore to someone else. If the person reports to you at your business, then this is your responsibility. Now, if you have someone else managing your business day-to-day and the employee works for him, he could do it. Or possibly both of you.

Virginia, where The Pot & Bead was located, is an "at will" employment state. This means that with the exception of a few illegal reasons,

I can fire an employee any time, for any reason. Most states are "at will" (check yours—your state's government website should point you to your state's Department of Labor office), but even still many employers choose to point this out in either the application, employee agreement, or both.

The remaining good employees still need training. Showing up on time, performing routine tasks, handling customers—good employees do these things—but a business owner wants and strives for not simply good, but excellent employees. Excellent employees go above and beyond. Excellent employees are, to a large extent, cultivated by the business owner. This means once you have some good employees, your job isn't done. There is always room to turn these good employees into great and excellent employees through ongoing interaction and training. It means that as an owner, you can't sit back and let things happen. You have to know what's up in your business and provide constructive critiques when things aren't the way you'd like them to be.

In Part I, I wrote about how I didn't yell or get overly upset with my employees, but there is one thing that seriously ruffled my feathers and caused me to get on their case: an employee turning away business!

At the end of an employee's shift, they were required to write a short shift report about what they did while they worked. One day before the start of summer, one of my employees wrote in his report about how someone called from a school wanting to bring in thirty kids to summer camp. He told them we couldn't do that based on the fact that our "official" description of summer camp classes was that they were for a maximum of twenty children (even though the store seats forty). The same day, he also told another customer that we couldn't accommodate a special request for a birthday party.

At least he wrote about these incidents in his report so I could correct them. I called the school back and they wound up booking their party. What my employee didn't realize was that the twenty child limit was somewhat arbitrary, set by me primarily so that the instructor wouldn't be overwhelmed or I wouldn't be scrambling to find a second instructor on short notice. But for a group like this, coming in with their own teachers, we could make special arrangements. We were also able to accommodate the other birthday party request, adding additional profit to that party. Imagine if he didn't tell me about these calls? If he didn't, I never would have called back, and we would have lost at least $300 in business between those two cases.

Right after that incident, I made sure that all my employees knew about it. We did some retraining on our party policies and accommodating special requests. It's good to train employees to think like you do: the best way to accomplish that is to explain why a policy exists in the first place. If they understand why you made a policy and why it made sense, then usually they are smart enough to know when breaking a policy is appropriate.

I had a lot to say about what I looked for when hiring in Part I of this book; finding good employees was always a challenge. Our application was four pages long, and after a couple of years, it needed some tweaks, especially the section on contacting the applicant. I added a second phone number, email address, and "how do you prefer to be contacted?" box. During an earlier round of hiring, I wound up with an application from someone who not only looked great on paper, but the employees in the store who accepted the application had good things to say, too. However, the phone number wasn't clear—I tried a couple of permutations, but no dice and I couldn't contact her!

I also started to receive many questions about why we didn't have an online application. Well, I had always insisted that possible applicants come into the studio. I believe that it helps weed out the folks applying on a whim. I added the ability to download the application on our website, but made it very clear that applicants must submit in person—we did not accept them via email or fax.

When I added the application download to the website, I took that as an opportunity to add some hiring hints and guidelines—to help applicants put in a good application and explain what we were looking for in a little more detail.

Here's the list and introduction directly from the website:

## HOW TO BE A SUCCESSFUL APPLICANT:

We pride ourselves on customer service and seek individuals that we feel will represent The Pot & Bead in the best way possible, helping our customers have a fantastic experience. Please read the following notes and guidelines before submitting your application:

1. We only accept applications at the store. We do not accept applications via fax, email, or any other method.
2. Due to the volume of applications typically received, we do not respond to every application. If your application meets our criteria, we will call you for an interview. This will typically happen within a few days to a week of receiving your application. If you've dropped off your application, you do not need to call to follow up.
3. Please make sure your application is complete. Applications that are missing items (phone number, references, social security number, signature at the end) or are incomplete in any other way will not be considered.
4. Please double-check your phone number! We have had applications from people we wanted to interview but their phone number was wrong!
5. Sixteen is the minimum age to work at The Pot & Bead.
6. We are not looking for artists. The staff at The Pot & Bead helps customers, stocks pottery, cleans, and runs birthday parties. We are looking for people who are customer service oriented.
7. It is STRONGLY encouraged that the applicant drops off their completed application themselves. We believe that if someone other than the applicant drops off the application, the applicant isn't really all that interested in working here.

After finding and retaining some great employees and after weeding out the bad, my next challenge was to ensure that my remaining great employees stayed with me while I either sold or closed The Pot & Bead.

Shortly before the summer of 2007, I was starting to have some real stress. I had seven employees at the time and was trying to manage the situation so I wouldn't need to hire any new employees in the next few months.

We had about 120 days of business left. Note that when I say 120 days, I'm referring to our last day of operation. My lease was up on October 31, 2007, but I needed time to sell the equipment and clean out so I decided that the last day for customers to paint would be September 30.

We needed to operate for another 120 days, including our fifth and final year of summer camp. The number of people registering for summer camp was low that year; I was late in getting the registration materials and advertising out, but I'm not sure if that's really what was responsible for slow summer camp sales that year. There were so many other options for kids and families in our area, we were having a problem being noticed.

With about 120 days to go, I wanted to try out some different things that had the potential to draw more business and get my employees excited: I decided we would paint our windows. Our lease said we needed the approval of the landlord, but at this point the landlord knew we were vacating so I felt that there was really no reason for me to go through the overly bureaucratic process to do something so simple. Also, other stores in the shopping center had paint on their windows. We had that precedent on our side.

I bought window paint and gave my employees some instructions on what I was looking for—the important thing was that it had to be visible from as far away as possible. Our retail space had windows in the front and in the back and we painted both. It took a little trial and error to get it right. Some colors didn't stand out on the background of the store; using the window space effectively was not intuitive for my employees so it took a couple of attempts to space out the letters evenly. We painted "Summer Camp" on the front window and "Paint Pottery" on the back.

The first few days after the painted signs were up, it did seem like we had more foot traffic through the store. When I was in the store, I thought that we had more people driving by the front and peering in. This was good for everyone's morale. I concluded that this added visibility was a good thing and my employees enjoyed painting the windows (but didn't always enjoy cleaning off the paint).

Scheduling myself and my employees that last summer was my number one concern. Before telling all of my employees about my plans to close, I had told my two key employees. They were the two employees who, at the time, worked the most and weren't leaving for college in the fall. I needed them to stick with me to the end, so I told them what was happening before everyone else.

Part of scheduling employees for the last few months also involved figuring out when our last day to paint was going to be and whether or not we would reduce hours. I decided that our last day to paint (or have a birthday party) would be on a Sunday to round out a weekend, and that the five or six weeks before then we would shorten hours. The reduced hours time period happened to coincide with a time when I knew I was losing four employees to college. I needed to make it until then with the staff I had.

In the meantime, I was still learning about managing employees and managing the business. While it was hard enough to control my own spending, controlling others proved to be even harder. After I went back to my "day job," I let one manager place some inventory orders from our main supplier. I gave her guidelines, including a spending limit. Well, at one point, she more than exceeded it—the bill on one invoice was more than double what I was expecting! Outside of exhibiting surprise and telling her not to do that again, I didn't do much. What I should have done was remove her ability to place orders immediately and call the supplier and ask if they'd take some items back, or at least ensure that our next orders were within my limit.

At the time, we were purchasing on vendor credit, meaning that in theory we were supposed to pay the vendor within thirty days of being billed. Originally, when we opened, I paid this vendor with an American Express card and I had to pay off the card each month. This was good, but when I started to try to purchase another studio (see Chapter 6 in Part I for that whole story) and was starting to struggle a bit financially, the supplier let me purchase pottery on thirty-day net terms. Well, I started to struggle paying that off every thirty days and the supplier let me build up a back log of about $20,000. Yep, I owed them $20,000. Later in 2005, I went back to paying them with a credit card, but there was still that $20,000 to take care of. I made a small lump payment once, and then kept making small biweekly payments. Three years later, when I was closing the business, I still owed $5,000. It's so easy to let something like this happen, especially when you're not starting out as a disciplined spender. Both you and your employees who have purchasing power need to have the same guidelines and discipline. This is all about training your employees and yourself.

In general, employees should not be acting on your behalf without explicit instructions. They are not expected to veer from that direction and this needs to be explained explicitly from the beginning. Otherwise, good employees who believe they are doing the right thing can get you into financial and even legal trouble. This is also something I learned the hard way.

Over the five years, we wound up not doing a huge amount of print advertising, but after the first two years in business, I settled on one print advertisement that I liked. I had signed my third yearly contract with the company that put out this particular ad but toward the end of that year, our sales started to drop significantly and this was one of the payments I fell behind on. I knew that the renewal for the contract was coming up and I was torn as to whether or not to renew.

The sales representative contacted me about renewing. In the past, we had always met and I signed the next year's contract. This time I didn't have time to meet with him and I told him that I was thinking about it. I didn't want to tell him flat out no just yet, but I hadn't committed to doing this either. I wasn't sure if my budget was going to allow print ads the following year.

One day, I received a call from an employee—the sales representative was in the store and looking for me. I was a little annoyed—I had told him I wouldn't be there. I told the employee to tell him to leave a copy of his materials. Well, when I did get to the store to pick this up, there was a signed contract. Yes. Signed. By my employee on "my behalf." I was upset but wound up not doing anything about it. My head said "okay, the decision has been made for you." I didn't think much more of it, and didn't realize that this wasn't a valid contract. I never gave my employee authority in writing to enter my business into any contract, which meant this was not a valid contract.

What I should have done was immediately tell the employee that this was wrong and I should have called the advertising company and had the contract canceled right away. It had terms that I never would have agreed to including a little clause saying something about if I was late on payments, I owed double. At that time, I was already behind on payments from the previous year's contract. Why would I agree to sign up to that? But I didn't notice it and didn't do anything and this became an issue.

Skip ahead to more than a year later when we were closing the shop. I still owed this vendor three payments from the contract signed by my employee. Well, the advertising company wound up filing a small claims suit against me for the amount of doubled payments. I wound up writing a defense to the suit, saying it wasn't my signature on the contract and that no employee has ever had the ability to sign for me. But the ads had been printed, so I did offer to pay for the original amount. The vendor emailed me and said he'd cancel the suit if I'd make the three original payments. I did and that was how that issue was settled out of court.

These experiences have simply trained me to be much more of a tightwad and nit-picky and conscientious than I've ever been in my life. A little too late in some respects, but I do learn from my mistakes and won't make the same ones again.

You might think this would lead a person to not trust her employees. I look at it like this: I set the expectations. Each time something unanticipated happened, I pointed it out, explained why and how it was wrong, and ensured that current and new employees were aware of it for the future.

The best way to handle expectations is to start on day one. On an employee's first day, he signed an employment agreement form. Over five years of business, my form grew from two short paragraphs that simply stated the employee's pay, their expected number of hours, that the first sixty days were probationary, and a huge list of itemized expectations from "being on time for your shift" to "no one other than scheduled employees are allowed in the store before or after business hours."

Now I would include a line: "Employees do not have the authority to sign contracts on behalf of The Pot & Bead," but I would also have a form to specifically delegate signature authority for times when I was temporarily incapacitated or out of town. This sounds like overkill but it can prevent problems in the future. I would also include a check and balance system like requiring two employees' signatures. If you have any questions or uncertainty about what to do here, check with your lawyer.

For most small businesses, payroll is the biggest expense after (or sometimes even before) rent. In my case, payroll was a little more than 20 percent of the cash that went out of my checking account. Look at it as not simply managing your employees, but as managing 20 percent or more of your money. It's worth your time and effort to get it right.

## No-Nonsense Tips and Tidbits:

- Make sure that your employees know how you want them to treat customers when they walk in the door. Don't assume they know—tell them.
- You are the HR department.
- Pay attention to how your employees are reacting to each other. If you suspect a problem, reach out to them. They may be too nervous or embarrassed to approach you. Don't assume everything is fine simply because no one is saying otherwise.
- How you present yourself to prospective employees on day one sets the tone for the relationship.
- Training never really stops. Employees will make a mistake. Don't be afraid to (gently) correct them and use that as an opportunity to ensure that the entire staff knows what's right and what you expect.

# Chapter 5

# The Internet—It's for Businesses Now!

When I originally wrote this, there weren't quite as many books on how to start an e-business or online-only business as there were on how to start a traditional brick and mortar (B&M) business, so if the former is what you want to do, you're in luck. You might already be overwhelmed with the information out there, but no matter what type of business you start, you need to maintain an online presence. That might be anything from ensuring that potential customers can find your address, phone number, and hours to having a full-blown e-store available.

About a year after opening, we flirted with starting an online store. Since our core business was pottery painting, this wasn't something that was easily translated into an online medium. Well, a little less than a year after opening, we offered a product attached to the beading side of our business: Italian charm bracelets, and we were lucky—we picked up on it while the trend was hot and sold quite a few online.

I purchased an online store software package from someone I had met through the chamber of commerce. At the time back in 2003, most online store packages were too expensive, too cheap, or too difficult to integrate seamlessly into one's website. Being the online geek I am, I really wanted to show off and have an online store. Most other paint-your-own-pottery studios didn't when we started and still don't have one. A few that sell finished wares do.

We did actually start the business with an online store component. The web company that hosted our website included a free e-commerce package. Since it was there, we set it up and attempted to sell some bead kits. We sold one. The e-commerce package was free but it was too cheap. It only allowed us to simply post a page of products. I felt that the online store wasn't professional enough so I didn't market it.

The year 2003 was also about the time the Italian charm bracelet fad hit the East Coast. Since we sold beads and customers made jewelry in the store, selling the Italian Charm Bracelets fit in pretty well with our line of product offerings.

With the Italian charm bracelet product selling well in the store, it looked like I had a good excuse to upgrade our online store software. This person I knew from the chamber, who was also new in his business, had developed a software store product. Since he was new and trying to grow his business, I was able to get a copy and have him set up the site for less than other professional e-commerce packages. The downside was that because his product was still new, it didn't have a lot of features I expected and made maintaining the online store a big project.

We sold a pile of the Italian charms for a while, but the problem was that there were hundreds of other online stores selling the same thing. Some were even selling them for less or selling copy-cat products.

It became a huge headache to manage. We received one-off orders and since we weren't selling much in the store anymore, we weren't ordering regularly from the manufacturer. Oh, and in the middle of this, the manufacturer changed hands and afterward their customer service declined. Frequently, individual charms were on back-order for unknown periods of time. It frustrated me and my customers. I eventually had to shut the online store down.

When it was obvious that the Italian charm bracelet fad was over, we stopped selling them in the store as well, but it was fun while it lasted and I still have my charm bracelet with my initials, my birthstone, a jeep charm, a Saturn charm, and a charm with a paint pallet on it.

If you have a brick and mortar business, it is helped by an online presence, which can help you expand, and so can an online store as long as it can hold its own. That means that you're not spending any more money on the online store than it's bringing in. Differentiating some of the issues and costs can be tricky, though.

Luckily, it's easier and cheaper now to get an e-store up and running than it was when I started out. Most e-commerce packages that come with a web hosting package are much better than what I had and packages that you pay for are cheaper and easier to work with than ever.

In your expenses and budgets, count the cost of only having a basic website and website hosting against your "normal" marketing or Internet expenses. Count the cost of anything else that's necessary for an online store against the online store. The money the online store brings in needs to cover these expenses. Think of this as a business within a business: it is in fact a division of your business; it requires a separate ledger for income and expenses.

But what if you're not open yet and you're trying to decide between an online store or a brick and mortar store? This isn't a straightforward decision to make and it's not easy to compare the two. Sure, you might sell the same product, but that doesn't make it the same business. One requires retail space, a lease, regular hours, etc. The other could potentially be run out of your home, in the evenings, without a set schedule while you hold down a full-time job.

There are many differences between online and physical stores. I've chosen what I think are the top three that need to be considered if you're trying to figure out which way to go. They are:

1. Startup expenses
2. Presence
3. Marketing

Startup expenses are the most obvious difference. If you're opening a retail store with a physical location, you need all the furniture and fixtures for that store. You may need to pay to outfit the space, like rearrange the walls and ceiling, put in new flooring, etc. You still need a website presence, which doesn't need to be much more than a business card. Startup expenses will likely run in the tens of thousands, maybe even be more than a hundred thousand dollars. Compare that to an online store that needs an investment of a couple thousand dollars (at most) for a decent website and enough to buy some inventory.

The second item on the list is presence. Presence is what I refer to as the face you present to people, as in when and where. A B&M store has store hours. This requires human presence during these hours, which puts either a limitation on yourself or requires you to have shift-working employees. Online presence doesn't require this; an online store is open 24/7, but the online presence still requires you to be available. Customers expect quick turnaround times on responses to email inquiries and expect order fulfillment to happen ASAP. Expect that any customer email needs to have a twenty-four hour response time. This means that while you don't need to be in one place all the time, you do need to be accessible or have someone who can stand in for you (if you take a vacation).

At the end of the day, your presence (online or B&M) is dictated by the expectations you've set for your customers. If you say you are open Monday through Friday 10 a.m. to 8 p.m., your store better be open. If you say that online orders are shipped within forty-eight hours, you better ship in forty-eight hours. Customers are easily upset if their expectations, which you set, are not met.

Marketing. This is the hardest and trickiest difference in online versus B&M stores and the part that I don't think many people consider when they're starting up their business. If you're a B&M, you have a physical store. Yes, to some degree this limits your physical reach. It's a safe bet that people aren't coming from across the country to be your customer. Depending on the level of specialty your business has, they might not even come across town, but likely there is a radius around your physical location where the majority of your customers live and work. The people who lived right around The Pot & Bead knew about us. To them, we stood out amongst our landscape; we were the only business of our kind in our shopping center and for a few miles around. We were unique within a certain area.

But the online landscape is different. When we sold the Italian charm bracelets online, we were one of hundreds, perhaps thousands, of online stores selling them. When I wrote this chapter, a search for "Italian charm bracelets" on Google returned 842,000 results. Think about this if you want to start selling online. How are people going to know about you? Here's the approach I would take: If I was interested in selling online, I'd look for a niche that wasn't being met currently. I wouldn't sell "clothing" (391,000,000 results on Google as of this writing), but I would think about selling "footsie flannel pajamas for adults" (713 results on Google today—already up from 174 results when I started writing this book).

For either business, online or B&M, you need to write a business plan. Too many people think that if they are starting an online business, they can do it part-time and cut corners. While it's true that lots of successful online sellers started part-time, it's not true that they cut corners. The most successful individual online sellers had a business plan, sales goals, and had researched their market and worked hard at it.

If you plan on doing both, you can include both components in one business plan, but still separate the financials. The original business plan for The Pot & Bead mentioned that we would use whatever opportunities we could find to sell online, but then we only included the cost of building and maintaining the website in our expenses and didn't include any estimated sales from an online store in the initial projections. Our initial projections were called "realistically conservative" by the banks and other people who looked at them. I was very proud.

Online store or brick and mortar—either way, you need a website. There are bazillions of books on websites and today there are more choices than ever on how to build one.

Hopefully by now, simply by being out in the world you know that a website is important. You probably even bought this book online (thank you, by the way). A website, or some online presence, is necessary for anyone in business. Let me rephrase that: You need to be able to be found. A full-up website that does everything is not necessarily needed as long as you can be found. This means your business might only need to be listed in some search engines or web-based business directories. Google has free business listings that you can set up on your own (see www.google.com/services). Your local town or county may also have a website where businesses are listed for free. Type the name of your town and state into a search engine and see what comes up. The Pot & Bead was located in Ashburn, Virginia. If I type "Ashburn, VA" into a search engine, two of the top ten results are places that are geared for local business listings. At the bare minimum, get your business's name, phone number, and hours of operation out there. In life, you're not only a business owner, but you're also a consumer. Think about how *you* find things when *you* need a new product or service. Are you using a phone book or are you looking more and more online? Ask your friends and family what they're doing. If you're putting together any kind of market survey of your product and service, include these kinds of questions.

Online is where I found several local lawn mowing and landscaping services for my house. I'm always at the computer and can't be bothered to dig out the heavy phone book. Plus, the phone book is a year old already and it's getting very expensive to list in there, so I'm not super confident in what I'd find. In a search engine like Google I simply type "landscaping" and my zip code, and boom, local business information comes up. That's all I need to find and hire the right service.

Finding your business online is one thing, but finding your website is another thing entirely, although it's related. Search engines like Google need to be able to find and index your web page. Making your page search engine friendly is known as Search Engine Optimization or SEO. It's a challenge for anyone or any business to wind up in the top ten or on the first page of a search engine's results.

For example, as I write this, I search Google for "paint your own pottery" and 510,000 results come up. My own business, The Pot &

Bead, was never on the first page of results; it was never even on the first five pages. But if I searched "Pot and Bead" or "The Pot and Bead" or even "Pot & Bead," my website always came up first. Same thing if one searched for "paint your own pottery, Ashburn Virginia." This was important because chances are the person searching was someone local, who knew about my business already and might not have known what my URL was or didn't remember the exact name of my business. They just wanted to find a website quickly so they could find out our hours or other information.

I gave up worrying too much about SEO a long time ago with The Pot & Bead because I was not trying to market to the country or the world, only locally. Most of those who looked at The Pot & Bead website, or needed to look, were local people who already knew we existed and just wanted store hours and directions. Yes, some local folks found out about our business through a random Internet search, but not a significant percentage. (I tracked "how did you hear about us" in the first couple years of business and the answer "via the Internet" was less than 5 percent.) If someone else is building your website, ask what they are doing to optimize your site for search engines. Do a little research on search engine optimization basics, so you know what they're talking about.

Once people find your business online, make sure they can actually find your business! As more people get net savvy and use online map websites or a GPS to find your physical location, it's important that you're certain they'll be able to use the information they read to find you.

We had someone call us once saying that she was having problems finding us. My employee explained how to get to us from her location, but the woman was adamant that we couldn't possibly be at our published address because that's not what was coming up on her GPS! I investigated a little and realized that if you put in our standard, advertised address, several GPS receivers and mapping applications were unable to find us. There was a modified address that could be found, which was also our "official" address according to the post office. Go to Google maps, put in your address, and see what happens. Google and other online maps allow you to embed maps directly into your website for free. I immediately changed our website to include that kind of map, replacing the hand drawn one I created years earlier.

Once customers and potential customers have found your website and your store, you need to ensure that they don't get away without giving you their email address. Email marketing is one of the best, low-cost ways to advertise and market your business.

Every page of your website needs a clear way for people to sign up for your email newsletter. You should also collect emails in your place of business or as you are out in the world networking with other people. "But I don't want to clutter up people's inboxes!" you say. Don't worry about this. First, people don't have to give you their email address. It's not like you're holding their first born hostage—you're only asking for their email address and they are free to say "no." Second, they always have the ability to opt out later since your email messages will come with a clear way to unsubscribe. Lastly, you're probably not going to send an email newsletter more than once a week. You might only send one once a month—enough so that you stay informative but not overwhelming and you don't become background clutter.

Before you start your email newsletter campaign, there are a few more questions besides how often to send. When during the week is the best time to send out an email newsletter?

There are studies about which day of the week and what time of the day is the best to send out marketing emails. Around the time I started my email campaign I had read that Tuesday through Thursday mornings were the best times to send emails. Over the last three years of my business, I was using an online service called Constant Contact, which kept lots of statistics each time a mailing went out. Here's what I learned:

Average email newsletter open rate: 20%

Open rate per day of week:
Sunday: 17.7%
Monday: 18.9%

Tuesday: 22.0%
Wednesday: 20.1%
Thursday: 24.6%
Friday: 24.4%
Saturday: 19.6%

What this told me was that for my business, days leading into the weekend were only slightly better if we wanted people to read our email newsletter than days at the end of the weekend leading into the start of the new week.

Of course, the email newsletter's content is extremely important, too. News, events, and specials are all good but consider other things that your customers might be interested in. Your email newsletter doesn't always need to be a direct call to action to make a purchase; you could give advice related to your services. For example, my email newsletter routinely gave tips and ideas on how to paint better. Clean humor is always good as are easy-to-read newsletters with bulleted lists like: "Top 10 reasons our product makes a great gift for (fill-in-the-blank)."

This chapter has touched ever so slightly on your business and the Internet but there are hundreds of books that in thousands of pages go into much more detail than I could ever hope to achieve here. I hope what you take away from this chapter is that if you are starting your business, plan an Internet strategy that is as integral to your business as anything else. Keep expanding and learning and tweaking. What is true about the Internet and how it fits in to your business today will almost certainly be different a few years from now.

## No-Nonsense Tips and Tidbits:

- Many things that I've written about business and the Internet are likely to be out of date by the time I submit this book to my publisher, or even by the time I finish this sentence. The best way to start figuring out what is current is to look and see what other successful businesses are doing. Start there.

- The trick is to have a solid online presence without it taking up *all* of your time!

- If selling online isn't your core business, it might not make sense to do it at all. Think carefully about this since it might take up more time that could be better focused on your core business.

- An online presence—at a minimum for people to figure out where you are located, what your hours are, and other key details—is necessary these days for *any* business.

- Everything else (a blog, an email newsletter, a Twitter feed, etc.) is optional and it might take some experimentation to figure out what is right for your business.

# Chapter 6

# Exit Strategy: Getting the Business Ready to Be Sold

I just got off the phone with my business broker; I've agreed to lower the asking price for my business. It's been listed on the market for a little less than a year. I had one major bite, but it didn't pan out.

It's early 2006 and I've been getting terribly anxious. Living the double life for the past year and a half has been hard. I need the income—I have a mortgage to pay —but the catch is that I'm not devoting the time and attention necessary to the business, which means the business suffers, and that makes it harder to sell.

## FINDING A BROKER

It was when I went back to work as an engineer that I first had the thought about selling my business. That was before Christmastime 2004, and I believed The Pot & Bead would be sold by the following summer.

After the New Year, I started looking for a business broker to work with. I didn't have to look too hard. Reputable and non-reputable brokers alike will frequently canvas businesses and give out their card—simply to let you know they're there if you're thinking about buying or selling. It's similar to how real estate agents send cards to your house. For some-one who was as busy as I was, I did somewhat appreciate this approach (assuming they're not pushy and *expect* a callback), so I called one of the guys who had recently dropped in.

Much like when you sell your house, you sign an agreement with a broker when you list your business for sale. This particular broker presented me with an agreement and I forwarded it to my lawyer for review. The lawyer gave a big thumbs down on the agreement—there was a clause saying that I would owe the broker a fee even if the business didn't sell!

Even though some brokers try to write in a clause like this, it's not the norm. If you don't think you can read through a contract on your own and pick up on these details, then definitely have a lawyer review anything before you sign. Whether you choose to use a lawyer or not, read the books listed in Appendix D on selling your business *before* you contact a broker.

I told the broker I wouldn't sign it—that clause had to be removed. The broker refused and then pulled a really sleazy ploy: he called me up saying that he had a potential buyer and that I needed to sign right away. My lawyer suggested that if that was true, he should be willing to let me sign an agreement *only* for this potential buyer; with no fee if it didn't work out. The broker refused, which told me that he really didn't have a serious potential buyer.

This all took place over more than a month, after which I was a little hesitant and not feeling rushed to find the next broker. Enter broker Number Two in the spring of 2005.

We met and I liked him much better; his attitude and his knowledge about the local area were extensive and his agreement didn't have wacky penalties if the business didn't sell during the term. I signed an agreement with him, putting the business officially on sale for $169,000. The agreement expired at the end of 2005.

How do you decide on the asking price for your business? If you asked ten specialists on the subject, you'd get ten different answers. This is illustrated quite nicely in Chapter 8 of *Buying Your Own Business* by Russell

Robb. In the book, Robb writes about multiples of earnings, cash flow, business valuations, and other techniques.

There is an emotional side to pricing your business, too. After all, I put a lot of hard work into the business. Shouldn't that count for something? In order to feel good about my asking price and to know what the lowest price I was willing to accept was, I put a spreadsheet together that listed all of my business debt at the time. I then compared that to different sale prices and what I would walk away with (if anything) at a particular sale price. Of course, I assumed that the sale price would have to be able to cover my debt (which at $169,000, it could). At the time, a sale price of $169,000 would have netted me around $20,000 after all the debt was paid, the broker was paid, taxes on the sale were paid, etc. It didn't seem like a lot, but it was something. I needed a sale price of at least about $130,000 to walk away with no debt. That was my lowest limit.

One method that books mention, but gloss over, is the method of looking for similar businesses that are currently on the market and examining their listing prices (and even the final selling price if you can find it). This gives you a good idea of what the market is willing to pay. There are a whole host of websites that list businesses for sale like bizbuysell. com. Scout them for similar businesses. This method is similar to how one prices their home for sale—taking into account neighbors' homes.

My agreement with the broker ran from the spring of 2005 until the end of the year. During that period of time, only one serious prospective buyer turned up. We met, and I never heard back after that.

Then in early 2006, we re-listed the business for a lot less: $99,000. By then, I was willing to take a loss on the business rather than continue to operate it, but I wasn't willing to take a complete loss. I had a business loan and other debt associated with the business that needed to be paid off. Anything not covered by the sale would be covered by me afterward. I didn't care if I didn't have extra money at the end, I simply didn't want the debt.

After being re-listed for about a month, I got the phone call I wanted to hear: "I have an interested buyer. We want to set up a meeting with you as soon as possible." We met the next night. The buyer had already shopped my store, as well as my local competition, and really liked my business.

The next steps were for me to send my broker updated financials. The broker asked for Profit & Loss statements (P&Ls) and my recent tax returns. The buyer would then put down a deposit. I also needed to start talking to my landlord about transferring the lease to a new owner.

Most leases include a transfer clause. I've included the full text of my lease in Appendix C for reference. The clause related to transferring a lease is Clause 15: Assignments.

In my anxiousness, I decided to ask the broker what he thought the chances were that the buyer would offer what I was currently asking or something close to it. The broker said that the likelihood was very small given the lack of real profit. He said to expect an offer that was maybe two-thirds of my asking price. I thought this was ridiculous, especially since net sales were good. One of the methods to price a business is to use a multiple of net or even gross sales. I had this method stuck in my head at the time. Two-thirds of my asking price was around $60,000 and was so much less than even ONE times my annual sales (which was approximately $180,000 in 2005).

I told him that my newly lowered price of $99,000 was firm. Anything lower than that was a waste of time. If I couldn't at least pay off my outstanding business loan, it wouldn't make sense. Besides, it was nearly summer—I had already done all the work to prepare and market for the upcoming summer camp including laying out money for advertising. At that time, I wasn't losing any money with the business and my current business debts (the business loan, credit cards) were being paid.

It didn't matter because the prospect never made an offer and that was the last truly serious interest I had for over a year.

Early on, I should have put much more effort into getting the business ready to sell. I did my best to take care of the day-to-day business while I was working full-time, but I didn't put the effort into trying to sell it. I thought that was what the broker was for. Maybe, but I could have and should have taken a more active role.

Whether or not you are the one actively selling your business, you do need to make sure it's ready to sell. It's the same as putting your house on the market: you typically clean up the place, fix some things, and put your best face forward.

If you're reading this and saying to yourself: "I'm not thinking about selling," it's still important for you to consider it. The best time to sell any business is when it's doing well. This means that your business should always be in top-notch condition. All those things that will help you sell will also help you run your business.

Any decent book on selling a business will have a section that discusses what to do to get your business ready for sale. Two excellent books are *The Business Sale System* and *The Complete Guide to Selling a Business*. In particular, Chapter 7 of *The Complete Guide to Selling a Business* goes into fantastic detail on preparing your business for sale—including how to restate your financial information.

To summarize what all the sources tell you, you need to:

1. Be up to date. This refers to your customer mailing list, gift certificate records, procedures, etc. These things should always be up to date anyway! If you are selling your business, you have no excuse to slack off in these areas.
2. Have a sales brochure. This is one of those things that I didn't do when I first started working with a broker. I thought he was responsible for marketing the business, not me, so I didn't bother. But I also didn't ask him what he was really doing to market my business.
3. Ensure that your financials are up to date. This is what a buyer is going to want to see.
4. Have a plan for the transition. Are you planning on offering training to the new owners? Decide what you're willing to offer. Some amount of management training is normal in the purchase price of a business.

Another important consideration when getting your business ready to sell is what to tell your employees. Do you or do you not tell your employees that you're planning on selling the business? Traditionally, business sales like mine are kept reasonably hush-hush. Why? Because it creates uncertainty, and you risk losing valuable employees. Employees keep the business running during the transition.

When I first planned to put my business up for sale, I told my manager, Diane. I told her because I needed her to be on board with my decision and help me keep the place in tip-top shape so it would sell. I told Diane that trying to sell the business was part of my plan to go back to work as an engineer. I knew I wouldn't be able to carry on two jobs indefinitely. Therefore I wanted it to sell, and sell quickly. In order to ensure that she would do a great job at keeping the place together on a day-to-day basis when I wasn't around much, I decided that if the business sold while she was still there, I'd give her a percentage of the profit of the sale. I thought this was good motivation for her to stick around and do a great job.

As it turned out, it really didn't seem to be much of an incentive to her. She still moved out of the area about six months later and before she left, had managed to tell almost everyone (employees and customers) about an impending sale. Should your employees know about a possible sale? Perhaps . . . Should the whole world know? No.

Apparently I wasn't explicit enough in explaining that this wasn't an appropriate topic for casual conversation. After she left and things died down with all that talk, I chose to tell no one except my immediate family.

## No-Nonsense Tips and Tidbits:

- Use the same scrutiny if you are hiring a business broker as you would any other service professional.
- Be wary of any agreements you are asked to sign. And don't sign if you're not comfortable with it!
- Don't assume employees don't know what information is and isn't for public knowledge. Explicitly tell them if there's something that is not to be shared.
- If you are interested in selling your business, *sell* it.

# Chapter 7

# At Lease's End . . .

It was near the end of 2006 when it dawned on me that there was no guarantee that selling the business would ever happen. I needed to be open to other alternatives. Up until then, I never thought I wouldn't be able to sell The Pot & Bead.

Here's what I knew as of the end of 2006: First, sales were down since I went back to a full-time day job. Sales were definitely proportional to how much money and effort I put into advertising and marketing. This should be obvious, but when sales are really good, it can be hard to know why. And for a small retail store, where word of mouth is crucial, there might be a tendency to believe that word of mouth is keeping the business going and advertising can be cut back.

Second (and this is the really embarrassing part), after sending Part I of this book to the publisher, I reviewed my lease and realized there really wasn't a five-year option like I thought. In fact, there was nothing. In Part I of this book, I wrote how important it was to have an option. This is one of the reasons I chose to put the full text of my lease in Appendix C. It's a very typical, standard lease that you can use to help compare and see what is normal and what is not.

I went back and looked at the notes that my lawyer had made when he reviewed the lease. I was concerned that maybe he did a less than thorough job and I didn't know enough to recognize that at the time.

Nothing in his notes pointed out that an option was lacking. I went back and looked at the email I exchanged with my former business partner and also with the leasing agent for the landlord—nothing. I even found the original lease proposal the landlord sent me before making a lease—still nothing.

This meant that when I went to call my landlord to try and renew my lease, I believed that I had no negotiating power whatsoever. The other thing I knew: rent had nearly doubled in the county where my business was located since I signed my original lease. I couldn't afford to pay double the rent. Even if sales were back at their peak, I didn't believe it was enough to support that kind of rent increase.

Worse yet, if I tried to sell the business, I'd be sticking the new owner with the same problem and if they had half a brain, they'd know it when they started to examine the business. It would be their responsibility to obtain a new lease.

At the end of 2006, I thought I was screwed—it was a very slow year when it came to anyone showing interest in purchasing the business and I seriously considered closing The Pot & Bead. My lease was set to expire in October 2007 and I had to be ready and prepare for this possibility that I would be closing the store at that time. It wasn't so bad except for the fact that I would still have an outstanding business loan, which I'd be responsible for.

There was one couple who I met back in May who were interested in buying the place but that went nowhere. That's all the activity that happened around my business until late that year. I still wanted to sell rather than close, but I'd made up my mind that if it didn't sell, I would close it when my lease was up.

Why? My priorities had changed. What I wanted to do in life had changed. I'd realized more about myself and what I love to do and am capable of. Most important: this was business, and the point was to make money. I had to face the fact that I was not making money. In fact, I was past the point where I was starting to lose money, which meant I was accruing more debt than only the business loan. Uh oh.

Sometimes you have to make really tough decisions. That's part of business ownership and life in general. When I decided that I would close, I was deciding that I would cut my losses. That's a hard and a very brave decision to make. But before giving up (no wait, I wasn't giving up, I was making a hard and necessary decision), I had to make sure I had examined all my options and had all the information possible to make a good decision.

One of those options was renewing my lease. I needed to contact the landlord to at least discuss the possibility. I wasn't sure if there was a better or worse time to start the negotiation process and I wasn't sure if it should be handled via phone or in writing. I was nervous because a fellow tenant in my shopping center claimed that he tried calling the landlord for months to try to renew his lease and that his calls were never returned. He said because of that, he had no choice but to close his store. Before I did anything, I emailed a friend, Julya Myers, who owns another paint-your-own-pottery studio, Amazing Art Studio, in Rockville, Maryland. Before she opened her cute little store, she worked in the commercial leasing business. Julya gave me some fantastic insight. She told me that a lot of new leases are written over the summer because folks want to be open for the holidays (gee—that's when my original lease was written and exactly why I was pushing to get it done in the summer of 2002). December through February is pretty much dead time. Julya also said I needed to watch the rate of turnover and available properties in the area to determine when a good time to approach the landlord was. If my shopping center was hot, I should start pursuing as soon as possible. If things were slow, then waiting till January was best. Vacancies in my own shopping center were also something to watch—the more vacant space, the greater the advantage I had when negotiating.

As for calling versus writing, Julya suggested I call and then follow up in writing. If I started running into an issue, I could give him a specific time period for contacting me, stating that I needed a new lease solidified in order to finish working on future projects. She also recommended that I start looking at other locations even if I had no intention of moving. Knowing what other options were available in the area at the time would put me in a stronger negotiating position. At the time, things were indeed slow; there was some empty space in my shopping center, so I would have until after the New Year to contact my landlord.

When there were about 120 days (four months) left on my lease, I decided it was time to tell my employees. I couldn't wait as long as I originally wanted to. I was going to make some changes, like shortening our operating hours for the summer and not reordering certain marketing materials. I thought it was better for them to know what was going on rather than speculate and create rumors. One by one, I took them aside and explained how I decided to not renew our lease. They were sad about it but understood.

Then, an unexpected thing happened. The next day I got an email from one of my employees, Susie. She was wondering if it made any sense in the world for her and her mom to purchase the business. I was shocked—I hadn't ever considered it. Well, that's not entirely true. I had considered the possibility of one of my adult employees taking over, but I didn't think it was realistic given that (I thought) they all had plans of their own for school and careers.

It turns out Susie, who had recently completed cosmetology school and was working a second job at a salon, wasn't interested in cosmetology as a career—it was something she was doing because until then she didn't know what she wanted to do. She still lived at home and her family had some experience in small business.

I emailed her back suggesting books she should read about the retail business, told her that taking it over was indeed a possibility, and that after thinking about it some more, if she and her mom were still interested, we should meet. We met a couple of days later to talk.

"How do we make this happen?" was the theme of the discussion. They definitely had a lot of enthusiasm for buying my business and I thought they were coming in with some good knowledge. Given that Susie had worked for me for a while, they weren't disillusioned about the status of the business. I had been very blunt when I told my employees I was closing. I told them that at the end of the day I wasn't making money with the business so renewing my lease didn't make sense for me. Susie and her mom understood that my marketing efforts for the business were minimal and believed that that was what the business needed.

After that meeting, they were going to write a business plan with the help of their accountant who would generate the financial parts. I let them know that time was running out—especially since I was going to have to do things like reduce hours, and in the near future even tell customers. I gave them the contact information of the leasing agent and even gave them some insight into the lease I had and what I would do if I was renewing.

The next day, I got a message from Susie with their accountant's email and he asked for some financial data. If you're selling your business, it's pretty standard to be asked for, and provide, some basic Profit & Loss Statements and even Balance Sheets for select periods of time.

Susie and her mom were so enthusiastic that they even came and helped me do inventory. We did inventory usually once a year around New Year's Day. While not as complicated as in other businesses (all we needed to do was count pottery pieces), it was a tedious job. I was thankful for the help.

My mother had always said to me: "Hope for the best, expect the worst." This was the feeling I had at least for the first week or so after we met. Their ability to purchase the business hinged on getting a business loan. Not knowing their financial situation, it was hard for me to judge how realistic getting a business loan was for them, but I was well aware that it always took longer than expected. I wasn't getting my hopes up too much.

It's funny how things happen and how things all seem to happen at once. In one week, I didn't get just one person asking me about purchasing my business. The day after Susie told me she was interested, I received an email from a woman, Tabitha, asking me if the rumor she heard from one of her customers that my place was up for sale was true.

Up until two weeks before that email, Tabitha owned a paint-your-own-pottery studio in a nearby town. It was close enough so that her business was technically competition, but far enough away that it wasn't a serious draw. She had opened about a year after I did in an area I had looked at, but didn't settle on.

She closed her shop prematurely and was looking to reopen someplace else. Apparently, she had landlord issues; issues that made mine look like nothing. The problems started from the beginning of her lease, when a burst water pipe caused her business to be closed for five weeks during the Christmas holiday season, and ended with ceiling tiles falling down in the middle of a birthday party.

We met over coffee and she told me all about her landlord woes and how she was unable to stay in her space anymore, especially after the ceiling tile incident. The ceiling tile problems were the result of HVAC (HVAC is the term used for Heating, Ventilation, and Air Conditioning) equipment not being fit properly for the size and use of the space. The equipment was fairly new but sized too small, and as a result was unable to keep the second floor cool in the spring. She had one of these cute, old former house buildings in a historic area and used both floors for her business. If it was only ceiling tiles falling during a party, that alone wouldn't be *too* bad. But some small animals had apparently made their home in the ceiling and didn't survive the heat either. When the ceiling tiles came down, yes, so did some dead squirrels. That was her final straw. She vacated the space that week, breaking her lease.

We talked about the possibility of her taking over my business. However, it didn't make sense for either of us. I was looking to completely sever my business ties to the area and she still had all the stuff (her own kilns and furniture) and even her own customer base. She was looking for a business partner and I was looking to get out of the business altogether.

Breaking a lease is not something one does lightly. You signed a contract and are obligated to meet your end of that contract. However, some situations do seem horribly unfair, like in Tabitha's case, specifically in regards to building and space maintenance.

My lease says that I'm responsible for *everything* inside the space. This is not unusual. A lease typically requires a guarantee from the tenant that the rent will be paid no matter what. When I realized I was losing money on the whole business, I too thought about closing early, but I was clearly responsible for the lease payments if I did. That would be additional debt for me. This makes sense for some people—buying out your lease is not unheard of.

What's the right thing to do? I checked in with a lawyer and he emphasized the importance of consulting with an attorney *before* you take any action. There are a lot of factors to consider: How much money is at stake? Would remaining on the premises be dangerous? Is it possible that a situation like this could be considered a "constructive eviction"? Depending on the laws of the state, a tenant may have the right to withhold a certain amount of rent or vacate the premises altogether.

Back at the store a month later, Susie and her mom decided that purchasing the business wasn't in the cards at the time. Susie's dad also owned his own business. While this was good in the sense that they knew and understood what it takes to run a small business, it was also too big a risk to have so much money and resources tied up in business ventures.

With four months to go until my lease was up, that was it—we'd be closing.

## No-Nonsense Tips and Tidbits:

- Selling the business is only one of several possible exit strategies a business owner should consider.
- Make sure you know what's in your lease. Review it periodically. Even if you have a lawyer review it, make sure you review it, too. Lawyers are imperfect people like the rest of us and might miss something.
- If you need to consider breaking your lease, consult with a lawyer before you take any action.

# Chapter 8

# Take My Business, Please!

It's November 2006. I met with my accountant this morning to discuss the future, or lack thereof, of my business. I have to face the truth and be honest with myself: sales are not good; they're actually down this year. (And the beginning of the holiday season isn't looking too good, either.) The stress is overwhelming. I tried to sell the business, but that hasn't worked out. I have to give serious consideration to the "C" word: Closing.

It could be worse. I could be facing the "B" word: Bankruptcy. Luckily, things are not *that* bad. I have debt but I am paying off the debt, so no "B." The fact that I am able to make payments toward my debts each month means that it's not appropriate for me to declare "B." In "B," typically any collateral that has been pledged to a debt is sold and the proceeds are used to pay off debt. In this case, the collateral was my mother's home. When I needed to refinance my business loan at the end of 2004 in order to buy out my former business partner, my mom's home was used as collateral.

My accountant confirmed what I already knew: I needed to close. My lease was up in 344 days. Yes, I'd started counting the days, but I couldn't simply let the days go by. I needed to have a plan, which is why I met with my accountant this morning to come up with a to-do list.

Why hasn't the business sold after more than a year and a half of "trying"? At the time, I believed the biggest obstacle was my lease—or lack of an option on it. With a little less than a year to go and no real lease option to speak of, anyone buying my business would have to take on some serious negotiations with the landlord. One of the reasons I thought I had to close was because rent had skyrocketed in this area, forcing many other people to close. Anything more than what I was paying would simply be too much. But I needed to know that for certain, so the first thing on my to-do list was to contact the landlord and ask him what the terms of renewing my lease would be.

While planning to close was a serious consideration going into 2007, it wasn't over yet—the business still could sell. I wasn't optimistic, but I wasn't giving up, either. I left that meeting with my accountant a bit depressed. Thinking about closing The Pot & Bead was not a pleasant reality to face, but at least I had a plan and some steps to take. I was not merely sitting and watching the clock count down.

I started on the to-do list my accountant and I wrote up right when I got home. I called my landlord, and to my utter shock, he quoted a rate comparable to what I was currently paying. Did this change anything? Should I renew the lease and then aggressively sell? I'll be honest, a part of me was hoping that the rate was going to be so high that it would make my decision to close the store really easy. Unfortunately, nothing is ever really easy.

Next on the to-do list was thinking about the products and services we were selling. For one, we sold a yearly membership. At some point we would have to stop selling those. Same thing with gift certificates. The policy at The Pot & Bead had always been that gift certificates never expired, so my accountant recommended that we should start putting an expiration date on them. Also on the to-do list: I needed to talk to the bank about refinancing my debt.

What about my staff? I decided that it was way too soon for them to know. I couldn't risk having them leave for another job early—the store did need to stay open for another 344 days. None of them would have problems finding another retail job, so I didn't need to worry too much about them, they'd be fine.

One other thing that my accountant recommended: call other pottery studios to see if they were interested in purchasing The Pot & Bead to expand their business in my area. I emailed the owners of the two closest pottery studios similar to mine to see if they wanted to expand; I had a great customer base to offer them. Chains and franchises (and franchise-chains) do have an economy of scale and are quite possibly the only brick and mortar businesses that can survive in this economic climate. I thought a lot about the economy of scale back when I first got into this business—I planned, expected, and hoped I'd be a small chain within five years. I still believe that had I achieved that, I'd be much more profitable. However, neither of the pottery studios was interested in purchasing my business.

The other variable that entered the closing decision equation: the day before I met with my accountant, I discovered that my local competition (that had opened within three weeks of me back in 2002) was also attempting to sell their business. They were listed on a businesses-for-sale website, and even though their name wasn't listed, it was easy to determine it was them based on certain characteristics of the listing such as location and the fact that it was a pottery studio.

This was good and bad news. The good part was that it gave me some information about their business, like gross sales and what they were paying for rent. (No-Nonsense note: If you're researching potential figures for your financial plan, scan through business-for-sale websites like bizbuysell.com. They will often post "gross sales" or "cash flow" numbers.) The bad part was the jealously that hit me. I tried selling my business for two years and couldn't. What if they could? I knew I had a better business; we had twice their gross sales (in our worst year)! Someone looking for a good pottery studio business to buy should buy mine!

My accountant suggested to list my business side-by-side with theirs—if I offered mine at the same price, but with gross revenues two or more times higher, mine looked like an excellent deal. But I never took that piece of advice; I never felt comfortable putting out revenue information (my mistake) and it wasn't too much longer after that that the business broker contacted me to let me know that someone else was interested in buying my business.

Two hundred and twenty-five days till my lease was up and an offer came in on the store. The broker who I wasn't officially working with anymore (since our contract expired a while ago) had emailed me a few times over the past few weeks claiming to have serious interest. I was very skeptical and tried not to get my hopes up. The broker told me a little about the potential buyer. It was a woman who had been in my store before with her kids. She was married, but the business was intended to be something she would do, not something "they" would do.

The offer was incredibly low—lower than I ever expected. Completely low. Did I mention it was low? It was unbelievable. I was hurt and insulted. I couldn't have opened this business for that price and there was no way I was going to sell my business for $35,000.

Or would I?

I got some advice from my accountant and family: I should definitely negotiate, but if they wouldn't budge, I would take the offer.

Within twenty-four hours of receiving the offer, I emailed the broker on a Tuesday. I explained to him that $35,000 was too low, especially given that his fee was $10,000, and proposed a counter offer. The broker's fee was 10 percent unless the purchase price was under $100,000—then it was a flat $10,000. At the time when I was listing the business for $159,000 and even lowering it to $99,000, this didn't seem that unreasonable.

I made two mistakes when I sent that email off. One, I didn't request a "return receipt" for the email and two, I didn't immediately follow up with a phone call. I spent all of Wednesday and Thursday biting my nails, wondering if they were going to counter or say that they were going to stick to the original offer (which expired that upcoming Friday). Well, come Friday morning, nothing, but I did get a short email from the broker late Friday morning reminding me about the expiration of the offer and asking me to call. So I called. He said he hadn't received my email.

I was shocked. I realized the two mistakes and was more than a little annoyed that he hadn't followed up earlier. Why was he waiting for me? Why didn't he try to contact me sooner? He didn't get paid unless the deal went through, so I thought it was in his best interest to ensure it happened. With a willing seller and a willing buyer, why wasn't he on top of things?

He said he would take my counter to the buyer and get back to me. I heard nothing the rest of the day. Unfortunately, I couldn't call him or anyone later that day. I was on a plane flying home from a trip related to my day job. The offer was expiring right about the time I was landing.

The next morning, after the offer had expired, I sent an email saying I was disappointed that I hadn't heard back. He replied saying that the buyer and her husband needed to think about it.

Monday morning, the broker forwarded me an email from the buyer. They were passing completely and suggested the broker not waste his time on them any longer; they weren't interested anymore at all.

I was flabbergasted. Wasn't some negotiation normal? Why wasn't the broker already jumping on them to at least get back to the original offer? He was going to give up just like that?

I finally got hold of the broker and explained that at the end of the day, I wanted and was willing to take $45,000 for the business. He offered to lower his fee by $5,000 and would get back to the potential buyer with a counter of $50,000.

Again, I waited for what was only a day or two but seemed like an eternity, and then had to make the effort to follow up with him. He said that the wife still seemed interested but had to check with her husband. The next day, the broker again forwarded an email from the buyer. She *was* interested but was having a hard time talking her husband back into it. That was a Friday. It was another long nail-biting weekend as I waited to find out what was going to happen. I had to spend an afternoon in my store, which was incredibly hard. My employees were asking me about our party packages and when we would change them up. I had to push them off, knowing that either the business would sell, or it would be closing soon. During all of this, my landlord kept calling me about renewing my lease!

After the weekend, I heard from the broker. It seemed like they were going to buy the place and would get back to the broker on Tuesday. I breathed a nervous sigh of relief. I didn't have a signed offer, so this wasn't a done deal yet, but I didn't worry about it too much Tuesday and Wednesday since I was busy with other things.

Thursday came and I still hadn't heard anything. I again took the initiative and emailed the broker to ask if there was any progress. He emailed me back and said that the buyer really was passing (apparently, she was unable to convince her husband back into the deal) and that he wanted to do one last push to sell my business in the next month. I was livid. When the heck was he going to tell me this?

After spending an evening ranting to my significant other and my dad, the next day I wrote the broker back telling him exactly how disappointed I was and how I thought he had done an awful job at communicating with me. I also wrote that if we were going to continue working together, there were a few conditions he had to agree to.

He wrote back a defensive email, ignoring the conditions and not saying whether or not he agreed. In his reply, he forwarded an email from the buyer in an attempt to prove that he was on top of things, but in fact, proved me right since the last email he received from the buyer was that Tuesday, and here it was, Saturday. If he received this on Tuesday, he was definitely *not* prompt in getting back to me.

I emailed back and ended the relationship right there. (Note that I could do this easily because we did not have a signed agreement that was in effect; our agreement had expired a while ago.) I emailed my accountant looking for a new broker recommendation. He said he only knew of horror stories; he didn't know of anyone he could recommend. Friends had been telling me for a while not to use a broker. Broker or no broker? That is the question!

It happened that at about the same time, I was speaking with the leasing agent from my landlord's company. She had someone interested in buying my "stuff" when I closed. I was interested in getting out sooner and wondered why he wouldn't simply buy my business—why only the stuff? That meant he wouldn't get my name, my website, my $3,000 channel letter sign, my logo, my customer mailing list, etc. But whatever. I was willing to entertain this possibility and the leasing agent was willing to try to encourage this individual to buy the whole business and do it sooner rather than later.

I told her a little about the deal that had recently fallen through and asked her if she could recommend a broker. She said I didn't need one. I asked about all the work they do that I don't have time for, like making sure things get transferred properly, etc. She said I only needed a lawyer to draw up the bill of sale, she would take care of the lease and assist the new guy with the transfer of utilities and such, and that was it. She said she had been in commercial real estate for twenty years and was adamant that I didn't need a broker.

I didn't look for a new one and probably never will work with a broker again. In researching for this book, I tried very hard to find someone with a positive broker experience to share. Most people I've spoken with had only negative things to say. That's probably because many people treat the broker the same way I did—as someone who would go away and only come back when they had an offer in hand, instead of treating the broker like a partner.

I did finally meet someone who had a positive experience and I think that's because she took the approach of treating the broker like a partner in her business. Grace Wolf, who owns Clay Café Chantilly, a pottery studio like mine in Chantilly, Virginia, has bought and sold five businesses. She used a broker three times: twice to buy a business and once to sell one. The times that she was the buyer, she found the business on an Internet listing and had to go through the seller's broker. But the time she was the seller, she used a broker she met through her local chamber of commerce. She described the process of finding a good broker was exactly like how one goes about finding a good real estate agent or banker: ask people who've successfully bought or sold a business and ask commercial lenders who they know and would recommend.

When Grace sold her business through a broker, the broker explained the entire process he planned on using before she signed a contract. They discussed a time frame, so both sides understood how long things would take, so there were no surprises. Grace was very happy with this experience. At no time did the broker take any actions without her prior understanding and approval. She said that he also had some very creative ideas on how to market her business. It was not only standard listings, the broker did some direct mailings and they even held an open house at the business.

At the end of the day, Grace said that the broker was very responsive and even though the sale took a little longer than she would have liked, she got top dollar from the business and was very happy. The sale took fourteen months, which Grace said was average for that type of business (a franchise).

Her situation was a little different than mine because it was a franchise. In her case, as it is with most franchises, the franchisor needs to approve the potential buyer, which adds additional time for the sale. My broker, like hers, should have vetted prospects and let me meet them right away. Then, the potential buyers would have to put down a deposit and sign a letter of intent, but could always back out within thirty days (or automatically if they were not approved by the franchisor).

Finally, I asked Grace about whether or not her employees knew that her business was for sale. She said she was private about it and recommends keeping everything private until there's a contract, unless an employee is going to buy the business. She couldn't think of any upside in letting employees know.

When I examined the emails that the broker had forwarded to me from the potential buyer, I noticed that I had her full name and email address. (I'll call her Jane here). I checked my customer database and sure enough, Jane had visited to my store a few times. I decided I was very interested to hear her side of what happened, for this book. I had the opportunity to get her perspective, so I decided to contact her.

I was still livid that the deal fell through—but I was upset with the broker, not her.

The last email he had forwarded to me said that the buyer *never expected* a counter; she expected me to accept the offer right away. This could only have come from discussions with him, so the broker discussed it with the buyer, but not me. When I said I wanted to counter, and counter high (it's high if you think of it in terms of a percentage of their original offer), why didn't he tell me, "Adeena, in my discussions with Jane, she doesn't believe you're going to counter, so this may be a bit of a shock"? Instead, when I told him of my counter, he simply said, "I'll pass that on."

I emailed Jane, telling her that I was interested in her side of the story and was not contacting her to reopen negotiations. She responded that she'd be happy to meet and we set up a date and time. She was right on time and very personable. I think the owner of a small business becomes the face of that business, so having a demeanor that is friendly and outgoing is important, and she had all of that.

I asked her what happened. How did she meet the broker? How did she find out about The Pot & Bead? She had first been to the store with her Mom's Club the summer before. She loved it. Several months later, she decided that she was interested in owning a business. Her research took her to a website that listed businesses for sale.

She looked through all the listings in the county and came across one that was a "Pottery and Craft" studio—it sounded to her like it was The Pot & Bead. She contacted the listing broker and asked if it was, but he couldn't give out that information until she signed an NDA ("Non-Disclosure Agreement"). This is good. A Non-Disclosure Agreement is a document that helps to protect the secrets of your business. (It's not a guarantee; it's a warm fuzzy since you're relying on people to simply honor their signature.) When she signed the NDA, the broker told her yes, it was The Pot & Bead.

Thus began the process of further looking into my business. Jane said she had always felt pressured by the broker. He kept pressuring her to put down earnest money before giving out detailed information. I do agree with the broker on this item. Earnest money can be returned to the buyer; it's not lost. It demonstrates the seriousness of the buyer.

She said she did communicate with the broker about what she was willing to offer on the business and that she wasn't interested in paying any more. She said that the broker communicated back an expectation that what she wanted to offer was going to be just fine.

Right up until she made the offer, her husband wasn't involved much in the process. He trusted her to do whatever she needed to. But once I made a counter, that's when he perked up and got involved. Why did I counter when the broker led them to believe I wouldn't? This completely destroyed the husband's trust in the situation. He then asked to look over whatever numbers were available, and he looked at other nearby studios. He even camped out in front of my studio one day to see the traffic. Unfortunately for me, he picked the wrong day; a day and time when school was in session. For a business centered around kids and families, we were always slow when school was in session.

So the husband decided no, and there was no going back after that.

When I met Jane, she was still enthralled with the shop and I thought she was fantastic. She would have been a terrific new owner. During our discussion, she asked a lot of "what if" questions, and we started talking about my lease. She was saying something and then added "and since you have your lease for three more years . . ." to which I said "Huwha?" Apparently, the broker told her I had already renewed and secured my lease for three more years. My jaw hit the floor. This was an outright lie and one that Jane said was key in her decision making process.

Not only had I not renewed my lease, the broker was well aware of that fact. It was his job to contact the leasing agent with the landlord to help secure a lease for the buyer. I asked (emailed) him on more than one occasion when this would be done and he always said after we had an agreement. I was talking occasionally with the leasing agent throughout this process and knew that the broker never contacted her. And the broker darn well knew that the furthest I got with the landlord in discussions about renewing my lease was limited to an estimate of the cost.

I left my meeting with Jane even sadder that it didn't work out and more upset with the broker than ever.

There are several lessons to take out of my bad experience that could be put to good use if you decide that working with a broker is the right thing for you. This applies whether you're in the buyer or seller position:

- Communicate. Follow up all important emails with a phone call and follow up all important phone calls with an email.
- Ensure that in any written agreement there are no penalties to you if you don't buy or sell.

- Ensure that in any written agreement you can cancel early with no penalties.
- If the above isn't an option, then make the agreement short-term; you can always renew later. You'll get some resistance on this item—the broker will tell you that it takes time to market a business and find good buyers. This is true, but be honest and up front with the broker; you want to see how well they are marketing your business before making a longer commitment. If the broker won't work with you on this, treat that as a warning sign.
- Ask lots of questions about how the business will be marketed. Will it be listed on websites? Which ones? Newspapers? Will the broker be preparing a brochure of your business (they might not, especially if you're able to negotiate them down to a smaller than normal fee)? If not, they should be more than willing to distribute the selling brochure you make.
- Ask them to share with you listings of your business. When they are marketing your business, you want to see the listing on websites or in newspapers.
- References are truly as important here as with any other service business. Get some references and make a couple of phone calls.
- Ask about other businesses the broker is also trying to sell at the moment. This is a catch-22 because if they're trying to sell a lot of good businesses, it means that you might have yourself a good broker, but it also probably means that they might not devote enough time and attention to your business.
- Related to the above: Make sure the business broker you work with is selling businesses in your class. If the broker routinely sells businesses that typically go for $1,000,000 or more and your business lists for $200,000 or less, it's a pretty good bet that he's not going to work as hard for you since his net commission will only be 20 percent of what he's used to getting on a deal.

The last thought I want to leave you with before closing out this chapter is this: A business broker is like any other service professional. If you don't believe that he or she is working hard enough, if you're dreading giving them their commission, then it's time to end the relationship and find another broker.

## No-Nonsense Tips and Tidbits:

- If you need to close up a business, face that decision head-on.
- Business-for-sale websites might give you some insight into competition or potential competition.
- Always follow up important emails in *any* situation. It is perfectly appropriate to make a phone call to say: "I sent you this email and wanted to confirm you received it."
- Use caution if you are going to use a business broker. Get solid references and be sure they are earning their commission.

# Chapter 9

# For Sale, by Owner

With about seventy-five days left to operate my business, I found out that my closest competitor was going to close in the summer of 2007. Apparently, they weren't able to sell their business either. They had opened up about two weeks before we did; I talked a little bit about this in Part I and how their existence only encouraged us to be better. It was okay for there to be two stores in the town, and it was okay for people to go to both, but we wanted to make sure people came back to us.

I found out they were closing through a Google Alert I had set up. The alert had picked up an article in a local newspaper describing how they were closing over the summer. Wow. It's not every day you find out something so dramatic about your closest competitor.

(Note about Google: Go to www.google.com/alerts and set up an alert with your business name and your competitor's names. Google will then email you anytime these names, or other keywords you choose, show up in a news article or blog. It's very helpful for keeping tabs on your business and industry. Plus, it's great to know if people are blogging about you!)

I had mixed emotions about their closing. Yes, it was great that they were closing because I really wanted to experience what business would be like without them, but I knew I was planning to close, too. I had an idea. What if I could stay open a few more months? Just through the busy holiday season? How awesome would that be to have the whole holiday season to myself? (Actually, when I first mentioned their closing to one of my employees, her first words to me were: "Does this mean we'll stay open?") And most important: Could I make a last push to try and sell the business? With my closest competition gone, and a landlord willing to be flexible rather than sit on empty space, the business might be attractive again.

There were two main things I had to consider:

1. Would this make sense financially?
2. Would my landlord let me stay open for a few more months without a new five-year commitment?

The financial part was easy enough to figure out. I estimated our sales through those months based on previous years. I estimated expenses and figured out what my total financial picture would be if I closed up when my lease was up versus closing a few months later. The numbers worked out; unless sales were a lot less than the previous year, it looked like staying open made sense financially. At the end of the day, I believed that I would be in less debt after we closed later (the actual numbers are in Chapter 3—we were close).

I also needed to ask if my significant other could handle it (or handle a stressed out me for a few more months and continue to put our other plans on hold) and asked my accountant for a sanity check. They both thought it made sense.

The next step was to ask my landlord. Several months earlier I had informed him that I wasn't planning on renewing my lease, which meant that they probably were looking for a new tenant to take my place. If they had already found someone, I would be out of luck.

Their first reaction was that they wanted me to sign on for another full year. I wasn't prepared to do that; I'd already made other plans with my life that didn't necessarily include remaining tied to the area. I told them that a year wasn't possible; I was only interested in a few more months. I also explained to them that I was interested in the opportunity to try and sell the store again, which would keep the business as a tenant for a longer period of time.

I spoke to the leasing agent on the phone and she told me that they had a meeting coming up and she'd bring it up to see if she could get a few more months approved. I emailed her around the time I thought this meeting was happening to see what was up; my drop-dead date was fast approaching. I had already told my employees I was planning on closing and I was going to need to announce it to the world pretty soon.

A week later, I heard back. I was approved to go on a month-to-month lease. Fantastic! But it wasn't a done deal until it was in writing. I needed this in writing and a few other items. I needed to make sure my rent wasn't going to go up—that was the biggie. I also used this as the perfect time to ask for some leeway on a few things in my lease that were very limiting, namely, the restrictions on our opening hours and what we could do with our windows.

My original lease said that we had to be open at least from 11 a.m. to 7 p.m., seven days a week. For most of the five years we were open, this wasn't a problem, but in the last few months, I wanted to cut the hours. I already did that at the beginning of our last summer, it was a way to save on payroll (and on a little stress). A couple of additional hours a week when I knew my cell phone wouldn't ring with a problem was something I was looking forward to.

As for the windows, that last summer I decided to paint them, as I wrote about in an earlier chapter. We were an art studio, so it made sense to paint nice designs and messages on the windows (even though the lease said I couldn't do things like that without the landlord's approval). I decided to do it anyway and suffer whatever the consequences were. It turned out that painting the windows was a great idea. Almost instantly, there was an increase of new customers in the store. As part of the lease renegotiation, I asked to be allowed to continue to do this. In this renegotiation, I was also trying to work on some of my old personal issues with following up on communications; meaning that I would wait an appropriate amount of time, but then I would take the initiative and follow up.

While these details were being worked out with the landlord, I let my employees know about the progress I'd made. This got them excited, which was fantastic. I waited as long as I did to tell my employees about closing to begin with because my main concern was morale. I still had a business to operate and the attitude of my employees while they worked really set the tone. Also, nothing is final until it's final.

When I originally told my employees about closing, I told them that I wasn't ready for customers to know and that I was a little paranoid about them finding out. I'm glad I had that attitude, because with the possibility of staying open, it was good that customers didn't know we might close.

Customers don't always digest information correctly. My competitor was closing with July 29 as their last day, but at least two weeks before that, we had customers coming to our store claiming that the other place was already closed, when it really wasn't. That's exactly why I didn't want the word that we might close to get out too early. Customers might then assume we were closed and not bother to find out if we were closed *for real* or not.

It took about two weeks before I had something from the landlord in writing regarding the lease. When I communicated with the leasing agent she said I needed to put my "requests" in writing and she would stick it in my folder. She implied that my requests weren't going to be a big deal. That night, I wrote the request letter, emailed her, and followed up with a hard copy through snail mail.

I received a letter back from the landlord about a week later. It stated that the month-by-month was approved, but for no longer than a year. They agreed to my request for flexible hours and said that it was up to the property manager about the windows and that they were forwarding my letter on to her. Yay!

I reset my mental countdown clock. It was the middle of August 2007. We had recently finished summer camp, and two weeks after that began the slowest month of the year. If we survived that, we'd be good till Christmas. My plan was to work hard to sell the place all on my own— no broker this time. I set a deadline; I needed a buyer by December 1 who would take possession on January 1. Keeping the store and my lease past the end of January was simply not what I wanted.

It was time to get a move on planning out the next few months. First, I had to understand what my goals were.

1. Make money.
2. Sell the store.

I began writing a list of things to do to achieve both of those goals. In the make money department, I made a list of free or nearly free marketing ideas and ways to keep expenses down. See *Marketing Your Retail Store in the Internet Age* in the Reading List, it's full of helpful and inexpensive marketing ideas. We also cut back some of our services to help simplify things (we stopped "special orders" unless they were large and trimmed our party packages). This helped keep us focused on our core business: selling pottery to paint.

Next, I had to think about how I was going to market and sell the store itself. I started making a two-page brochure, highlighting the important features of the business. I had read somewhere in an article about doing this. I knew that I was going to openly tell everyone that the store was for sale. I'd start by telling my close friends, family, and business associates. My employees already knew. Then I needed to tell customers, put it on the front page of the website, and tell people right in our store.

I began to give a tiny bit of thought to what would happen when someone seriously expressed interest in buying the business. I knew I needed an NDA (a Non-Disclosure Agreement), but then what?

Then it dawned on me: I really knew nothing about how to market and sell my business. If you read Part I, you know that I tried *buying* a business, and I had read books all about that. Didn't some of those books talk about selling a business, too? I had to have something on my bookshelf. The day before I was headed out of town for a few days, I looked through my collection of business books—there was a chapter here and a chapter there, but nothing really comprehensive. A trip to the bookstore took care of that and I was kicking myself for not doing this before I ever hired a broker two and a half years earlier.

I plowed through the books pretty quickly. I knew pretty much what was in them but I needed to see it all laid out in writing. The books had samples and templates of all kinds of forms and even a sales agreement (but this was starting to be a little eerily familiar; in Part I of this book, I wrote about how I lost a pile of money trying to purchase a store). But this was different, right? This time, I was the seller and I was a little smarter about things.

I used the templates in the book to come up with a Confidentiality Agreement and a short "Buyer Questionnaire." I also expanded my sales brochure by a page and decided that it did make some sense to put my asking price right on the brochure. I was asking for $59,000 for my business. Then I was ready to email it to everyone I knew locally.

I did that and within twenty-four hours received a response. Someone wanted to talk to me about the business. He introduced himself as a real estate agent who worked with commercial clients, so I suspected that he wasn't necessarily interested in the business himself, but thought it still was worth sitting down over a cup of coffee to discuss.

I did, and my initial instinct about him was correct. He was interested in being a broker for the sale, albeit at a lower rate than the previous broker (6 percent versus 10 percent). It was an interesting conversation, but I was a little disappointed. I wasn't looking for a new broker.

Within a week, I had two other people email me looking for more information. I emailed both the Confidentiality Agreement and Buyer Questionnaire and asked them to return this before I passed out anymore detailed numbers or information. One got the forms back to me right away, one didn't. It turned out that the one who did was a "scout" for a friend. If the business was interesting, he'd pass it on to the friend who was looking to buy a business.

The one who didn't respond right away followed up a week later. She said that her husband was an accountant and only cared about the numbers. I re-sent the agreements and said that both she and her husband needed to sign them. Immediately, I got them back from the husband, but not her. I emailed her saying that I needed a signature from her, too, before I would share any numbers. She wrote back saying that they had already changed their minds; they didn't like the location and didn't like the fact that another studio was opening up nearby.

Another studio? Yep! A franchise that for two years had been threatening to open up nearby on and off again, was on again. One of my employees visually confirmed a "coming soon" sign on the actual retail location. But this time, I wasn't too worried. With my closest competition gone, this was still less competition than I had in the past, and they were going to be located a bit further away than the competitor that had recently closed. At least this couple told me they dropped their interest before I shared anymore financial information with them.

Speaking of which, exactly what was I going to share? In the past, when working with the broker, I would share my P&Ls, my actual Profit & Loss statements. I learned that this was a mistake. The books I read both talked about a P&L "restatement." This meant that I didn't have to share *every* detail or my *real* P&L with a prospective buyer at this stage.

Examples that the books gave were similar to this one: Let's say I went to my trade studio's annual convention and the business paid for it. While it's a legitimate business expense, it's an optional one. Therefore, I don't have to include it as an expense when I show a potential buyer my expenses. However, the books implied that you let the prospective buyer know that it's a "restatement" and that they should understand that these optional expenses are omitted.

One book discussed preparing a "memorandum" and this is what I did. I included all the actual income and all the *necessary* expenses I had during the past couple of years. I also included some other data like information regarding my lease payments and I highlighted the fact that sales had improved in the past couple of months. I passed the memorandum on to the "scout" who had signed my Confidentiality Agreement. The verdict: without a long-term lease in place, they weren't interested.

I received a few more inquiries. Some other people were willing to sign my Confidentiality Agreement and received the memorandum. No one else went any further than that. For each one who wound up not pursuing my business, I tried to find out why. At least one other individual was concerned about my lack of a lease. I tried to explain that the landlord was in a position to work with a new tenant, and also that I would pursue and get the lease contingent on a sale. That didn't help.

Someone else was apprehensive about the number of hours I was putting in. She also had a full-time job. I explained that I was only actually putting in a couple hours a week; not much to speak of. I knew that I was leaving out an important fact—I believed the store needed more attention, not less, to be successful.

Then, in late September, I was contacted by someone I knew through my chamber of commerce. I'll call him Jason (not his real name, of course). He said that in passing, he heard a rumor that I was selling the store and was interested if that was true.

I agreed to meet him for coffee and told my family about it. They were thrilled that I was taking a meeting, but I wasn't too excited. I knew who I was meeting and I didn't picture him as someone truly interested in the business. I thought he was only interested if the store was making a pile of money and as soon as he found out that it wasn't, he'd lose interest immediately.

At the meeting, he signed my Confidentiality Agreement and I gave him the memorandum to look at. He admitted that he wasn't a financial guru and was going to take it to his financial advisor and lawyer to review, but he wasn't discouraged by what he saw. He already owned a small business *without* a retail front. He was looking for an opportunity and he believed he had found it with The Pot & Bead.

I left that meeting pleasantly surprised, but I refused to get my hopes up. He came back a week later and asked for some more detailed financials. I contacted my accountant—what else could I provide at this stage? My accountant recommended passing on the Schedule C (which is used to report profit or loss from a business, typically used by sole proprietors) from my tax forms. Jason also told me that he was already meeting with banks about financing and would contact the landlord about leasing the space *and* leasing the space next door!

We met again and he had a pile of new questions. He also had a huge, thick file of research. He showed me his plans for taking the space next door. He'd started a business plan, he'd printed out my recent email newsletters and pages from my website, and he had been in my store on a Saturday when I wasn't there; he introduced himself to my employees and told them that he was trying to buy the place.

I already knew about his visit to the store. When it happened, one of my employees had sent me a text message. I was a little freaked out. What if they said something wrong? By wrong I mean that deals can be fragile and people's minds fickle. What if the store was too slow? What if it was too messy? What if their attitudes sucked that morning? I had my employee call me to tell me all the details. She told me that they discussed how no one wanted the place to close and how he said that "it wouldn't if he had anything to do about it." Phew. I was nervous about everything, but I was very pleasantly surprised and extremely encouraged by his enthusiasm.

When we met again, I tried to express that at this point I was ready for some kind of commitment: a letter of intent or offer letter and a deposit. He was just as interested as I was about moving forward and would talk to his lawyer about drawing up a letter.

A couple of days later I hadn't heard anything, so I emailed him and said that I needed the offer letter within a week. I said that I did have other interests to pursue. This was true. Susie's mom hadn't given up on my business and had recently contacted me about pursing a partnership arrangement. Not my favorite idea because it meant I would still have ties to the business, but I was considering it. It was still better than closing the place. I didn't really like applying that kind of pressure on Jason. I'm not a sales person and I hate pressuring people, but it was necessary at this point. I got a call from him a little while later, but before he saw my email. He said he was going to try and have an offer letter by my deadline.

At home, Dave, my significant other, was telling me that I needed to put more pressure on Jason. I didn't think that was right; I thought Jason was being very sincere, so when he called and asked if I would meet his wife, I thought that was a great idea and decided that Dave needed to come and meet them, too.

Starbucks played host to us again. Dave and I got there a little early that Saturday morning. There was a young boys' soccer team that had taken over the inside of the coffee shop. It was loud and there was only one seat available. We decided to sit outside, even though it was a little cooler than we liked. On the way out of the store, the parents of the kids were blocking the path. I chuckled internally—it wasn't only an issue at my store. When a large group comes in to a smaller place, they take over and forget that other people are around. We excused ourselves and got through.

Jason and his wife showed up and we all had a very nice chat. It was the best thing for Dave; he left feeling just as comfortable with the buyer as I was and believing that he was honest and sincere. We talked about an offer letter and deposit coming on Monday. Great!

Monday came, it was getting close to 5 p.m., and I hadn't heard anything. Should I call? Would that be too pushy? Should I wait? My normal reaction in a situation like this was to wait, but what I've learned over the past five years is that in situations like this, when half my brain is telling me to wait, I need to ignore that and push myself a little to take some initiative.

So I did—I called. Jason had just gotten home and apologized for not calling me before I did. He said he had met with his lawyer and the lawyer was writing up a Letter of Intent (LOI). He needed to check his messages to see if it was ready for him to pick up. We agreed to meet on Wednesday evening. I was glad I called. I felt better. I would have sat there and stewed for who knows how long if I didn't. It was funny, though. He called back about fifteen minutes later and wanted to express again how serious and committed he was to this deal.

Let's talk about his lawyer for a second. First of all, I also knew him through the chamber of commerce. Second, he's a lawyer looking out for his client's best interest (in theory). I respect that. But I was incredibly nervous that the lawyer was going to talk my buyer out of the deal. When we discussed the LOI that evening, the buyer mentioned that his lawyer wanted to hold the deposit in escrow. I said I'd get back to him about that; I didn't know if that was right or not.

I went back to my books to see what they said about the deposit and what one did with it when they had it in hand. They said nothing. I knew that an escrow was normal, but how does that get set up and who does it? I had no idea.

I contacted my accountant to see what he knew. He said it was fine for Jason's lawyer to set up the escrow account, but that I ought to have a copy and record of the transaction. I needed to hold some proof and have a way to access the escrow should it legally become mine.

That Wednesday, I had the LOI in hand and provided a written response to it, clause by clause. Overall, it didn't express a clear end date or a clear closing date and that was my main concern. I understood why. Jason was dependent on financing from a bank, and without that, he couldn't commit to a closing date.

Based on my feedback, he had his lawyer update the LOI and a few days later, the week before Thanksgiving, I had my letter. I reviewed it and signed it in his presence. There was only one thing that needed a tweak: the number of days for the due diligence. We changed the wording to make it clear that once the LOI was signed, a twenty-day due diligence period began. Five business days after the LOI was signed, I was supposed to have a Purchase Agreement in hand for the full asking price: $59,000. That was right after Thanksgiving (we agreed not to count Black Friday as a business day).

The contract was a couple of days late because Jason wasn't having luck with bank financing. I finally did receive a Purchase Agreement in mid-December. It was fine except for the lack of a specific closing date.

I was supposed to go on vacation. We talked about meeting when I got home, but then I sent Jason an email—I really needed this whole thing to close by the end of the calendar year so I could close my books and move on. The last thing I wanted was to be operating my business at all in 2008 which meant I would have business taxes to deal with a year later in 2009. It was Jason's problems securing bank financing that were slowing things down.

Jason had an alternate financing option. In a few months he'd be able to draw (penalty-free) from his 401(k). At this point, I said that I would accept 10 percent of the purchase price at closing, and $1,000 a month for a few months until the balance could be paid. I said I would gladly accept this if the deal was completed by the end of the year. It made sense to him and he said he and his lawyer would work on it and we'd have something to look at when I returned.

The week I got back was hellish. I played phone tag with Jason all week. Could he have some more financial info? Sure. His lawyer was inaccessible here and there. Uh, ok. Can we meet tomorrow? Ok, great! Uh, I don't have the contract yet, can we meet tomorrow?

I was supposed to meet with Jason at the very end of the week on Friday. On Friday—the Friday before Christmas—I didn't hear from him. I left a voice mail. Saturday—no word—I left another voice mail and reminded him that I was in town all week and off from my day job so I was completely available. But in my head, I was starting to panic. He had been so responsive, why wasn't he calling me now? What if he was thinking about backing out at this point? What was I going to do? Make another push to sell the place? Close? I was so stressed out, on the verge of freaking out by the end of Sunday, and I still hadn't heard anything.

On Monday, Christmas Eve, I got the relief call. The lawyer was still working with the landlord. A couple of things needed to be approved with the lease and then they were good to go. Jason and his lawyer wanted the contract to be dependent on the lease being accepted. That was perfectly fine with me. When would I see the contract? I needed to see it before closing day when it would be signed, of course. Jason said I would see it the day or two after Christmas.

A few days later, on the 27th, I spoke with Jason. He had some bad news and good news for me. The bad news was that we weren't going to be able to close on the contract on the 31st. The whole thing with the landlord was taking too long. He had just gotten off the phone with his lawyer who had spoken with the landlord's lawyer. The changes they wanted to make to the lease needed to go to the "committee" to be approved. It was going to be two or three weeks before we knew about their acceptance.

The good news was that he was in possession of an executable contract. Upon acceptance of that contract, he would give me a *nonrefundable* deposit toward the purchase price. He was doing this as an act of goodwill. He knew I didn't want to be running the business into 2008 and he saw this deposit as covering one month of rent; the amount of time I would still possess the business.

When he dropped off the contract for me to review, it was executable any day after that. I had some information to provide: a Schedule of Assets and a breakdown of how the sales numbers were allocated. This is also referred to as Asset Allocation and it's not necessarily a requirement for a Sales Agreement, but it means that you and the buyer agree how things are allocated for tax purposes. One of the books in the Reading List, *The Complete Guide to Selling a Business*, has a great chapter on tax issues associated with selling a business, including how to understand and deal with Asset Allocation.

I picked up and reviewed the contract and it all seemed reasonable. Specifically, I reviewed it against the clauses in *The Complete Guide to Selling a Business*. I sat there the next morning wondering if I needed to call a lawyer or not. Anytime I've not used my own lawyer, things didn't work out well, but every time I've used a lawyer, things didn't necessarily work out fantastic either, and I was out a lot of money, too. Had I learned my lessons in the past? Yes, I was smart. I needed to take the time to be diligent about reviewing my own documents and would not spend money on a lawyer in this case. Done.

Next, I had to get together my Schedule of Assets, which became the first attachment to the Sales Agreement. This was simply a list of all the tangible items that were part of the sale. As for Asset Allocation, Jason and his lawyer gave me the ability to freely allocate the purchase price among four categories: inventory, equipment, goodwill, and non-compete.

The following Monday, New Year's Eve, we both signed the Sales Agreement and I accepted the non-refundable deposit. We would close by the end of the month—no later than January 31st!

Everything was fine for the first two weeks into the New Year. I was excited and even somewhat relaxed for the first time in a long time. Then in mid-January, one of my three employees gave notice that she was quitting at the end of the month. Crud. Three employees working the number of hours they were working was the bare minimum staffing situation I felt we could have. I needed to hire someone new unless Jason wanted to be on the schedule for those hours in February. He would be in training, but he would save on payroll. We did pay employees for the training period, so whenever we needed to hire there was a big hit to payroll for the first three to four weeks.

I slapped the "help wanted" sign on the front door (at least I could start gathering applications) and went home to email Jason about the situation. While I had agreed to write up the next month's schedule, it was going to be his business, so he definitely had a say in how we'd proceed. I told him that normally, I would be looking for applicants, interview, then hire, and start training right away. But it could take a couple weeks to find someone, so it was likely that a new person wouldn't be joining the staff till February. Jason would bear the cost of the extra payroll.

I heard back from Jason and unfortunately he had some bad news of his own. Bank number six had turned him down for a loan. He was exhausted and said that he was very sorry, but he wouldn't be the new owner of The Pot & Bead.

Of course, this hit me pretty hard, but I wasn't going to give up that easily. I responded by asking him about his previous backup plan, i.e., using his retirement money that he was going to have access to in a few months. I also offered to lower the price by $10,000. Instead of waiting for him to email me back, I called to follow up. I wasn't going to sleep well that night if we didn't have a conversation.

"Adeena, you're making it hard for me to say 'no.'" That was the good news. The bad news: he wasn't really sure about this yet. Unfortunately, January 2008 wasn't a good time for the market. All of our 401(k)s, IRAs, and such were all down about 20 percent since the peak the previous October, which meant that his retirement savings were a lot less than when he had the original idea, so he was a little hesitant to use these funds. I couldn't blame him.

We finished the conversation agreeing that he would get back to me by the end of the upcoming weekend. The contract we had signed was still valid even though it said that it was dependent upon him finding bank financing, but it really didn't matter where the financing came from. That, along with a change to the purchase price, was easily modifiable. I was okay with him taking the time to think about it some more and hopefully he would come back with a positive answer. I wasn't optimistic and I didn't like that I was back to thinking about my only other option: closing.

## No-Nonsense Tips and Tidbits:

- Keep track of your business presence on the web, your competitors, and your industry in general by using Google Alerts (www.google.com/alerts).
- Be ready to respond to changes.
- You should always run big decisions by the people in your life who it will affect the most (like a significant other) and also by those you trust to give you unbiased opinions.
- In addition to starting and opening a business, there are several books out there that will help you if you plan to sell. Read some of these even if you plan to have a broker or someone help you sell your business. They will give you an idea of what to expect and what questions you should be asking.

# Chapter 10

# Closing the Business

It's January 29, 2008. In the past twenty-four hours I've told a handful of people that we'll be closing The Pot & Bead next month. Pretty much everyone, including my mother, employees, coworkers, and friends tried to express their sympathies to me, but the thing is, at this point, I'm no longer sad about closing—I'm actually feeling quite relieved.

It was late last week that I received the final notice and decision from Jason. He wasn't going to be able to buy the business. In the week leading up to that, I made the decision that if he wasn't going to buy, I needed to close. It's very simple at this point. I'm losing money. To turn around and court another buyer to get a sale could take months. I'm losing too much money to give it that time. There is no guarantee it would work out that well and I'd be back stuck where I am now, with even more debt.

I feel good and relieved about this decision mostly because things are back under my control. I'm also listening to my gut this time, which is telling me that this is right. It feels right.

Closing a business was as new a thing to me as opening a business was all those years ago, but there didn't seem to be as many books and resources available on how exactly to do it. I did do a Google search and all that yielded was a pile of companies that helped to liquidate your business—for a fee. My business was too small for that kind of service. This was going to be another do-it-yourself type of activity.

211

The first thing I did was make that ever-important list—my closing checklist. Having a to-do list is a pretty powerful thing. It's a road map and a plan. Having a plan to execute takes some of the stress away from any large project that needs to be accomplished. People wonder how I get so many things done at once. Having manageable to-do lists is definitely a helper. "Open my business" is not a good item for a to-do list, but "write the intro to my business plan," "register a URL," and "file for business license" are. The closing checklist outlined everything from closing out all my utility accounts to informing customers and shutting down the website.

Let's say you're already a fellow business owner and you've been caught in the uncertain economy, and maybe your life outside the business has changed due to marriage or divorce or illness. Your goals and desires aren't the same as what they were when you started your business and you're not making the kind of money you thought you would be by now. You're asking yourself the same question I asked myself for the last two years: How do you know when it really is time to close? Good question. Sometimes a situation is so overwhelming and you're so underprepared that you don't see the answer.

That was the case with my friend Mike. He and his wife owned some rental property. For the purposes of the property, they were business partners. Mike's wife had a little experience with flipping properties and had enough luck at it, so the two of them went in deeper and bought a couple of duplexes. But they never had a real strategy for their business and got caught in the market downturn.

They made several mistakes getting involved in this business from the start:

- There was no clear understanding of each partner's responsibilities.
- At the beginning, Mike didn't feel entirely comfortable getting involved—he wasn't listening to his gut.
- When the rest of life got difficult (illness, family issues), they let things go with the business a little.

When I spoke to Mike, they were at the point where it was time for them to get out of this business. Even though the thought was in the back of their heads, they needed to come up with a concrete plan on how to get out—an exit strategy. It's not always as simple as putting up a "for sale" sign when in the interim, there are things to manage and bills to pay.

They did have the ability to undo at least two of the mistakes made above. First, they still needed to sit down and delineate each person's responsibility going forward. Given that they were not only business partners, but husband and wife, they could potentially benefit from some outside advice. A Small Business Development Center is able to assist in these situations.

Next, they should have regained control of their business and lives by coming up with a plan, writing it down, and outlining all the steps it would take to get there. They needed to agree on their goals: sell the property, no matter what the cost? Keep the property until the economy picks up and ensure that it's rented?

Mike said that one of the problems at the beginning was they weren't conservative enough in their initial estimates of expenses. They didn't allow for the fact that in their business there was a lot of possibility for "open-ended" expenses, in other words, expenses that increased without their control such as taxes and utilities.

The good thing was that after having had the property for some time, they were in a better position to estimate expenses and put together a budget for the next year or two, or however long they needed to decide on their short-term goals and exit strategy.

My own goal for the last month that The Pot & Bead was open was to make a clean break and liquidate as much stuff as possible. I had to decide on a specific day to close and a specific day that would be the last painting day and then get the word out quickly.

I gave the landlord the required thirty-day notice. Remember that I was on a month–by-month lease at this point, so I didn't owe any additional rent past then. Most people in my situation would run out their lease but that had happened five months prior. I was on a month-by-month and could leave anytime with thirty days' notice.

February 29 was the day we needed to be out of the space. I scheduled the 28th and 29th to move out and clean up, which meant the 27th was the last day for operating hours. It was also the last day I'd have employees and the last day I'd cut payroll checks.

As a paint-your-own-pottery studio, we needed to set a date to have our last birthday party and last painting day, since it normally took a week to get the finished pottery back to people, so February 17 became that day.

I had to make the schedule for my remaining two employees for the month of February and let them know what was going on. I reduced the hours as much as was feasible, including closing one day a week (since I didn't have the staff to be open seven days a week anymore).

On February 1, 2008, we announced to the rest of the world that The Pot & Bead was closing. We put signs around the store, updated the website, and announced it in our email newsletter. Then the liquidation "everything must go" sales started and people came out en masse for them. I used Craigslist (an online classified listing website) heavily to announce the sales and specific items for the sale.

On the 28th, I rented a truck and everything that didn't sell came home. Cleaning up the space wasn't difficult considering we didn't have any significant damage. After we let the landlord know we were going to leave, the property manager sent a letter that outlined what to expect when vacating the property. It referred me to sections in my lease (Articles 22 and 52) that dealt with "Property at Tenants Risk" and the "Surrender of Premises."

Several items needed to be completed before turning over the space back to the landlord. These included surrendering the space in broom clean condition with all trade fixtures removed and/or disposed of off the property; walls and floors patched; security systems disabled; and all signage, interior and exterior, removed; and having the utilities taken out of my name and the accounts placed in the landlord's name. I made an appointment with the property manager to turn over the keys. The only issue that wasn't clear was my sign on the outside of the building. He said that we could remove it or he could have it done and charge us around $400. We said we'd do it. This was money-saving time, not money-spending time.

Unfortunately, this whole process was like pulling off a Band-Aid very slowly—you want it to be over but it's not. In fact, even after we left the space, it wasn't over. But things felt better with each thing checked off the to-do list. Electric out of my name: check! Kilns sold: check!

After the actual closing, it was time to reassess. I still owed taxes, still owed some vendors, still had credit card debt associated with the business, and still had a business loan. I had close to $100,000 in debt.

The liquidation sale took care of a little more than $10,000 of it. It's amazing that people will come out in larger numbers for a sale. At the right price, stuff moves. We sold the two large kilns and pretty much all the rest of the furniture. I sold most of the remaining inventory to another local store. Everything else came home to be sold off at yard sales and through eBay.

Taxes were going to be due in March, and again there would be quarterly taxes due in April, and then the following year, there would be taxes. In other words, closing the business didn't mean I was completely free of it—I'd be dealing with "leftovers" well into the following year. But with the business closed, I finally turned off my cell phone without feeling pangs of guilt and looked back over the last six years. I thought about the goals I had back in 2002 when I started and what I should have done differently.

## No-Nonsense Tips and Tidbits:

- It's okay if you have to close a business. It does not mean you are a failure or a bad person. It means you took a risk and it didn't work out as planned. That's what taking risks is all about.
- The hardest part about closing a business might be dealing with any resulting debt.
- Do not forget about your taxes after you close a business!

# Chapter 11

# So You Still Want Your Own Cute Little Store

You've read this entire book of good and bad, and you still want your own cute little store or other small business. You've decided that you can handle the bad in order to get the good. Kudos! You're on your way.

Before you rush off, answer the following questions for yourself (No-Nonsense Tip: not all of them have right or wrong answers):

- Why do you want your own cute little store? List the reasons.

  _____

  _____

  _____

- What is your current financial situation?

  _____

  _____

  _____

- In order to support yourself and possibly your family, do you need to continue to take in whatever income you take in now? (If the answer to this question is yes, but you still want to go into business for yourself, start working NOW on reducing your debt and building up a savings cushion that can carry you through the first year of your business.)

_____

_____

_____

- Do you have a spouse or significant other who would be involved (even indirectly)? Have you spoken with him or her about your idea and desire?

_____

_____

_____

- Have you discussed this idea with your friends/family? What was their reaction?

_____

_____

_____

- Are you in good physical shape? (Do you eat right and exercise?) If the answer is no, consider working on this. Even if your business will not have you on your feet the whole day, the better physical condition you are in, the better you will be able to handle any stress that comes your way!

_____

_____

_____

- How organized are you? Would you be able to organize all of the papers and documents yourself, or will you need the help of a personal organizer?

_____

_____

_____

- Who is currently selling the product/service you want to offer? Who would be your competition? How will you be better than them?

  _____

  _____

  _____

List of things to have before opening or purchasing a business:

- a business plan!
- zero (or as close as possible) debt
- supportive family and friends

Remember that there is list of ongoing responsibilities that you as the owner will constantly have to deal with:

- employee management
- customer service/appreciation
- marketing
- paying the bills
- finding new ways to boost sales
- keeping track of financials, inventory, customers, etc.

# Chapter 12

# The Final Word: Why Exactly *Are* You in Business?

"Business is always personal. It's the most personal thing in the world."

—Michael Scott, *The Office*

I opened The Pot & Bead with a single goal: to become a small chain as quickly as possible. Sounds reasonable, right?

Less than a year after I opened I was at a ceramic association trade show. One of the speakers was a very dynamic and interesting individual and an expert in retail. Before and after his talks, I had some short side discussions with him and had mentioned to him my goal of starting a chain. He flat out told me it was a mistake—that too many small business owners do what I thought I wanted to do: expand too quickly.

I don't take blunt criticism well and rebutted with how organized I was, how all my procedures were set up, how I was building a brand. He chortled and said that a lot of folks in my position needed to simply concentrate on building the business in the single location instead.

What he was trying to say went in one ear and out the other, partly because I wasn't listening and partly because he wasn't saying what he meant. My goal should have been profitability and it took me another four years to figure that out.

It sounds obvious. Any business exists to make a profit, right? Well, a lot of business owners make the mistake of thinking that profitability is so obvious a goal that anything they do is because they want to be profitable. Wrong. And it may have cost me my business.

Having a goal of a small chain wasn't all bad. It forced me to set things up from day one in a fairly organized fashion. Before we opened the doors, I had the first set of operational procedures written. We had developed a logo and were committed to the brand. These are all good and necessary things.

The problem was that in seeking multiple stores, I wasn't actively thinking about profitability. Yes, I tracked sales numbers. I tried to create incentives with my employees and other things to draw in more business. I marketed and advertised. I mistakenly thought that once I had multiple stores, profitability, as a function of scale, was inevitable.

Throughout the first year, while I was so focused on the second store, I overspent. I thought that if I was going to be a larger business, I had to act like it and set myself up that way. I was not as tight with the purse strings as I should have been. I spent too much on consultants (like one that tested my employees for their skills in order to test new potential employees for matching skills) and miscellaneous "little things" that weren't necessary. I thought that because I was a new business, I wasn't supposed to be profitable yet so my spending was okay.

I didn't feel the need for a sounding board to bounce ideas off of or at least to get positive affirmation that I was making right decisions, even the small ones. Should I buy this new set of shelves? At the time, I made the purchase instead of mentioning it to someone who might have said simple words like: "Are you sure?" which might have been enough to make me wait a day, which might have been enough to make me change my mind.

It wasn't until I realized that a second store wasn't going to happen in my time frame that I started to rethink my goals. And still I didn't get it right. My next goal was to cut expenses. Again, this is a good thing, but cutting expenses doesn't lead to profitability because it doesn't necessarily increase profit. The message is that a business's first and foremost goal is profitability. All else is secondary.

How does one achieve profitability? It's so simple, it's silly: money in needs to be more than money out. The trick is to be able to control *both* sides of that equation. Money out is controlled by budgets and being thrifty and creative and not letting others force you into making bad decisions with your checkbook. It's about penny pinching and remembering that there is no guarantee that every dollar out will find its way back to you.

Money in is within your control, too. It's about having a product or service that is worth what someone will pay for it. It's about having a product or service that is better than your competitors'. It's about pricing that product or service what it's worth (don't simply undercut competitors if your product is better). Then it's about getting the word out so people know that you and your product or service exists.

It took me more than five years, more debt than I ever wanted to be in, and some other bumps and bruises to figure this out. Hopefully you're much smarter and are on the road to profitability right now.

Before you start thinking about any of the "buts": "but the economy is bad," "but costs are rising," "but I have no money to spend on marketing to attract new customers and generate sales," remember that you are still in charge and in control of your business and your destiny. You might have to make some hard decisions and change how you've always done things, but if you've come this far, to the point that you own your own business, then you've proven, at least to yourself, that you have some drive and the will to succeed, and you can!

Take a break, take some breaths, and start making a list of the things you can do, the books you can read, the resources at your disposal. One book I didn't read until I was closing up was *Streetwise Small Business Turnaround: Revitalizing Your Struggling or Stagnant Enterprise* by Marc Kramer. Even if you don't feel that your business is in need of a "turnaround," I highly recommend this one as another "don't get caught making these mistakes" book.

You're in business because you believe in your business and in yourself. It's not an editorial mistake that I included the same quote at the beginning of this chapter that I included in the Introduction. Business is indeed very personal. It's true when you work for someone else—anyone who takes pride in their work and accomplishments has made business personal. It's even more true for the entrepreneur. Your business is your baby. It's your creation. You take care of it, you nurture it, and you see it through good times and bad. You want everyone else to see the good in your business and you are easily devastated by the bad (whether or not others see that).

I hope one of the things that you take away from this book is that it's a memoir of a business—a business that was very personal and touched all other aspects of my life. I'm thrilled that I had my business as long as I did. I made plenty of mistakes, learned a lot, and have been able to share those experiences with others and will continue to do so.

If I did it again, what would I do differently?

I've realized that it really is all about controlling money. I would have controlled my money and improved my spending habits dramatically. These last two sentences can be said in so many different ways, each one of them true: managing cash flow, controlling expenses, cutting back expenses, etc.

Other things that I might have done differently include the fact that when I was ready to sell, I would have been more open and public about it and would have done it with much more gusto.

While yes, there are things I would do differently, there are a bunch of things I did right and would do again. I've summarized the good and the bad into two lists that I hope prove useful to you in your business venture:

## No-Nonsense Tips and Tidbits:

Things I did right and would do again:

- Have a business plan.
- Have the business plan reviewed by an organization like the SBDC (Small Business Development Center).

- Have an accountant work with me from the start of the business.
- Have a written partnership agreement.
- Have store procedures in place before opening.
- Be ready to hire employees right away.
- Be committed to the brand right away.

Things I did wrong, wouldn't do again, and hope you avoid:

- Didn't control spending. (How to fix: Second-guess every spending decision.)
- Didn't have back-up funds. (How to fix: Use a "pay yourself first" method to build up a savings cushion.)
- Didn't cut my losses earlier. (How to fix: Seek out more impartial advice and trust your gut.)
- Focused too much on a second store and not the profitability of the first one. (How to fix: Focus on profit, not the idea of the larger business.)

If you remember only a few words from this book, I hope it's the following:

It *is* about money—that's your livelihood.
It *is* personal—it's your business.

Best Wishes and Good Luck!

# APPENDIX A

# Timeline

Building a business, and more important, exiting a business doesn't happen overnight. This appendix is the timeline of significant events in the life of The Pot & Bead.

One interesting note: it only took about six months to get the business up and running, yet it took more than three years to exit.

## 2002

March—The idea for The Pot & Bead is born! Business plan writing begins.

June—Started to meet with the bank that would grant the first business loan

June—First met with leasing agent for what was to become the home of P&B

July—Received loan commitment letter from bank

August—Quit my "day job"

September 9—Lease executed

September 16—Loan completely executed

October 1—Took possession of the space

October 12—Open for business

October 24—First two employees start

# 2003

February 1–2—Held very successful Grand Opening event

April 7—Overnight burglary

June 15—Found out about another paint-your-own-pottery business for sale; started looking into possibly buying it

August 1—Took possession/started running the business with intent to sign sales agreement for the second store on the 8th

October 26—Abandoned that business

December 26—Letter from landlord about overdue Common Area Maintenance (CAM) that was twice my monthly rent

# 2004

April—Started to buy partner out after realizing that the original agreement of 50/50 ownership wasn't holding up

September—Started to have thoughts about returning to a full-time engineering career

October—Finally agreed on partner buyout terms

November 15—Wound up in hospital unexpectedly for almost a week; on bed rest for two weeks following that; business is unaffected

December—Partner buyout complete

December 13—Started new full-time job; I am no longer available during the day, during the week

# 2005

February—Tried to list business with first broker

April—Started conversations with new broker

May—Listed business for $169,000

July—Met with potential buyer; didn't go anywhere

# 2006

March—Lowered the asking price of P&B to $99,000
April—Sent my first book, *Cute Little Store,* to publisher; met with one couple interested in the business; didn't go anywhere
July—*Cute Little Store* published!
December—First glimmer of interest in the business since April; didn't go anywhere

# 2007

March—Received first official (and extremely low) offer on business; deal expires; I sever contact with business broker
May—First local competitor closes
July—Other local competitor closes; business picks up
August—Landlord agrees to extend lease month-by-month for up to a year
September—Announce that P&B is for sale by owner; asking price: $59,000
October—The Pot & Bead is five years old! Hold big birthday party
October, early—Met with potential buyer
October 31—Original lease expires; now on month-by-month
November 16—Letter of Intent signed with buyer
December 31—Sales Agreement signed; with non-refundable deposit accepted!

# 2008

January 16—Discover that buyer will not be able to finance purchase; sale isn't going to happen
January 27–29—Decide to close at end of February 2008; notify landlord; notify employees

February 1—Announce to the world that P&B is closing
February 17—Last day to paint pottery
February 27—Last day with operating hours
February 29—We are out of the space
March 2008 and beyond—Dealing with the resulting financials

# APPENDIX B

# Business Plan

This is the original business plan for The Pot & Bead. It is presented in full, only without the resumes and with my former partner's name changed. We didn't have a lease yet, so there are a couple TBDs related to our lack of space and several places refer to a town that we didn't end up going with—we wound up a few minutes away.

## The Pot & Bead, LLC
*Contemporary Ceramic and Beading Studio*

### EXECUTIVE SUMMARY
#### Company Overview

This business plan was prepared for *The Pot & Bead, LLC*, a newly formed limited liability company. The mission of the company is to sell unpainted bisque (prefabricated pottery) for customers to paint, and beads to craft with in a contemporary studio setting. This business venture has been modeled after several successful studios nationwide offering similar products and services. Ms. Adeena Mignogna and Mr. John Johnson are the joint owners and sole members of the company. The retail store will be located in the TBD shopping center in Leesburg, VA.

#### Market Need

Painting your own pottery has become a nationwide craze that fulfills the artistic desire within both young and old. The alternative studios offer the appeal of blending the best elements of arts and crafts classes (hands-on creativity), coffeehouse sociability, and boutique shopping (with personalized creations to bring home) in one unique environment. *The Pot & Bead* will take this proven concept of painting your own pottery one step farther with the addition of adding a beading element into the same studio environment.

Research by the owners of *The Pot & Bead* have identified that the arts and crafts industry is currently exhibiting major growth. Research on existing studios has shown that these businesses are very profitable and are expanding store locations to take advantage of this trend in self expression. (Source: *Glazenfyre* studio; *Clay Café* studios; *Our Name Is Mud* studio; etc.)

The appeal of crafts, especially beading and painting bisque (unglazed ceramics) has grown steadily over the past decade (Source: *Georgies*, a CA studio which specializes in helping new studios). The roots of this business were firmly laid in the trendy, affluent areas of LA in the early 90's, with many celebrities jumping on the bandwagon to paint and create their own masterpiece. The creativity trend has grown eastwards with many stores flourishing in affluent suburban and urban neighborhoods. Many college educated families with children are looking for wholesome family entertainment that allows both parents and children to express themselves creatively while enjoying a fun time together.

## Type of Business

*The Pot & Bead, LLC* will sell unpainted bisque (unfinished ceramic which has been pre-fired but requires final glazing) for customers to paint and beads for customers to craft distinctive homemade jewelry, both in a studio setting. *The Pot & Bead* will also provide services such as children's parties, scout and brownie troop evenings, school field trips, charity event hosting, as well as a range of finished pottery in the studio and for sale on a website. *The Pot & Bead* considers itself to be a retail establishment in the crafting and entertainment industries.

## Company / Business Summary

*The Pot & Bead LLC* was organized as a Limited Liability Company on May 24, 2002 in the state of Virginia. It is a startup business owned and operated by Adeena Mignogna and John Johnson, co-owners of *The Pot & Bead LLC*.

## Financial Summary/Objectives

The financial plan and analysis section of this document details the projected operating results, financial position, cash flow, and contingency plan. It is expected that cash flow will be positive beginning in the early part of the second year of operations.

## Management Overview

The company is to be run by Adeena Mignogna and John Johnson. The combination of management experience, marketing, business and analytical skills, together with the enthusiasm and energy of Ms. Mignogna and Mr. Johnson make them uniquely qualified to run a business of this type. Mr. Johnson is a seasoned Manager in the aerospace industry where he has worked for large, small and start up organizations. He has had executive decision making responsibilities and has a successful track record of managing programs within the planned budget and schedule. Ms. Mignogna's interpersonal skills, computer, accounting, graphic design and engineering background are ideally suited to run the day to day operations of *The Pot & Bead* and oversee marketing and promotional activities. Two of the key ingredients for any retail establishment are customer satisfaction and business acumen, both Ms. Mignogna and Mr. Johnson are very personable and from their professional and academic backgrounds have a high level of management, analytical and business experience.

## Product, Service and Competition

*The Pot & Bead* will sell ceramic bisque for customers to paint and beads to craft, all in the studio. The store will also carry a limited offering of pre-painted ceramics. The product and service emphasis will focus on personal creativity in a fun, friendly and family atmosphere; a place where families, couples, groups and individuals can relax while enjoying a rewarding and satisfying experience. *The Pot & Bead* will provide more crafting opportunities than other local contemporary ceramic studios. Whereas other contemporary studios are typically dedicated to ceramics,

231

this store will carry a full line of beading supplies and other crafting activities. *The Pot & Bead* target customer will be the parent of the child, who will be persuaded that quality and value are the essence of *The Pot & Bead's* products and service. In addition, the level of service that the store will provide will be unparalleled in the area.

## Funds Requested

The amount of startup funds requested (in the form of a loan and line of credit) is $90,331, with the terms to be agreed upon. Those funds, in combination with the $12,000 of owner startup equity will be sufficient to purchase store fixtures, make leasehold improvements to the store, acquire inventory, provide working capital for the first several months of operation, and generally provide for the many expenses and contingencies related to the startup of a retail establishment. The owners have contributed $12,000 of their own equity to startup the business. The total startup funding consists of $53,486 in startup costs and $36,845 in working capital.

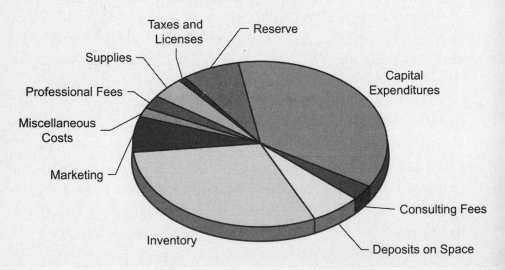

**Startup Expenses**

| Capital Expenditures | $19,439 |
|---|---|
| Consulting Fees | $1,700 |
| Deposits on Space | $3,400 |
| Inventory | $16,300 |
| Marketing | $3,517 |
| Miscellaneous Costs | $1,080 |
| Professional Fees | $1,300 |
| Supplies | $2,450 |
| Taxes and Licenses | $300 |
| Reserve | $4,000 |
| **Total:** | $53,486 |

*Figure 1 Startup Expenses*

## COMPANY BACKGROUND

### Identification of Market Opportunity

In the very lucrative crafting industry, a successful niche to be filled by *The Pot & Bead* is meeting the need for family entertainment and children's activities in the Leesburg and Loudoun County areas. By offering several crafting activities as well as parties involving those activities and by providing advice and other significant value-added services, *The Pot & Bead* will be able to compete against the very few contemporary studios in the Northern Virginia area. *The Pot & Bead* can meet this demand for family activities by offering a variety of crafting products in a fun, friendly and sociable atmosphere with a conveniently located store just outside of downtown Leesburg.

The demographics of Leesburg are very promising for the store. Leesburg, located in Loudoun County, is a prosperous suburb of Washington, D.C. Leesburg and Loudoun County have experienced a high population increase over the past decade and the population of Loudoun County is expected to nearly double between 2000 and 2010. More than 80% of the households in Loudoun County are single family structures and there is a strong family orientation.

The town of Leesburg has an eclectic atmosphere, mixing old world historic charm with new, upscale, residential neighborhoods that attract many professional families. Leesburg and the surrounding areas attract many families partly because of the historical roots and family atmosphere where they can enjoy their precious resource of free time. Loudoun County is one of the fastest growing areas of the country (Source: *Leesburg Today* and US Census Bureau), and due to this population growth does not offer sufficient family and children's party events.

Contemporary Ceramic Studio Association (CCSA)[1] data suggests that each 'paint your own pottery' studio can support a population of 50,000. *The Pot & Bead* located in Leesburg meets this requirement. There exists a limited number of activities for children's parties in Leesburg and Loudoun County; there are none offering the products and services of *The Pot & Bead*. However, the phenomenon of crafting, in particular the 'paint your own pottery' concept, is thriving in Northern Virginia. Research on several similar studios revealed their stores to be highly profitable, (*Clay Cafe* is even opening a second store in Chantilly in April 2002; their primary location is in Falls Church) the Fairfax *Paint Your Own Pottery* studio has been visited on several occasions by the owners who have found the place to be full of children's parties, Boy Scout evenings, individual painting and small family get-togethers. The closest store to Leesburg will be the one opening in Chantilly in April 2002, but the location of this store is far enough away from Leesburg to not affect *The Pot & Bead's* attractiveness. There are also several elementary, middle and high schools in the surrounding area, which yields a potential customer population of several thousand children (source: Loudoun County School demographics 2000) whom require after school activities, weekend parties, and general family fun things to do.

Loudoun County, and in particular the Leesburg area, is an excellent market opportunity for the services and products offered by *The Pot & Bead*. With no nearby competitor (closest one 25 miles away) *The Pot & Bead* is well positioned to attract customers from a very populated, affluent, and family oriented market.

---

[1] The CCSA is the professional trade organization for studios of this type. *The Pot & Bead* is a member studio.

## Business History

*The Pot & Bead* is a startup business. The owners have initially capitalized the company with $12,000 of equity. Ms. Mignogna and Mr. Johnson have incorporated the entity as a Limited Liability Corporation and have signed a letter of intent for a TBD year lease on a 1,500-square-foot space located at TBD in Leesburg. In planning the start up of this business, Ms. Mignogna and Mr. Johnson have carefully researched the successful business model provided by the Contemporary Ceramic Studio Association (CCSA) and *Georgies* (a California based studio supplier who has also written a manual for new studios), both used by many studios nationwide.

*The Pot & Bead* has also hired Elisa Waldman, owner of *Paint, Glaze & Fire*, a successful studio operating for 5 years near Kansas City, as a consultant during the startup phase. As part of this consulting service, *The Pot & Bead* has been able to the operating financial data of Ms. Waldman's studio. Ms. Mignogna and Mr. Johnson also spent two days in training at the end of May at *Paint, Glaze & Fire*.

## Growth and Sales Objectives

With the demand for family-oriented activities forecasted to grow proportionally to the population growth, Ms. Mignogna and Mr. Johnson have worked with Tom Butler of Butler Consulting Group, Inc. to devise a 5 year sales plan. The plan assumes that first year revenues for *The Pot & Bead* will total $115,764. Based on industry data2, the first year sales goal appears to be reasonable. The forecasted sales for the next five years are shown below.

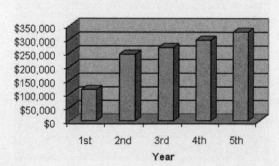

**5 Year Sales Forecast**

---

[2] Actual sales data has been collected from studios operating successfully over the past several years.

## Legal Structure and Ownership

The company is organized as a Limited Liability Company in the state of Virginia. Ms. Mignogna and Mr. Johnson's decision to organize as an LLC was driven by the possible tax benefits and corporate advantages such as limited liability. Ms. Mignogna and Mr. Johnson have filed all the necessary paperwork and have acquired all the appropriate permits to conduct a retail establishment.

## Company Location and Facilities

The store is a 1,500-square-foot space located at TBD in the town of Leesburg, Virginia. Leesburg and the surrounding vicinity of Loudoun County have a population of approximately 150,000 people (source: US Census Bureau). This shopping center and surrounding establishments cater to families and children, the type of customers *The Pot & Bead* seeks.

The TBD shopping center can best be described as TBD.

*The Pot & Bead* unit will be equipped with several tables and chairs for painting and crafting as well as a "bead bar." The "bead bar" is a bar like structure with stools where customers can sit and bead and request beads from a shelf. The store will also have a single counter, cash register and a variety of fixtures, shelving, and excellent lighting. A bathroom will be available for customers. The front face of the store has several large windows which can be decorated with shelving for product displays that will change with the seasons. In the back of the store is a room to house two firing kilns and act as storage area. The store and its contents will be protected by an alarm system that will be monitored by TBD.

Ms. Mignogna and Mr. Johnson will also be purchasing Quickbooks to use as an accounting, inventory control and Point of Sale software solution. They intend to be able to accept major credit cards through a credit card processing service both in the store and on the website.

The store will be open from 11:00 a.m. to 7:00 p.m., Monday through Thursday, 11:00 a.m. to 10:00 p.m. on Friday and Saturday, and 12:00 noon to 5:00 p.m. on Sundays (TBR). The store will be closed on holidays.

## Plans for Financing the Business

The owners have contributed $12,000 of their personal savings to get the business started. In addition, Ms. Mignogna and Mr. Johnson estimate that another $90,331, in the form of a $61,316 loan and $29,015 line of credit, will be needed to properly launch the business.

# OWNER'S BACKGROUND

## Background on Ms. Mignogna

Adeena Mignogna will be one of two owners and managers of *The Pot & Bead*. Adeena brings a variety of experience to the business. As an engineer, she has a great deal of experience working with suppliers, managing employees and at a variety of analytical tasks. Adeena also has a great deal of managerial experience beginning in college when she managed her college radio station, WMUC-AM. This experience involved many activities including managing budgets and directing more than 50 employees at a time. Her retail and sales experience includes several years as a cashier in grocery stores and working in restaurant kitchens.

Ms. Mignogna has been involved in many activities with children over the years including face-painting at outdoor festivals, religious education instruction and participation in several mentoring programs. Adeena graduated from the University of Maryland College Park with B.S. degrees in Physics and in Astronomy. Adeena is 28 years old, in excellent health, and is married.

Adeena will work full-time in the store and act as the day-to-day manager of *The Pot & Bead*.

## Background on Partner John

John will be one of two owners and managers of *The Pot & Bead*.

## Other Key Employees

In the early days of the business, Ms. Mignogna and Mr. Johnson anticipate that part-time help will be hired. The local market provides an ample supply of good part-time help (high school and community college students).

Although not employees of the business, *The Pot & Bead's* accountant, Tom Bulter of Butler Consulting Group, Inc., will be consulted regarding tax and finance issues and [name deleted] will be available for consultation on legal issues. *The Pot & Bead* has also hired a consultant, Elisa Waldman to assist with the startup of the business. Ms. Waldman is the owner of *Paint, Glaze & Fire*, a studio operating successfully for five years near Kansas City. Finally, *The Pot & Bead* website will be designed and maintained by Chronoclysm.com. No additional expertise will be needed.

## MARKET ANALYSIS

### Summary

By all accounts, both the crafting and entertainment industries are in a growth phase. Higher household incomes mean more disposable income, and educated parents are realizing more and more the value of creative outlets for children.

Leesburg is the county seat of Loudoun County, and is approximately 35 miles west of Washington, D.C. Leesburg and the surrounding area have a population of over 150,000. It is recognized as one of the fastest growing cities in the Northern Virginia area. Loudoun County is home to AOL, MCI/Worldcom, Orbital Sciences Corporation, as well as many new and established businesses. The residents are a mix of native 'Loudouners' and new, younger professionals looking for a fun, family friendly environment where they can start to call 'home'. The area has several elementary, middle and high schools with a K-12 population of 45,000 thousand.

As far as the Loudoun County area is concerned, there is a lack of family-oriented and kid-centered activities. Families currently need to travel a half hour or more for most entertainment and activities.

On the average, each 'paint your own pottery' store serves a population base of 50,000 people. These stores tend to be located in a variety of different locales from downtown or historic areas to strip malls. Most tend to locate where the majority of foot traffic comes from families with young kids.

238

To measure the market potential and demographic data (e.g., average household income, number of households, and number of businesses), the owners have contacted the local chamber of commerce, public library, city and county governments. They have also extensively visited existing local and non-local 'paint your own pottery' studios to determine what products and services they offer and what they charge.

## Industry Analysis

Despite the healthy growth rates experienced in the entertainment industry in recent years, competition in the entertainment industry is generally considered intense. People have disposable income to spend and retailers/etc are competing for those dollars. It is estimated that the local market spends more than tens of millions of dollars on entertainment annually. At the moment, the Leesburg and Loudoun County areas consist of highly-educated people and there is a lack of entertainment outlets without having to drive far. It is expected that over the next several years the competition for entertainment dollars in the Loudoun county area will become quite intense.

From census, marketing surveys, and entertainment industry data, the size of the Leesburg and Loudoun County market for entertainment dollars is approximately several million dollars per year. It is expected to grow proportionally to the population growth. *The Pot & Bead's* first year forecasted sales goal represents a fraction of a percent of the market.

## Target Market

The market that will be targeted by *The Pot & Bead* are suburban middle-to-upper-middle class families with young children. These customers are presently limited in their selection of entertainment choices in Leesburg and the surrounding area. The closest movie theatre is in Sterling, located 15 miles from Leesburg. This market is typically college educated and somewhat discerning in their choice of entertainment for their children. For example, an afternoon crafting a personal creation would be much preferred over an afternoon spent at *Chuck E Cheese's*, a pizza and entertainment establishment located in Herndon,

VA. This is true for individual family outings as well as the more lucrative children's parties.

The average expenditure for *The Pot & Bead* will be $22-26 per visit, this compares favorably with an afternoon at the movie theatre where a ticket, popcorn, and beverage for a small family can range from $25-$45. The $22-26 per visit cost is extremely affordable for this market group. The defined market can easily be convinced of spending a couple of hours crafting, as *The Pot & Bead* offers a unique brand of fun and family together time. The market in the Loudoun County area has not been penetrated at all; the closest 'paint your own pottery' studio is located in Chantilly, a 35-45 minute drive from Leesburg.

## Customer Profile

Although the ultimate consumer of the store's goods and services are children and young adults, the parents of the children are the final decision makers and the ones spending the money. Therefore, this plan's customer profile is that of the parents.

| | |
|---|---|
| Average Age: | Late 20s to early 50s. |
| Income: | Annual household income exceeding $55,000. |
| Family status: | Full nest with some of the children between the ages of 3–teenage. |
| Geographic location: | Resident of Loudoun County. |
| Occupation: | Mostly white collar and professional. |
| Attitude: | Strong belief that children's activities are fun and should be diverse. |
| Motives for buying: | Strong desire for spending quality time with their children and hosting children's events. |

## Major Competitors and Participants

There are no stores of this type currently in Loudoun County. The only major competitor at this time is *Clay Café*, located in Chantilly VA, about 25 miles away (a 35–45 minute drive). Other competitors with local 'paint your own pottery' stores are *Clay Café* located in Falls Church and *Paint Your Own Pottery* located in downtown Fairfax. A smaller, traditional pottery studio, *Pottery By Hand*, is located in Round Hill. None of these competitors offer crafting activities other than pottery.

Competing entertainment activities for children's parties such as *Chuck E Cheese* do not currently exist in Leesburg or in Loudoun County.

There are no known plans for a crafting studio of this type to enter Loudoun County at this time. *The Pot & Bead* will have the local children's activity market virtually to itself. With the appropriate promotional and advertising approach *The Pot & Bead* will easily attract the minimum number of customers to make a very successful business.

The Contemporary Ceramic Studio Association (CCSA) is the trade organization for 'paint your own pottery' studios. As such, they are a great resource for new and existing studios. The CCSA is an excellent source of information and although a great number of studios are opening up across the nation this year, none except for *The Pot & Bead* are planned for Loudoun County. *The Pot & Bead* is a registered member studio of the CCSA.

To remain competitive as the area and market grows, *The Pot & Bead* will expend energy and advertising dollars to emphasize the fun and value of the party services, capitalizing on the easy access and short drive time to downtown Leesburg from all the surrounding neighborhoods.

## Market Segmentation

The segment of the crafting market that *The Pot & Bead* intends to attract can be understood in the following ways:

First, these consumers recognize the appeal of having their children express their creativity in a simple manner by painting their own pottery piece or fashioning a small beaded item.

Secondly, they do not want to spend a vast amount of time buying all the required equipment (paint supplies, bisque, beads, wire etc) and then sitting down figuring out how to make it a fun experience. They would much rather prefer the turnkey approach of showing up, sitting down and just watching their children create a masterpiece. *The Pot & Bead* is also conveniently located within minutes of the surrounding residential neighborhoods. This no hassle, easy, and fun experience will be fondly remembered and frequent visits will follow, especially when a birthday or other celebration event is being planned.

Thirdly, children are getting more sophisticated in their entertainment choices. This sophistication has been spurred on by the Internet generation and the variety of children's TV shows targeted at the very young, young, pre-teen, and teenager audiences. Children are also fascinated by the instant gratification that painting and beading offers. This self expression can lead to increased self esteem and character building.

*The Pot & Bead* also offers one stop shopping for pre-finished items that can be used as gifts for a variety of occasions. *The Pot & Bead* will provide a wide selection of unique pottery and jewelry not found in any other local gift retailer, and at very reasonable prices.

## Projected Market Growth and Market Share Objectives

The store's projected market growth is about 10% per year for product sales. Sales projections are based on data provided by studios which have been operating in areas with similar demographics for the past five years. *Paint, Glaze & Fire* is one such studio operating in a prosperous suburb of Kansas City.

# PRODUCT / SERVICE OFFERING
## Product / Service Summary

*The Pot & Bead* will sell unpainted pottery (known as bisque) for customers to paint in the studio. The store will also sell beads and supplies for beading in studio. Parties for both children and adults will be a primary service provided.

*The Pot & Bead* will offer over 200 varieties of bisque and several hundred types of beads. The types of bisque selected for painting will be based on the CCSA's surveys of the most popular items sold elsewhere in similar stores. Types of bisque will be changed routinely in order to keep customers interest high. Seasonal items will also be available throughout the year. The types and variety of beads are based on a bead kit that has been developed by *Art & Soul* of New Caanan, CT. *Art & Soul* is the only other multi-use studio in the US offering both pottery and beading. *Art & Soul* has assembled this kit to satisfy the many children and adults who enjoy this form of crafting.

## Product / Service Uniqueness

The uniqueness of *The Pot & Bead's* products can be summarized as follows:

- No other crafting studio in the Northern Virginia area offers both pottery and beading.
- There are no similar places in Leesburg which accommodate child and adult craft-based parties.

The experience and qualifications of the co-owners, together with their customer relations skills, help make this venture unique and gives a definite competitive advantage to the business.

## Product / Service Descriptions

The store will be selling multi-crafting opportunities for individuals and for parties at reasonable prices. The major product lines will be as follows:

- Paint your own pottery
- Beading—customers can make jewelry and other items in-studio
- Children's Parties
- Adult Parties
- Instruction in painting and beading techniques
- Limited amount of pre-painted ceramics
- Pre-painted ceramics and beads available on an e-store

## Competitive Comparisons

The competition for crafting and entertainment dollars will initially come from places outside of Leesburg and Loudoun County where families must now travel to for children's parties and activities. *The Pot & Bead*, primarily because of its location advantage, will easily be able to compete in this marketplace. The other stores of this nature in Northern Virginia are single craft stores. No store in all of Northern Virginia currently offers the diversity of both pottery and beading. *The Pot & Bead's* pricing will be in line with other studios in Northern Virginia and other areas across the country with similar economic characteristics. Finally, a competitive feature that could have a significant impact is that customers will receive a level of service and advice that will be available at *The Pot & Bead* but is not available at the discount or superstore.

In summary, *The Pot & Bead's* services and products will be distinguished from its competitors by the following four major differences:

- Conveniently located to Leesburg and Loudoun County
- Offering both pottery painting and beading
- Owners with both business management and technical (Internet, web page generation, computer literate) backgrounds
- An e-store for selling pottery and beads on line

# MARKETING PLAN
## Creating and Maintaining Customers

*The Pot & Bead* will attract and maintain its customer base by offering competitively priced services and products. *The Pot & Bead* will also demonstrate, through hard work and a customer driven approach, that the business can entertain and provide hours of enjoyment for adults and children in its contemporary studio.

Since *The Pot & Bead* is a startup, it will spend a good portion of the first year creating a customer base. This will be done through the publicity generated by the grand opening, efforts by Ms. Mignogna and Mr. Johnson to network within local neighborhoods, schools and local corporations, and through newspaper advertisements. The newspaper ads will emphasize *The Pot & Bead* high quality and great value message. Word of mouth will also play a significant part as visitors to the store experience the high quality, value priced products.

*The Pot & Bead* also plans to conduct a survey in the Leesburg area to determine the best ways to reach potential customers.

Maintaining customers can and will be done by upholding the following standards:

1. Provide excellent service and knowledgeable advice to consumers.
2. Provide a welcome and relaxing, family-oriented atmosphere.

All first time customers will be asked to fill out a small sheet of paper to go with their piece so that *The Pot & Bead* can collect email address and other useful data. This data will be maintained and email addresses in particular will be used as a very inexpensive way to send out promotional materials.

Building on the successful advertising strategies described by the CCSA, *The Pot & Bead* will vary its approach to finding new customers on a monthly and seasonal basis. By maintaining a finger on the pulse of its customers, eliciting feedback, and maintaining strong community relationships, *The Pot & Bead* will maintain and broaden its customer base.

Repeat business is a primary goal of *The Pot & Bead*.

## Product Pricing Strategy

*The Pot and Bead's* services and products will be priced to be competitive with the marketplace. The owners of *The Pot & Bead* understand the pricing strategy of its competitors and will monitor their pricing to stay competitive.

*The Pot & Bead's* products will be priced roughly in line with other studios which typically charge a flat cost for the bisque the customer chooses plus a sitting fee which covers paint, use of brushes, etc. On average, bisque will be sold for four to six times the wholesale price. Studio sitting

245

fees will be $6 per hour with a maximum per day cap. Beading activities will be priced similarly; the main difference is that there will be a flat $5 sitting fee. There will be several levels of service for parties, with a step pricing structure. For example, a $12/child party may include pieces of bisque of $5 in value plus time and a $15/child party may include pieces of bisque of $6 in value plus time and a birthday cake.

Prices will be evaluated periodically to ensure that they are in tune with what the local market can bear.

## Product Positioning

*The Pot & Bead* brings some clear alternatives to the entertainment sector. The most important features of the business are the creativity and personal expression it fosters for its customers. The beading and 'paint your own pottery' combination is a unique offering in Northern Virginia. By combining these two proven forms of artistic entertainment *The Pot & Bead* is well positioned to take full advantage of the popularity of the crafting market.

The customer will view the personal creativity offered by beading and painting as an excellent alternative form of entertainment, one where the enjoyment outlasts the experience.

In addition, all the items in the studio are non-toxic, very safe and easy to work with. Care by the owners on the pottery and beading selections are determined by extensive lessons learned from similar stores around the country and by informative product comparisons found in the trade association CCSA materials. The beading selection is a proven combination of all popular styles that have been previously researched by *Art & Soul*, the only other combination pottery and beading store known in the country.

The retail cost of a single pottery piece ranges from a few dollars to fifty dollars depending on the size and type of the item (e.g., tiles are approx. $4, large vases can be in the range $40-$50). This finished cost is comparable to a production item found in a department store, but lacking in any kind of self expression and personalization.

Ms. Mignogna and Mr. Johnson maintain that the best positioning for the store will be to promote the following theme: "explore your artistic side in a fun-filled, family atmosphere." This will be *The Pot & Bead's* message.

## Sales and Distribution Plan

The sales and distribution of the products will be through the retail setting and via a store web site. The store will be located adjacent to the historic district of Leesburg. This area is extremely busy with a tremendous amount of automobile and foot traffic.

## Promotional Strategy

The initial promotional strategy will consist direct mail marketing, press releases and media marketing. This will include advertising the business in local newspapers (*Leesburg Today* and *Loudoun County Times*) and producing flyers which describe the opening of the store. Local journalists will be sent press releases and information packets about the grand opening of *The Pot & Bead*. It is believed that *The Pot & Bead* is unique enough to the area to garnish interest as a profile piece for the local papers.

The flyers will be distributed in the many residential neighborhoods in and around Leesburg. These flyers will offer discounts for first time clients towards a free sitting feel or some discount on the price of an item. For groups of five or more this discount will be increased.

Each customer's information will be recorded in a database for future email announcements. *The Pot and Bead's* website will also be used to promote business (see section on Internet Strategy).

Brochures, calendars and business cards will be distributed to local schools, brownie and scout groups, local soccer teams, and women's social clubs.

It is intended that each year a charity event will be sponsored by *The Pot & Bead* where well known local artists will paint items to be sold off in the store with the proceeds going to charity. Local celebrities (the mayor, etc.) will also be invited to come in and paint for free and the items added to the charity sale. By becoming a good citizen in the community the store hopes to gain respect and increase public relations. *The Pot & Bead* also plans to become an active member in the Loudoun Council of Arts.

*The Pot & Bead* plans to advertise "special event nights" routinely. Some of these event nights may include "Ladies' night" or "Date night," etc.

Customer response will be tracked in order to tailor advertising more appropriately to maximize the use of *The Pot & Bead's* advertising budget.

## Internet Strategy

The website URL is: www.potandbead.com. The site is registered to Ms. Mignogna for at a minimum the next year and *The Pot & Bead* has contracted with a web hosting service, [name deleted].

*Chronoclysm.com* will be developing and maintaining the website. The website shall contain engaging content and will be constantly evolving to keep up with consumer interest and to keep customers coming back. The majority of websites for stores of this type are poorly integrated, do not contain an e-store and provide limited reasons for consumers to return to the site. *The Pot & Bead's* website will strive to take advantage of the Internet's potential to increase its customer base and generate additional revenue.

The site will contain information about the store including upcoming events, specials, coupons, Frequently Asked Questions (FAQ), location, hours, products and services offered and contact information.

*[name deleted]* maintains and tracks site usage. These statistics will be useful in marketing (i.e., a coupon page may be looked at 1000 times, but the coupon is never seen in the store—that coupon/promotion is not working).

The e-store, a secondary source of revenue for *The Pot & Bead*, will sell some pre-painted ceramics, beads and beading kits. The beading kits are pre-packaged projects whose instructions can be downloaded by a customer.

*The Pot & Bead* plans to maximize all sources of free advertising on the web by registering with search engines, posting on existing message boards and becoming listed in all local online directories.

## Financial Plan and Analysis

The following sections contain forward-looking statements that represent Management's best estimate of the most likely financial performance of *The Pot & Bead*. These estimates are based on market research, consultation with experts with knowledge of the industry, and actual vendor proposals. Actual financial results may vary significantly from the projections.

## Initial Capital Requirements

Initial investment will consist of up to $12,000 in cash from Ms. Mignogna and Mr. Johnson. Other initial investment may come from friends and family of the two principal owners. Remaining funding will come from debt financing through a commercial lending institution. Application will be made for loan guarantees through the Small Business Administration. Based on current projections, working capital requirements for the first year of operation will require funds totaling seven months of rent plus payroll expense. It is anticipated that cash flows from the business will be sufficient to fund the other cash requirements of the company. The total startup funding requirement through debt will be $90,331, consisting of $53,486 in startup costs and $36,845 in working capital.

## Operating Costs and Cash Flows

Operating costs and cash requirements for the first year are detailed in the Appendix. The largest monthly expenses will consist of payroll costs, followed by rent and cost of goods sold. It is anticipated that first year revenue will be insufficient to cover first year operating cash requirements by approximately $37,000. The difference will be funded via additional borrowing on the debt facility used for startup funding. Monthly cash flows will turn positive early in the second year of operation.

## Revenues

Based on discussions with people with similar businesses, the average sale per customer was approximately $22 in the late 1990s. Although a higher per customer revenue figure could be assumed reasonably, for purposes of this presentation, $22 will be the average revenue per patron. Management assumes a gradual ramp-up in customer traffic, with only six customer purchases per business day in the first month of operation. By the 12th month, daily customer count will grow to approximately 29 as a result of the marketing efforts of the company. A detailed revenue projection for the first year of operation appears in the appendix.

## Financial Projections

Monthly financial statements and annualized statements for five years are presented in the appendix. The model assumes that the business will remain in a single location for the five-year period, with no expansion into other locations. Monthly profitability will occur at the end of the first year of operation, with profitability growing annually.

## Contingency Plan

In the event that revenues and cash flows fall short of the budget, Management has several options available to conserve cash.

- Defer payroll. Since the bulk of the company's monthly expenses consist of payroll to an owner, payroll may be deferred if necessary.
- Additional investment. Initial investors may be called upon to provide additional operating funds for the company.
- Reduce inventory. Purchases of bisque and supplies may be deferred.
- Additional debt.
- Sale of the business.

# Appendix C

# Financial Data

## OPERATING COSTS

The following table details the operating costs for the first year of operations.

| | 1 | 2 | 3 | 4 | 5 | 6 | 7 | 8 | 9 | 10 | 11 | 12 |
|---|---|---|---|---|---|---|---|---|---|---|---|---|
| Bank/Credit Card Chg | $50 | $50 | $50 | $50 | $75 | $75 | $75 | $100 | $100 | $100 | $150 | $150 |
| Beading Supplies | $20 | $20 | $20 | $20 | $20 | $20 | $100 | $100 | $100 | $100 | $100 | $100 |
| Bisque | $576 | $1,020 | $1,056 | $1,296 | $1,620 | $1,296 | $1,536 | $2,520 | $2,016 | $2,256 | $3,120 | $2,736 |
| Electricity | $160 | $160 | $240 | $320 | $320 | $320 | $400 | $480 | $480 | $560 | $640 | $640 |
| Insurance | $50 | $50 | $50 | $50 | $50 | $50 | $50 | $50 | $50 | $50 | $50 | $50 |
| Loan Payment | $1,958 | $1,958 | $1,958 | $1,958 | $1,958 | $1,958 | $1,958 | $1,958 | $1,958 | $1,958 | $1,958 | $1,958 |
| Marketing | $500 | $500 | $500 | $500 | $500 | $500 | $500 | $500 | $500 | $500 | $500 | $500 |
| Misc | $500 | $500 | $500 | $500 | $500 | $500 | $500 | $500 | $500 | $500 | $500 | $500 |
| Other Supplies | $200 | $200 | $200 | $200 | $200 | $200 | $200 | $200 | $200 | $200 | $200 | $200 |
| Owner's Salary | $6,013 | $6,013 | $5,831 | $5,831 | $5,831 | $5,831 | $5,831 | $5,831 | $5,831 | $5,831 | $5,831 | $5,831 |
| Professional Fees | $500 | $500 | $500 | $500 | $500 | $500 | $500 | $500 | $500 | $500 | $500 | $500 |
| Rent | $1,700 | $1,700 | $1,700 | $1,700 | $1,700 | $1,700 | $1,700 | $1,700 | $1,700 | $1,700 | $1,700 | $1,700 |
| Sales/Use Tax | $143 | $252 | $261 | $321 | $401 | $321 | $380 | $624 | $499 | $558 | $772 | $677 |
| Staff | $0 | $555 | $555 | $555 | $555 | $555 | $555 | $555 | $555 | $555 | $555 | $555 |
| Utilities | $320 | $320 | $320 | $320 | $320 | $320 | $320 | $320 | $320 | $320 | $320 | $320 |
| Total: | $12,689 | $13,798 | $13,742 | $14,121 | $14,550 | $14,146 | $14,606 | $15,938 | $15,309 | $15,689 | $16,897 | $16,418 |

Annual Operating Costs  $177,904

# CASH REQUIREMENTS

Detailed Revenue Prediction for First Year of Operations

The following table gives the projected daily, weekly, and monthly revenue during the first twelve months of operations.

| Item | Classification | Cost |
|------|----------------|------|
| Cash Register | Capital Equipment | $300 |
| Chairs/stools | Capital Equipment | $500 |
| Coffee Machine | Capital Equipment | $50 |
| Computer | Capital Equipment | $2,000 |
| Counter | Capital Equipment | $500 |
| Credit Card Equipment | Capital Equipment | $250 |
| Dipping Racks | Capital Equipment | $50 |
| Dipping Tank | Capital Equipment | $100 |
| Fax Machine | Capital Equipment | $100 |
| Kiln Furniture Kits | Capital Equipment | $300 |
| Kiln Shelves | Capital Equipment | $400 |
| Kiln Vents | Capital Equipment | $624 |
| Kilns | Capital Equipment | $3,340 |
| Lighting | Capital Equipment | $1,000 |
| Phone Setup | Capital Equipment | $75 |
| Safe | Capital Equipment | $250 |
| Seats | Capital Equipment | $2,000 |
| Security System | Capital Equipment | $1,000 |
| Shelving | Capital Equipment | $800 |
| Sign | Capital Equipment | $2,000 |
| Software | Capital Equipment | $750 |
| Stereo System | Capital Equipment | $300 |
| Tables I | Capital Equipment | $900 |
| Tables II | Capital Equipment | $600 |
| Venting | Capital Equipment | $250 |

*Continued.*

| Item | Classification | Cost |
|---|---|---|
| Wiring | Capital Equipment | $1,000 |
| Training Workshops | Consulting | $1,700 |
| Security Deposit on Space | Deposits | $3,400 |
| Bead Counter | Inventory | $1,500 |
| Bead 'Kit' | Inventory | $9,600 |
| Bisque | Inventory | $4,000 |
| Glaze & Underglaze | Inventory | $1,200 |
| Grand Opening Advertising | Marketing | $1,500 |
| URL Registration | Marketing | $17 |
| Website | Marketing | $2,000 |
| Books | Other | $450 |
| CCSA Registration | Other | $195 |
| CCSA Startup Manual | Other | $35 |
| Wholesaler's Catalogs | Other | $400 |
| Accountant Fees | Professional | $200 |
| Attorney Fees | Professional | $1,100 |
| Brushes | Supplies | $200 |
| Business Supplies | Supplies | $1,000 |
| Cleaning Supplies | Supplies | $200 |
| Misc. Tools & Supplies | Supplies | $750 |
| Packing Supplies | Supplies | $300 |
| Business Licenses | Taxes and Licenses | $300 |
| Unknown/Other | | $4,000 |
| | **Total**: | $53,486 |

# Monthly Financial Statements for First Year of Operations

| | Month 1 | Month 2 | Month 3 | Month 4 | Month 5 | Month 6 | Month 7 | Month 8 | Month 9 | Month 10 | Month 11 | Month 12 |
|---|---|---|---|---|---|---|---|---|---|---|---|---|
| Revenue | 3,168 | 5,610 | 5,808 | 7,128 | 8,910 | 7,128 | 8,448 | 13,860 | 11,088 | 12,408 | 17,160 | 15,048 |
| Cost of Goods Sold | 796 | 1,240 | 1,276 | 1,516 | 1,840 | 1,516 | 1,836 | 2,820 | 2,316 | 2,556 | 3,420 | 3,036 |
| Gross Margin | 2,372 | 4,370 | 4,532 | 5,612 | 7,070 | 5,612 | 6,612 | 11,040 | 8,772 | 9,852 | 13,740 | 12,012 |
| Operating Expenses: | | | | | | | | | | | | |
| Payroll and Fringe | 6,013 | 6,538 | 6,386 | 6,386 | 6,386 | 6,386 | 6,386 | 6,386 | 6,386 | 6,386 | 6,386 | 6,386 |
| Rent and Utilities | 2,180 | 2,180 | 2,260 | 2,340 | 2,340 | 2,340 | 2,420 | 2,500 | 2,500 | 2,580 | 2,660 | 2,660 |
| Selling, General, Admin | 1,743 | 1,852 | 1,861 | 1,921 | 2,026 | 1,946 | 2,005 | 2,274 | 2,149 | 2,208 | 2,472 | 2,377 |
| Total Operating Expenses | 9,935 | 10,600 | 10,508 | 10,647 | 10,752 | 10,672 | 10,812 | 11,160 | 11,035 | 11,175 | 11,519 | 11,424 |
| Operating Income (Loss) | (7,963) | (6,230) | (5,976) | (5,035) | (3,682) | (5,060) | (4,200) | (120) | (2,263) | (1,323) | 2,221 | 588 |
| Interest Expense | 633 | 622 | 612 | 601 | 590 | 579 | 569 | 558 | 547 | 536 | 526 | 515 |
| Depreciation | 324 | 324 | 324 | 324 | 324 | 324 | 324 | 324 | 324 | 324 | 324 | 324 |
| Net Income (Loss) | (8,196) | (6,853) | (6,587) | (5,636) | (4,272) | (5,640) | (4,768) | (678) | (2,811) | (1,859) | 1,696 | 73 |

# Annualized Statements for 5 Years

| | Year 1 | Year 2 | Year 3 | Year 4 | Year 5 |
|---|---|---|---|---|---|
| Revenue | 115,764 | 244,530 | 268,983 | 295,881 | 325,469 |
| Cost of Goods Sold | 24,168 | 51,050 | 56,155 | 61,771 | 67,948 |
| Gross Margin | 91,596 | 193,480 | 212,828 | 234,110 | 257,521 |
| Operating Expenses: | | | | | |
| Payroll and Fringe | 76,445 | 87,911 | 101,098 | 116,263 | 133,702 |
| Rent and Utilities | 28,960 | 30,987 | 33,156 | 35,477 | 37,961 |
| Selling, General, Admin | 24,834 | 26,573 | 28,433 | 30,423 | 32,553 |
| Total Operating Expenses | 130,239 | 145,471 | 162,687 | 182,163 | 204,216 |
| Operating Income (Loss) | (38,643) | 48,008 | 50,140 | 51,947 | 53,306 |
| Interest Expense | 6,889 | 4,635 | 3,090 | 1,545 | 773 |
| Depreciation | 3,888 | 3,888 | 5,888 | 9,888 | 9,888 |
| Net Income (Loss) | (45,532) | 43,373 | 47,050 | 50,402 | 52,533 |

**Commenting on the business plan now:**

Five years later, I'm still very proud of this business plan. It ensured that we thought through things from the beginning and enabled us to get the lease and business loan necessary to start the business.

A business plan should still be a living document and while I made an updated version in early 2003, a few months after we opened, I didn't keep it up much beyond that. I didn't have a plan and certainly didn't have an exit strategy.

That turned out to be one of the two things missing from this plan: the exit strategy and explicit goals of profitability. The financial plan shows profit after the first year but the rest of the plan doesn't explicitly support that. The rest of the plan justifies the existence of the business and shows that we did as much homework as possible ahead of time, but it didn't show a commitment to profit, to return on the investment of time and money.

# APPENDIX D

# Lease Clauses

This appendix contains the full lease that I signed when I started The Pot & Bead. The purpose of including it here is to give you an idea of what a real commercial lease looks like. This is a fairly standard, one-sided lease for a commercial property. Names and addresses are of course deleted and I added some of my own notes at the end of several clauses.

## SHOPPING CENTER LEASE

### INDEX

| Article | Title |
|---------|-------|
| 1 | PREMISES |
| 2 | TERM |
| 3 | RENT; DEPOSIT |
| 4 | INTENTIONALLY DELETED |
| 5 | GROSS SALES |
| 6 | NOT A JOINT VENTURE |
| 7 | RESTRICTIVE CLAUSE |
| 8 | ANNUAL OPERATING COSTS |
| 9 | REAL ESTATE TAXES |
| 10 | ADDITIONAL RENT |
| 11 | UTILITIES |
| 12 | INTENTIONALLY DELETED |

13    USE OF PREMISES

14    CONDUCT OF TENANT'S BUSINESS

15    ASSIGNMENT; SUBLETTING

16    REPAIRS BY LANDLORD

17    MAINTENANCE AND REPAIRS BY TENANT

18    CHANGES TO THE SHOPPING CENTER

19    PERSONAL PROPERTY TAXES

20    ALTERATIONS AND TENANT'S
          IMPROVEMENTS

21    NOTICE OF NON-LIABILITY

22    PROPERTY AT TENANT'S RISK

23    INSURANCE

24    DAMAGE

25    CONDEMNATION

26    RULES AND REGULATIONS

27    PARKING AREAS AN OTHER FACILITIES

28    PERFORMANCE BY TENANT

29    LANDLORD'S REMEDIES UPON DEFAULT

30    LAWS AND ORDINANCES

31    ROOF RIGHTS

32    SIGNS

33    SUBORDINATION

34    ESTOPPEL CERTIFICATES

35    HOLD-OVER

36    NOTICES

37    LANDLORD'S LIABILITY

38    DELAY

39    QUIET ENJOYMENT

40    APPLICABLE LAW

41    WAIVERS

42    NO RECORDING OF LEASE

43    REMEDIES CUMULATIVE; NO WAIVER

44    NO OPTIONS

45    HEADINGS AND INTERPRETATION

46    PARTIES; ASSIGNS AND SUCCESSORS

47    MODIFICATION

48    SEVERABILITY

49    NEGOTIATED AGREEMENT

50    MORTAGEE PROTECTION CLAUSE

51    ENTITY TENANTS

52    SURRENDER OF PREMISES

53    SURVIVAL

54    LANDLORD'S RIGHTS

55    SHOWING OF PREMISES AND LANDLORD
      ACCESS

56    SPECIAL STIPULATIONS

Exhibits
A     Site Plan
B     Rules and Regulations
C     Ownership of Tenant
D     Sign Criteria
E     Landlord's Work

# SHOPPING CENTER LEASE

THIS LEASE is made this 9th day of September, 2002, (the "Lease Date"), by and between (i) [name deleted] (hereinafter "Landlord") and (ii) THE POT & BEAD, LLC, a Virginia limited liability company (hereinafter "Tenant").

# WITNESSETH:

## 1. PREMISES.

(a) For and in consideration of the rent hereinafter reserved, payable in lawful money of the United States which shall then be legal tender of all debts, public and private, and the mutual covenants hereinafter contained, Landlord does hereby lease and demise unto Tenant, and Tenant does hereby hire, lease and accept from Landlord, an area containing approximately 1,247 square feet (the "Premises") in the building erected (or being erected, as the case may be) in the [name deleted] Shopping Center (the "Shopping Center"), located at [address deleted], all upon the terms and conditions hereinafter set forth. The Premises is cross-hatched on the site plan attached hereto as Exhibit A and by this reference made a part hereof. Said Exhibit A sets forth the general layout of the Shopping Center and location of the building in which the Premises will be situated, and shall not be deemed to be a warranty, representation or agreement on the part of the Landlord that said Shipping Center is or will be exactly as indicated. Landlord reserves the right to change, increase or reduce the number, composition, dimensions or locations of any parking areas, pylon signs, service areas, walkways, roadways, buildings, (including permanent and temporary kiosks) or other common areas in its sole discretion and may make alterations to existing buildings or construct additional buildings within the Shopping Center from time to time.

(b) Landlord agrees that within a reasonable time after the execution hereof, it will commence, and thereafter with reasonable diligence carry forward to completion, the construction of the Premises in accordance with the description of Landlord's Work described in Exhibit E attached hereto and made a part hereof, (all such items are hereinafter collectively referred to as

"Landlord's Work"). Construction of the Premises by Landlord shall be deemed to have commenced when work has been begun on Premises. Under no circumstances shall Landlord be liable to Tenant in damages for any delay in commencing or completing the Premises. Landlord shall have the exclusive right to determine the architectural design and the structural, mechanical and other standard details and specifications of Landlord's Work, including without limitation the type of materials and the manufacturer and supplier thereof.

(c) Landlord's construction of the Premises shall be conclusively deemed to be substantially completed on the date Landlord mails to Tenant a certificate of Landlord's representative that the Premises have been substantially completed in accordance with the description of Landlord's Work on attached Exhibit E.

(d) Tenant agrees to submit to Landlord for approval within 30 days from the date of execution of this Lease, complete drawings and specifications for all improvements proposed to be constructed by Tenant in the Premises in accordance with attached Exhibit E. Landlord agrees to promptly return the drawings and specifications to Tenant with Landlord's notice of (i) approval, (ii) approval subject to required revisions or comments, or (iii) disapproval. If Landlord has approved Tenant's drawings and specifications with comments, Tenant agrees to return to Landlord within 15 days of date of receipt of said drawing specifications, revised drawings and specification showing information or reasonable changes required by Landlord.

(e) Tenant will commence the work required to be done by it not later than forty-five (45) days after Landlord's approval of Tenant's drawings and specifications, which time shall be extended by a period of time equal to the time required by Landlord to complete the Landlord's Work, if the same is not then complete.

Tenant shall pay all sums due for Tenant's construction and/
or fees payable by it in connection therewith prior to the date
Tenant opens the Premises for business.

## 2. TERM.

(a) The term of this Lease shall commence on the Lease Date and
shall end sixty (60) months after the expiration of the "Abatement
Period," as defined in Article 3; provided, however, that in the
event the Abatement Period expires on a date other than the last
day of a month, the term of this Lease shall continue for the
number of months set forth above from the first day of the first
full calendar month following the expiration of the Abatement
Period.

(b) The term "Lease Year" as used herein shall mean a period of twelve
(12) consecutive full calendar months. The first Lease Year shall
begin on the Rent Commencement Date (or on the first day of
the calendar month following the Rent Commencement Date if
said date is other than the first day of the month), and each succeeding Lease Year shall commence upon the anniversary date of
the beginning of the first Lease Year.

(c) The parties agree that they shall execute an agreement specifying the Rent Commencement Date and the date of termination
of this Lease and such other matters as Landlord may require.
Tenant agrees, to execute and deliver to Landlord said agreement
within five (5) business days after receipt of written notice from
Landlord. If Tenant fails to execute and return any such agreement to Landlord within such five (5) day period, then Landlord
shall be entitled to collect from Tenant, as liquidated damages
with respect to such default of Tenant in addition to Minimum
Rent and other amounts payable hereunder, as Additional Rent,
an amount equal to one-half of one percent (1/2%) of the amount

of Minimum Rent then payable under this Lease, for each day Tenant delays in returning the requested agreement to Landlord.

## 3. RENT; DEPOSIT.

(a) Commencing with the Rent Commencement Date, Tenant shall pay "Minimum Rent" for the Premises in accordance with the schedules set forth below. The "Rent Commencement Date" shall be the Lease Date. The Minimum Rent shall be payable to Landlord or its designated agent in advance, in equal monthly installments, without notice or demand therefore, and without deduction, recoupment or setoff, with the first monthly installment to be due and payable no later than the Rent Commencement Date and each subsequent monthly installment to be due and payable on the first day of each and every month following the Rent Commencement Date during the term hereof. If the Rent Commencement Date is a date other than the first day of a month, Minimum Rent (together with all other charges payable hereunder) for the period commencing with and including the Rent Commencement Date until the first day of the following month shall be pro-rated at the daily rate of one-thirtieth ($1/30^{th}$) of the fixed monthly rental or other charges and shall be due and payable on the Rent Commencement Date. Notwithstanding the foregoing, if Tenant complies with the provisions of this Article 3 set forth below, all Minimum Rent and Additional Rent payable by Tenant pursuant to Articles 8 and 9 of this Lease shall be abated during the period (the "Abatement Period") beginning on the Rent Commencement Date and ending on the first to occur of: (i) the date Tenant opens for business in the Premises, or (ii) ninety (90) days after the date Landlord delivers the Premises to Tenant. The foregoing abatement of Minimum Rent and Additional Rent (the "Rent Abatement") represents Landlord's contribution toward work required by Tenant to open for business in the Premises. The Rent Abatement is contingent upon

Tenant's delivery to Landlord, within thirty (30) days after the expiration of the Abatement Period, a statement, executed by or on behalf of Tenant (the "Abatement Certificate"), certifying that Tenant has expended a sum equal to or greater than the amount of the Rent Abatement in connection with improvements to the Premises (excluding, however, Tenant's personal property, trade fixtures and inventory), together with copies of bills, invoices, contracts and other information which shows that Tenant has expended an amount equal to or greater than the Rent Abatement in connection with constructing and/or remodeling the Premises. If Tenant fails to deliver the Abatement Certificate and supporting documentation to Landlord in accordance with the foregoing provisions of this Article 3, then Tenant shall not be entitled to the abatement of Minimum and Additional Rent provided for above, and Tenant shall pay to Landlord, within thirty (30) days after the expiration of the Abatement Period, the full sum of the Rent Abatement.

[**NOTE**: I didn't understand this clause at the time even though my lawyer did try to point it out to me. What it says is: if I was spending more than three months' rent on improvements to the space—which I was—I didn't need to pay rent for the first ninety days. There were two catches—one was the paperwork headache and the second was the end of the "Abatement Period," which in our case would have ended at the date we opened for business. We had some scheduling issues with the contractor and he wasn't able to complete the work until after we opened for business. Looking back now, I would have tried to have part (i) of the above removed. I had the potential to save $9,000.]

(b)(1) Tenant shall pay Minimum Rent in the amount of Twenty-Six Thousand One Hundred Eighty-Seven and No One-Hundredth Dollars ($26,187.00) per year in equal monthly installments of Two Thousand One Hundred Eighty-Two and Twenty-Five One-Hundredth Dollars ($2,182.25) each for the period commencing on the Rent Commencement Date and ending on the last day of the first Lease Year inclusive;

(2) Tenant shall pay Minimum Rent in the amount of Twenty-Seven Thousand one Hundred Three and Fifty-Four One-Hundredth Dollars ($27,103.54) per year in equal monthly installments of Two Thousand Two Hundred Fifty-Eight and Sixty-Three One-Hundredth Dollars ($2,258.63) each for the period commencing on the first day of the second Lease Year and ending on the last day of the second Lease Year inclusive;

(3) Tenant shall pay Minimum Rent in the amount of Twenty-Eight Thousand Fifty-Two and Sixteen One-Hundredth Dollars ($28,052.16) per year in equal monthly installments of Two Thousand Three Hundred Thirty-Seven and Sixty-Eight One-Hundredth Dollars ($2,337.68) each for the period commencing on the first day of the third Lease Year and ending on the last day of the third Lease Year inclusive;

(4) Tenant shall pay Minimum Rent in the amount of Twenty-Nine Thousand Thirty-Three and Ninety-Nine One-Hundredth Dollars ($29,033.99) per year in equal monthly installments of Two Thousand Four Hundred Nineteen and Fifty One-Hundredth Dollars ($2,419.50) each for the period commencing on the first day of the fourth Lease Year and ending on the last day of the fourth Lease Year inclusive;

(5) Tenant shall pay Minimum Rent in the amount of Thirty Thousand Fifty and Eighteen One-Hundredth Dollars ($30,050.18) per year in equal monthly installments of Two Thousand Five Hundred Four and Eighteen One-Hundredth Dollars ($2,504.18) each for the period commencing on the first day of the fifth Lease Year and ending on the last day of the term of this Lease.

(c) (1) Landlord hereby acknowledges receipt of Two Thousand Five hundred Ninety-Eight and Ninety-Six One-Hundredth Dollars ($2,598.96) which shall constitute prepayment of the first full month's rent, Real Estate Taxes and Annual Operating Cost charge as set forth below.

(2) Tenant has deposited with the Landlord the sum of Two Thousand Five Hundred Ninety-Eight and Ninety-Six One-Hundredth Dollars ($2,598.96) to be held by Landlord as security for Tenant's satisfactory performance of the terms, covenants and conditions of this Lease including the payment of Minimum Rent and Additional Rent.

(3) Landlord may use, apply or retain the whole or any part of the security so deposited to the extent required for the payment of any Minimum Rent and Additional Rent or any other sum as to which Tenant is in default, or any other sum due Landlord under the terms of this Lease, or for any sum which Landlord may expend or may be required to expend by reason of Tenant's default in respect to any of the terms, covenants and conditions of this Lease including any damages or deficiency in the re-letting of the Premises or other re-entry by Landlord.

(4) If Landlord uses, applies or retains the whole or any part of the security, Tenant shall pay to Landlord, as Additional Rent, an amount sufficient to replenish the security to its original sum within five (5) days after being notified by the Landlord of the amount due. Tenant shall be in default of this Lease if the amount due is not paid within the required time period.

(5) In the event of a sale or leasing of the Shopping Center or any part thereof, of which the Premises for a part, Landlord shall have the right to transfer the security to the purchaser or lessee and Landlord shall, upon such transfer, be released from all

liability for the return of said security; and Tenant agrees to look solely to the new Landlord for the return of said security; and it is agreed that the provisions hereof shall apply to every transfer or assignment made of the security to a new landlord.

(6) Tenant covenants that it shall not assign or encumber the security deposit given to Landlord pursuant to this Lease. Neither Landlord, its successor or assigns shall be bound by any such agreement or encumbrance or any attempted assignment or encumbrance.

(7) In the event that Tenant shall fully and faithfully comply with all the terms, conditions and covenants of this Lease, any part of the security not used or retained by Landlord shall be returned to Tenant after the expiration date of the term of this Lease and after delivery of exclusive possession of the Premises to Landlord; provided, however, that Landlord may retain all or a portion of the security until Landlord makes the final annual adjustments of Annual Operating Costs and Real Estate Taxes and ascertains Tenant's share of such amounts which accrued prior to the expiration of the term.

(8) Payment by Tenant of a lesser amount than shall be due shall be deemed to be payment on account, and shall not constitute an accord and satisfaction with respect to the underlying obligation. The acceptance by Landlord of a check for a lesser amount with an endorsement or statement thereon, or upon any letter accompanying such check, that such lesser amount is payment in full, shall be given no effect, and Landlord may accept such check without prejudice to any other rights or remedies which it may have against the Tenant.

[**NOTE**: These clauses on Rent say that I cannot withhold rent, ever. If the Landlord does something bothersome, I can't withhold even a portion of the rent. This is fairly standard in a commercial lease and sometimes surprising to new tenants.]

## 4. INTENTIONALLY DELETED.

## 5. GROSS SALES.

(a) The term "Gross Sales," as used herein, shall means the sum total, for each Lease Year, or portion thereof, of all sales of all goods, wares, merchandise, services or all other receipts whatsoever of all business conducted in, on, from or about the Premises, (including, but not limited to catalogue sales made at or from the Premises) by Tenant or any sublessee, licensee or concessionaire of Tenant whether for cash, credit or other consideration (without reserve or deduction for inability to collect) including, but not limited to such sales or services (i) as a result of transactions originating in at or from the Premises, whether delivery or performance is made from the Premises or some other place; and (ii) pursuant to mail, telephone, telegraph, closed TV circuit, so called "Dial-A-Buy" and other devices, automated or otherwise, whereby orders are received at the Premises. Each sale upon installment or credit shall be treated as a sale for the full price in the month during which such sales shall be made, irrespective or credit shall be treated as a sale for the full price in the month during which such sales shall be made, irrespective of the time when Tenant shall receive payment therefore. Gross Sales shall not include, however: (i) any sales tax, gross receipts tax or similar tax by whatever name called, the amount of which is determined by the amount of the sale made, and which Tenant or any sublessee or concessionaire of Tenant is required to account for, and pay over to, any governmental agency: (ii) transfers of merchandise made by Tenant from the Premises to any other stores or warehouses of Tenant, or (iii) credits or refunds given to customers for merchandise which was purchased from the Premises and thereafter returned or exchanged.

(b) Tenant covenants and agrees that (i) not later than the fifteenth (15<sup>th</sup>) day after the close of each calendar month of the term hereof, it will deliver to Landlord a complete, true and accurate report verified under oath by Tenant or by an authorized officer of Tenant, of all Gross Sales for such month and (ii) not later than sixty (60) days after the close of each Lease Year, and after the termination of this Lease or any renewal thereof, it will deliver to Landlord a complete, true, accurate fully audited report (the "Year End Report"), certified to be correct by an independent certified public accountant, of all Gross Sales for such year. The obligations contained in this Article 5 to report Gross Sales monthly shall survive the expiration or other termination of this Lease. If Tenant shall fail to deliver such report and such failure shall continue for ten (10) days after the date of written notice of such failure from Landlord, Landlord shall have the right thereafter to employ a certified public accountant to make such examination of Tenant's books and records as may be necessary to certify the amount of Gross Sales for said Lease Year, the certification so made shall be binding upon tenant and Tenant shall promptly pay to Landlord the cost of such examination of its books and records for said Lease Year and Tenant shall immediately be deemed to have released any and all options or rights granted or to be granted to Tenant under the terms of this Lease (including, without limitation, rights of renewal, rights to terminate or rights of refusal and any rights or privileges granted pursuant to any Special Stipulations included in this Lease). In addition Landlord may, at its option, elect to treat such failure to deliver said report within ten (10) days after written notice of such failure from Landlord as an event of default, in which event, in addition to Landlord's other rights and remedies, Landlord may elect to increase the Minimum Rent by an additional amount equal to fifty cents ($0.50) multiplied by the number of square feet of leasable area in the Premises for each such default.

(c) Tenant will keep, at its principal business offices located at the Premises or at such other place as Tenant shall designate in writing, complete, true and accurate records of all sales made on or from the Premises including but not limited to sales tax returns, canceled checks, bank statements, sales slips, Federal and State income tax returns, and all dated tapes from cash registers and/or any other mechanical or electronic device used for sales transactions. Landlord shall have the right to cause an audit (separate and distinct from the audit required to be made by Tenant pursuant to the preceding paragraph) to be made of the records of Tenant relating to its Gross Sales at any and all reason able times, and Tenant shall retain its records relating to such Gross Sales; provided that an audit with respect to any Lease year shall be commenced within three (3) years of the date of receipt by Landlord of the Year End Report of Tenant's Gross Sales for such Lease Year. If the actual Gross Sales exceed the Gross Sales set forth in the Year End Report by two percent (2%) or more, Tenant shall forthwith also pay the reasonable fees and costs of the audit, and Landlord shall also have the right to declare Tenant in breach of this Lease and avail itself of any and all remedies provided for herein, or available at law or in equity.

## 6. NOT A JOINT VENTURE.

Any intention to create a joint venture or partnership relation between the parties hereto is hereby expressly disclaimed.

## 7. RESTRICTIVE CLAUSE.

Tenant covenants that it will not own, operate or maintain, or directly or indirectly have any affiliation, investment or interest in, or other business or financial association with, any retail commercial store or establishment for retail sales or merchandise display, which is similar to or in competition with the business conducted in the Premises within a radius of five (5) miles from the site of the Premises, except those in operation as the date hereof as listed on the Exhibit attached, if any. For so long as Tenant shall own or have any interest in such other permitted locations, any change in the name, size, location, or the type of business conducted upon such other locations (within the radius above described) shall be deemed to be a breach of this Lease.

[**NOTE**: For the type of business I was in, the likelihood that I would want or desire to open a similar business within five miles was very small so I ignored this clause. But if you're in a business, such as a food or service business, that serves a lot more people and could be in each and every shopping center, so pay attention to this.]

## 8. ANNUAL OPERATING COSTS.

Tenant agrees to pay to Landlord on the first day of each month, in advance, during the term hereof, as Additional Rent, without notice or demand therefore and without any deduction whatsoever, an annual operating cost charge equal to one-twelfth $(1/12^{th})$ of its Proportionate share (as hereinafter defined) of the Annual Operating Cost (as hereinafter defined) of the Shopping Center. Tenant shall initially pay an estimated minimum annual charge of $2,992.80 per year, in equal monthly installments of $249.40 each. At any time during each twelve (12) month period, Landlord may retroactively re-estimate Tenant's proportionate share of landlord's Annual Operating Cost and may bill Tenant for any deficiency which may have accrued during such twelve (12) month period and thereafter Tenant's monthly installments shall also be adjusted. Within one hundred eighty (180) days (or such additional time thereafter as is reasonable under the circumstances), following each September 30th of each year, Landlord shall deliver to Tenant a statement of Landlord's Annual Operating Cost for such twelve (12) month period and the monthly installments paid or payable shall be adjusted between Landlord and Tenant, and Tenant shall pay Landlord or Landlord shall credit Tenant's account (or, if such adjustment is at the end of the term, Landlord shall pay Tenant), as the case may be within fifteen (15) days of receipt of such statement, the amount of any excess or deficiency in Tenant's Proportionate Share of Landlord's Annual Operating Cost paid by Tenant to Landlord during such twelve (12) month period. Failure of Landlord to provide the statement called for hereunder within the time prescribed shall not relieve Tenant of its obligation hereunder. The obligation to pay Annual Operating Cost accruing during the term shall survive the expiration or other termination of this Lease.

[**NOTE**: This "Additional Rent" is also known as Common Area Maintenance (CAM). Throughout the rest of the lease, you'll see other things that get thrown under "Additional Rent." Basically, the landlord had the right under this lease to pass off almost anything related to the shopping center to us tenants, with no limit.]

(a) (i) Tenant's share of Annual Operating Cost ("Tenant's Proportionate Share") for each full or partial fiscal year selected by Landlord during the Term shall be computed by Landlord by multiplying the amount of Annual Operating Cost by a fraction obtained by dividing the total number of square feet of space contained in the Premises by the total leasable retail area contained within all buildings in the Shopping Center from time to time, exclusive of any free-standing building the tenants of which are required by the terms of their leases to maintain common areas adjacent to their facilities.

(ii) If Landlord elects to assume responsibility for the HVAC Equipment pursuant to paragraph 17(a) of this Lease, then Tenant's Proportionate Share of Annual Operating Cost shall also include the costs and expenses incurred by Landlord with respect to the HVAC Equipment, which shall be determined by multiplying the total amount of Annual Operating Cost incurred by Landlord with respect to HVAC Expenses in the Shopping Center by a fraction obtained by dividing the total number of square feet of space contained in the Premises by the total leasable area contained within all other premises in the Shopping Center, from time to time, for which Landlord has, or has assumed, the responsibility of maintaining HVAC Equipment.

(b) Annual Operating Cost means the total cost and expense incurred by Landlord in maintaining public liability insurance, fire insurance with extended coverage, workers' compensation insurance, property damage or other insurance on the Shopping Center with such policies and companies and in such limits as selected by Landlord and in managing, operating, repairing, replacing and maintaining the Shopping Center, roof and the Common Facilities (as hereinafter defined), including all amounts charged by Landlord for any such services and work provided directly by Landlord and all amounts charged by other persons or entities, whether or not related to Landlord, and specifically including without limitation, the costs of gardening and landscaping; management, maintenance and service contracts; repairs; line painting; regulation of traffic; utilities; sanitary controls; removal of snow, trash, rubbish, garbage and other refuse; depreciation on equipment and machinery used in such maintenance, the cost of personnel to implement such services; servicing and maintaining the fire sprinkler system; legal, management and accounting fees; cleaning, maintaining, repairing and replacing the Common Facilities; and in providing security protection; at Landlord's option, reserve funds for the replacement of roof and parking lot facilities and for the HVAC Equipment if Landlord elects to assume responsibility for the

HVAC Equipment, as provided in Article 17; and an administrative fee equal to fifteen percent (15%) of Annual Operating Cost. It is understood and agreed that management fees may be charged by Landlord or any other person or entity on the basis of a specified percentage of the gross receipts derived from the Shopping Center or on any other basis, provided that, in the case of management fees charged by the Landlord, such fees shall not exceed the greater of five percent (5%) of gross receipts or the customary management fees charged for similar properties in the same geographic area.

(c) Common Facilities means all areas provided by Landlord, from time to time, for the common or joint use and benefit of the occupants of the Shopping Center and their employees, agents, servants, customers and other invitees, including, without limitation, management offices, community rooms, parking areas, parking decks, access roads, driveways, retaining walls, landscaped areas, truck serviceways, sidewalks, parcel pickup stations and, to the extent Landlord elects to service, repair, maintain and/or replace HVAC Equipment (as defined in Article 17) in the Shopping Center, all such HVAC Equipment for which Landlord has, or has assumed, responsibility.

(d) Landlord shall not be liable in any such case for any inconvenience, disturbance, loss of business or any other annoyance arising from the exercise of any or all of the rights of Landlord in this Article 8.

## 9. REAL ESTATE TAXES.

Tenant agrees to pay Landlord monthly during the term hereof, together with each monthly installment of Minimum rent or Adjusted Minimum Rent as Additional Rent, without notice or demand therefore and without any deduction whatsoever, one-twelfth (1/12th) of its pro-rata share (as defined below) of Real

Estate Taxes (as hereinafter defined), for each Tax Year (as hereinafter defined).

[**NOTE:** More "Additional Rent" here in the form of property tax.]

(a) Tenant shall pay upon being billed an estimated annual charge of $2007.67 per year, payable in equal monthly installments of $167.31 each. During the first Lease Year, in the event Landlord's mortgagee or the taxing authority having jurisdiction over the Shopping Center bills and requires payment of Real Estate Taxes in advance, Tenant's pro-rata share shall be due and payable upon being billed by Landlord in addition to the monthly payment set forth herein, which payment shall be applied to the following Tax Year. At any time during a Tax Year, Landlord may retroactively re-estimate Tenant's pro-rata share of Real Estate Taxes and may bill Tenant for any deficiency which may have accrued during such Tax Year, and thereafter Tenant's monthly installment shall also be adjusted. Within one hundred twenty (120) days after Landlord's receipt of tax bulls for each Tax Year, or such reasonable (in Landlord's determination) time thereafter, Landlord will notify Tenant of the amount of Real Estate Taxes for the Tax Year in question and the amount of Tenant's pro-rate share thereof. Any overpayment or deficiency in Tenant's payment of its pro-rata share of Real Estate Taxes for each Tax Year shall be adjusted between Landlord and Tenant, and Landlord and Tenant hereby agree that Tenant shall pay Landlord or Landlord shall credit to Tenant's account (or, if such adjustment is at the end of the term, Landlord shall pay Tenant), as the case may be, within fifteen (15) days of the aforesaid certification to Tenant, the amount necessary to effect such adjustment. The failure of Landlord to provide such certification of the amount of Real Estate Taxes within the time prescribed above shall not relieve Tenant of any of its obligations hereunder. The obligation to pay Real Estate

Taxes accruing during the term shall survive the expiration or other termination of this Lease.

(b) Tenant's pro-rata share of Real Estate Taxes shall be determined by multiplying the total amount of Real Estate Taxes paid by Landlord for each full or partial Tax Year (less contributions paid by any tenants operating under ground leases in the Shopping Center and contributions by tenants of any supermarkets, department stores, junior department store, or other "anchor" or "major" tenants of the Shopping Center) by a fraction, the numerator of which is the total gross leasable area ("GLA") contained within the Premises, and the denominator of which is the total GLA contained within all buildings within the Shopping Center, exclusive of (i) any free standing buildings or ground leased areas and (ii) any space occupied by a supermarket, department store, junior department store or other "anchor" or "major" tenant of the Shopping Center.

(c) The term "Real Estate Taxes" means all taxes, rates and assessments, general and special, levied or imposed with respect to the Shopping Center land, building and improvements of which the Premises are a part, including all taxes, rates and assessments, general and special, levied or imposed for schools, public betterment, general or local improvements and operations, and taxes imposed in connection with any special taxing district and all fees, charges and assessments payable by Landlord under the provisions of the Declaration for Ashburn Village recorded in the land records office of Loudoun County, Virginia in book 959 at page 874, as amended from time to time. If the system of real estate taxation shall be altered or varied or any new tax or levy shall be levied or imposed on said land, buildings and improvements, and/or Landlord in substitution for Real Estate Taxes levied or imposed on the Lease Data on immovables in the jurisdiction where the Shopping Center is located, then any such new tax or levy shall be included within the term "Real Estate Taxes." Should any governmental taxing authority acting under any regulation, levy, asses or impose a tax, excise and/or assessment however described (other than an income or franchise tax) upon against, on account of or measured by, in whole or in part, the rent expressly reserved hereunder, or upon the rent expressly reserved under any other leases or leasehold interest in the Shopping Center, as a substitute (in whole or in part) or in addition to any existing real estate taxes on land and buildings or otherwise, such tax or excise on rents shall be included within the term "Real Estate Taxes." Reasonable expenses, consisting of attorney fees, consultant fees, expert witness fees and similar costs, incurred by Landlord in obtaining or attempting to obtain a reduction of any Real Estate Taxes shall be added to and included in the amount of any such Real Estate Taxes. The term "Real Estate Taxes" shall not include taxes, rates of assessments levied against portions of the Shopping Center that are encumbered by leases, from time to time, the terms of which require the tenant to pay the full amount of said charges levied or assessed against the premises leased thereunder. Real Estate Taxes which are being contested by Landlord shall nevertheless be included for purposes of the computation of the liability of Tenant under this Article; provided, however, that if Tenant shall have paid any amount of increased rent pursuant to this Article 9 and Landlord shall thereafter receive a refund of any portion of any Real Estate Taxes on which such payment shall have been based, Landlord shall pay to Tenant the appropriate portion of such refund. Landlord shall have no obligation to contest, object to or litigate the levying or imposition of any Real Estate Taxes and may settle, compromise, consent to, waive or otherwise determine in its discretion to abandon any contest with respect to the amount of any Real Estate Taxes without consent or approval of Tenant.

(d) The term "Tax Year" means each twelve (12) month period established as the real estate tax year by the taxing authorities having lawful jurisdiction over the Shopping Center.

## 10. ADDITIONAL RENT.

Any amount required to be paid by Tenant hereunder and any charges or expenses incurred by Landlord on behalf of Tenant under the terms of this Lease shall be considered Additional Rent payable in full on the data and upon the same terms and conditions as the next succeeding installment of Minimum Rent next falling due hereunder after Tenant knows, or has reason to know, that any such sum is due and owing. Any failure on the part of Tenant to pay such Additional Rent when and as the same shall become due shall entitle the Landlord to the remedies available to it for non-payment of rent. Tenant's failure to object to any statement, invoice or billing rendered by Landlord within a period of thirty (30) days after receipt thereof shall constitute Tenant's acquiescence with respect thereto, and such statement invoice or billing shall thereafter be deemed to be correct and shall be an account stated between Landlord and Tenant. If Tenant requests that Landlord prepare, review, or execute any document, consent or waiver in connection with this Lease or otherwise, Tenant shall be obligated to pay to Landlord, as Additional Rent a fee, in the amount set forth on a fee schedule adopted by Landlord from time to time, to compensate Landlord for the cost of reviewing and processing and such request, and Landlord shall not be obligated to process any such request of Tenant until Tenant has paid Landlord the applicable processing fee. Landlord will supply Tenant with a copy of Landlord's then current processing fee schedule upon Tenant's request. Nothing herein shall be deemed to require that Landlord consent to, execute or approve any document, consent or waiver submitted to Landlord by Tenant notwithstanding Tenant's payment of the applicable processing fee. In addition to all liens upon and rights of setoff or recoupment against any money or property of Tenant by law, Landlord shall have, to the extent permitted by law, a contractual security interest in and a right of setoff against all deposits, moneys or other property of Tenant now or hereafter in the possession of or on deposit with Landlord. Each such security interest or right of setoff or to enforce such setoff and/or security interest or by any delay in so doing. Every right of setoff and/or security interest shall continue in full force and effect until such right of setoff and/or security interest is expressly waived or released by an instrument in writing executed by Landlord.

## 11. UTILITIES.

Tenant shall be responsible for and shall promptly pay all water rent, gas, electricity and other utility bills (including sewer charges, tap-ins, hookup and connection charges) for utilities used or consumed in the Premises as the same shall become due commencing on the first to occur of (i) the date Tenant occupies the Premises, or (ii) the Rent Commencement Date, it being understood and agreed that Tenant shall promptly make all required deposits for meters and utility services connected with Tenant's use of the Premises. Charges for the foregoing shall commence on the date Landlord delivers possession of the Premises to Tenant. In no event shall Landlord be liable to Tenant or any agent, servant, licensee or assignee of Tenant for damages or otherwise for curtailment or suspension of any utility services, in the event of default by Tenant under this Lease, or due to repairs, action of public authority, strikes, acts of God or any other cause whatsoever, whether similar or dissimilar to the aforesaid.

## 12. INTENTIONALLY DELETED.

## 13. USE OF PREMISES.

The Premises shall be used and occupied by Tenant solely for the purpose of operating a retail store (i) selling unpainted, pre-fabricated pottery for customers to paint and (ii) selling beads to craft distinctive homemade jewelry, both in a studio setting and for no other purpose whatsoever and Tenant further agrees to conduct its business in the Premises under the name or trade name of The Pot and Bead. The Premises shall not be used for any illegal purpose or in violation of any law or regulation of any governmental body, or in any manner to (i) create any nuisance or trespass; (ii) annoy or embarrass Landlord or any other tenant of the Shopping Center; (iii) vitiate any insurance carried by Landlord; (iv) alter the classifications or increase the rate of any insurance on the Premises; (v) allow any noise or odor to emanate from the Premises; or (vi) violate the Certificate of Occupancy issued for the Premises.

## 14. CONDUCT OF TENANT'S BUSINESS.

Tenant shall open for business in the Premises on or before the expiration of the Abatement Period, and shall thereafter continuously, actively and diligently operate its said business on the whole of the Premises, in a high quality and reputable manner, from at least 11:00 AM to 7:00 PM Monday through Sunday of each week, if applicable law permits the Shopping Center to be open on Sundays. Tenant shall be permitted to close its business in the Premises on all Federally recognized holidays. Tenant shall maintain a full staff of employees and a full and complete stock of merchandise at all times, shall use a cash register or other similar device for transacting sales, and shall maintain displays of merchandise in the display windows, if any, and keep such display windows and Tenant's store signs well lighted from at least dusk to 11:00 PM each day so as to maximize the Gross Sales produced by Tenant's business. Tenant shall warehouse, store and stock only such goods, wares and merchandise as Tenant intends to offer for sale at retail in or from the Premises, and as permitted under this Lease. Tenant will not place or maintain any merchandise, refuse or other articles in any vestibule or entry of the Premises, on the sidewalks or corridors adjacent thereto or elsewhere on the exterior of the Premises or obstruct any driveway, corridor, sidewalk, parking area, mall or any other common area. Tenant will not conduct or permit to be conducted any auction, fictitious fire sale, going out of business sale, bankruptcy sale or other similar type sale in or connected with the Premises. In any and all of its printed or visual advertising in relation to the Premises, Tenant shall use the insignia or other identifying mark, if any, of the Shopping Center, as designated by Landlord form time to time. Tenant agrees that actual damages to Landlord resulting from a failure of Tenant to operate in the Premises in accordance with the provisions of this Lease (including, without limitation, damages resulting from the adverse impact on the sales and percentage rental payable to Landlord by other tenants of the Shopping Center), will be difficult to ascertain, and therefore, at Landlord's option, in addition to all other rights and remedies available to Landlord for breach of this Lease, Tenant shall pay to Landlord for the failure of Tenant to observe and perform the covenants of this Article 14 (in amount equal to one hundred percent (100%) of the Minimum Rent otherwise payable hereunder for each month during which such a breach occurs, since the parties hereto agree that it is difficult, if not impossible, to ascertain precisely the damage caused to Landlord by a breach of the obligations contained in this Article, and that this provision for liquidated damages represents a fair and reasonable provision by the parties.

[**NOTE:** The first version of this lease did not have the additional sentence about being able to close on federally recognized holidays. It said I must be open 11 a.m. to 7 p.m., period. I should have argued that not all the other businesses had this restriction—some were closed on Sundays, for instance.]

## 15. ASSIGNMENT; SUBLETTING.

(a) Neither Tenant, nor any of its permitted successors or assigns, shall transfer, assign, mortgage, encumber, or, by operation of law or otherwise, pledge, hypothecate, or assign all or any of its interest in this Lease, or sublet or permit the Premises, or any part thereof, to be used by others, including, but not by way of limitation, concessionaires or licensees of Tenant, without the prior written consent of Landlord, in each instance, which consent shall not be unreasonably withheld by Landlord. Any such subletting or assignment shall be referred to as a "Transfer," and the person to whom Tenant's interest is transferred shall be referred to as a "Transferee."

(b) The prohibition against any Transfer without the prior written consent of Landlord shall apply, without limitation, to the following circumstances, each of which shall be deemed a Transfer; (i) if Tenant or any guarantor of this Lease is a corporation (other than a corporation, the outstanding voting stock of which is listed on a "national securities exchange," as defined in the Securities Exchange Act of 1934), and if shares of such corporation are transferred by sale, assignment, bequest, inheritance, operation of law or otherwise (including, without limitation, a transfer to or by a receiver or trustee in federal or state bankruptcy, insolvency or other proceeding), so as to result in or make possible a change in the present control of such corporation; (ii) if tenant or any guarantor of this Lease is a partnership, any change in control or ownership of such partnership; (iii) any transfer by sale, assignment, bequest, inheritance, operation of law or other disposition of all or substantially all of the assets of Tenant or any guarantor; (iv) any other change in ownership of Tenant, any guarantor of this Lease or business operated by Tenant; or (v) any subletting or assignment which occurs by operation of law, merger, consolidation, or reorganization or any change of Tenant's corporate or proprietary structure. In no event may Tenant assign this Lease, or sublease the Premises, if Tenant is in default under this Lease.

(c) In the event that Tenant desires to effect a Transfer hereunder, Tenant shall give Landlord written notice (the "Transfer Notice") thereof. To be effective, the Transfer notice shall be accompanied by Tenant's check, payable to the order of Landlord, or Landlord's Agent, in an amount equal to the greater of (i) $1,000.00 or (ii) one percent (1%) of the Minimum Rent to compensate Landlord for the cost of reviewing the proposed Transfer and specify the proposed Transferee, and the proposed terms of the Transfer, and contain such information about the proposed Transferee, its experience, its financial situation, its methods of operation, its contributions to the tenant mix of the Shopping Center, and its impact on the Shopping Center, as a prudent businessman would require in making the Transfer decision. Tenant specifically agrees to apprise Landlord of any adverse or negative information in its possession concerning the proposed Transfer and the proposed Transferee. The Transfer Notice shall also contain a certificate by Tenant (or an officer or general partner of Tenant if Tenant is a corporation or partnership) of all "Transfer Consideration" (as defined below) payable in connection with the proposed Transfer. Within sixty (60) days of the receipt of the Transfer Notice Landlord shall, by written notice to Tenant, elect: (i) to permit the proposed Transfer (ii) to terminate this Lease; (iii) to sublet with the right to further sublet from Tenant for the balance of the term of this Lease (a) all of the Premises, or (b) only so much of the Premises as Tenant proposed to Transfer, at the same rental as Tenant is obligated to pay to Landlord hereunder; or (iv) to deny consent to the proposed Transfer, in which event Tenant shall continue to occupy the Premises and comply with all of the terms and conditions hereof. In the event that Landlord fails to give Tenant written notice of its election hereunder within the specified sixty (60) day period, Landlord shall be deemed to have denied its consent to the proposed Transfer.

(d) If this Lease is Transferred, the Transferee shall assume by written instrument all of Tenant's obligations under this Lease and such Transferee, at least thirty (30) days prior to the effective date of the Transfer, shall deliver to Landlord the proposed sublease, assignment and assumption agreement or other instrument evidencing the Transfer and the Transferee's undertaking to perform Tenant's obligations under this Lease. All of such documents shall be subject to Landlord's prior written approval. After any Transfer of this Lease, Tenant shall continue to be liable hereunder, and shall not be released from performance hereunder. In addition to the Rent reserved hereunder, Tenant shall pay to Landlord all monies, property and other consideration of every kind whatsoever paid or payable to Tenant in consideration of or related to such Transfer and for all property transferred to the Transferee, as all or part of the consideration including, without limitation, fixtures, other leasehold improvements, furniture, equipment and furnishings (collectively, all of the foregoing monies, property and other consideration shall be referred to as the "Transfer Consideration"), but excluding bona fide consideration paid for transfer of Tenant's property. Following a Transfer of this Lease, Landlord shall not be required to send the named Tenant any notice of default by the approved Transferee.

(e) Any Transfer without Landlord's consent, whether as a result of any act or omission of tenant, or by operation of law or otherwise, shall not be binding upon Landlord, and shall confer no rights upon any third person. Each such unpermitted Transfer shall, without notice or grace period of any kind, constitute a default by Tenant under this Lease. The acceptance by Landlord of the payment of Rent following any Transfer prohibited by this Article 15 shall not be deemed to be a consent by Landlord to any such Transfer, an acceptance of this Transferee as a tenant, a release of Tenant from the performance of any covenants herein contained, or a waiver by Landlord of any remedy of Landlord under this Lease, although amounts actually received shall be credited by Landlord against Tenant's rent obligations. Consent by Landlord to any one Transfer shall not constitute a waiver of the requirement for consent to any other Transfer. No reference in this Lease to assignees, concessionaires, subtenants or licensees shall be deemed to be a consent by Landlord to the occupancy of the Premises by any such assignee, concessionaire, subtenant or licensee. Notwithstanding anything in this Article or any decision of any court to the contrary, it shall be deemed reasonable for Landlord to refuse consent to a Transfer if, at the time Landlord's consent is requested, other premises in the Shopping Center suitable for that prospective Transferee's use are (or soon will be) available.

(f) If Tenant is a corporation, limited liability company or partnership, Tenant represents that the ownership and power to vote its entire outstanding capital stock or partnership interests belongs to and is vested in the persons listed on Exhibit C. The foregoing provisions of this paragraph (f) shall not apply to a publicly held entity described in clause (i) of paragraph (b) of this Article 15.

## 16. REPAIRS BY LANDLORD.

Landlord agrees to make all necessary repairs during the term of this Lease or any extension thereof, to the roof of the Premises and all necessary structural repairs to the exterior walls and foundations, (exclusive of doors, door frames, door checks, other entrances, windows and window frames) provided such repairs are not made necessary through the misuse of the same by the Tenant or the negligence of Tenant, its agents, servants, contractors or employees, and provided that Tenant shall give Landlord written notice of the necessity for such repairs. Landlord shall not be liable to Tenant for any damage caused to the person or property of Tenant, its agents, employees or invitees, due to the Premises or any part or appurtenances thereof being improperly constructed or being or becoming out of repair, or arising from the leaking, of gas, water, sewer or steam pipes, or from electricity, or from any other cause whatsoever. Tenant agrees to report immediately in writing to Landlord any defective condition in or about the Premises known to Tenant which Landlord is required to repair, and failure to so report shall make Tenant liable to Landlord for any expense, damage or liability resulting from such defects. Landlord hereby reserves the exclusive right at any time and from time to time to install, use, repair, inspect and replace pipes, ducts, conduits and wires leading through or located adjacent to the Premises and serving other parts of the Shopping Center in locations which do not materially interfere with Tenant's use thereof. Landlord's right hereunder may be exercised by Landlord's designees. If any excavation shall be made or authorizes to be made upon land adjacent to the Premises, Tenant shall afford to the person causing or authorized to cause such excavation license to enter upon the Premises for the purpose of doing such work as Landlord shall deem necessary to preserve the building located upon the Premises from injury or damage and to support the same by proper foundations, without any claim for damages or indemnification against Landlord or diminution or abatement of rent. Landlord shall not be liable in any such case for any inconvenience, disturbance, loss of business or any other annoyance arising from the exercise of any or all of the rights of Landlord in this Article 16.

[**NOTE**: I really didn't appreciate this section when I signed the lease. Basically, the landlord is responsible for the maintenance of nearly nothing. Anything and everything inside the space was my responsibility. This is fairly standard with a commercial lease.]

# 17. MAINTENANCE AND REPAIRS BY TENANT.

## Tenant covenants and agrees:

(a) That it shall maintain the interior of the Premises (including necessary and periodic repeating) together with all electrical, plumbing and sewage facilities (including free flow up to the main sewer line and grease traps, if any), heating, air conditioning and other mechanical installations therein, exterior and interior of all doors, door frames, door checks, other entrances, windows and window frames in good condition and surrender same at the expiration of the term, in the same good order in which they are received, damage by reasonable wear and tear and acts of God excepted. Landlord shall be under no liability for repair, maintenance, alteration or any other action with reference to the Premises or any part thereof, or repair, maintenance, alteration, replacement or any other action with respect to any exterior doors, plumbing, heating, electrical, air conditioning, or other mechanical installation therein. Tenant shall promptly repair at its own expense any damage (whether structural or otherwise) to the Premises caused by any construction or alterations performed by Tenant or bringing into the Premises any property for Tenant's use, or by the installation or removal of such property, regardless of fault or by whom such damage shall be caused, unless caused solely by the negligence of Landlord or its employees, officers or agents. Notwithstanding the foregoing, Landlord may, at its option, upon not less than thirty (30) days notice, elect to assume responsibility for the mechanical portions of heating, ventilation and air conditioning equipment (the "HVAC Equipment") which serves the Premises and which is located on the roof or in another location outside the Premises, and the routine servicing thereof, in which event the costs and expenses incurred by Landlord in maintaining, repairing and/or replacing the HVAC Equipment shall become an

Annual Operating Cost for purposes of Article 8 of this Lease, except that Tenant's Proportionate Share of expenses related to the HVAC Equipment shall be as set forth in paragraph 8(a)(ii).

[**NOTE:** The landlord did not elect to take responsibility for the HVAC. If there are any clauses like this in a lease, try and discover what the landlord will or won't do ahead of time. In this case, it meant budgeting for HVAC maintenance.]

(b) That it shall be responsible for the removal and disposition of Tenant's refuse and rubbish from the Premises and the Shopping Center. In order to facilitate the systematic and orderly removal of such refuse and rubbish, and in order to coordinate the hours during which such service is performed for the various tenants and the use of the loading areas, Landlord shall have the right, from time to time, to select one or more independent contractors for the removal of refuse and rubbish. Upon request by Landlord, Tenant agrees to employ the contractor designated for the area in which the Premises is located for the removal of refuse and rubbish. Landlord agrees that the rate to be charged for such service shall be computed upon sound business practices and consistent with industry practice. The removal and disposition of Tenant's refuse and rubbish as aforementioned shall be subject to constant supervision and approval by Landlord. If at any time Landlord at its sole discretion, determines that removal and disposition is less than satisfactory, Landlord or its agent or an independent contractor selected by Landlord may contract to have removal and disposition completed to its satisfaction. Any charges under such circumstances shall be Tenant's responsibility due within ten (10) days as Additional Rent. Tenant shall not permit the unsightly accumulation or placing of rubbish, trash, garbage, debris, boxes, cans or other articles of any kind or description whatsoever in the Premises, or in the area immediately surrounding the Premises, or in any other part of the Shopping Center. Tenant shall store all rubbish, trash, garbage, debris, boxes, cans or other such items, in fireproof containers approved by Landlord during such time that elapses between removals from Premises.

[**NOTE**: Trash removal—this was never a pleasant topic. We shared a Dumpster with several other tenants, a couple of whom were restaurants and generated an amazing amount of trash, especially on weekends. Several times over the five years additional rent was added for extra trash pickups and cleanups around the Dumpster area. That cost was split between me and my fellow tenants.]

## 18. CHANGES TO THE SHOPPING CENTER.

(a) Exhibit A sets forth the general layout of the Shopping Center. Exhibit A is not and shall not be deemed Landlord's representation or agreement that all or any part of the Shopping Center is, will be, or will continue to be, configured as indicated therein. Landlord also reserves the right to enlarge the area of the Shopping Center by adding additional ground thereto from time to time and, whether or not so enlarged, to construct other buildings or improvements in the Shopping Center at any time and from time to time and to make alterations thereto or additions thereto and to build additional stores on such building or buildings and to build adjoining the same, and Tenant shall have no interest of any kind whatsoever in the said additions of additional stores or adjoining buildings.

(b) Landlord shall have the right, at any time and from time to time, to (i) make alterations or additions to, any buildings or other improvements in or about the Shopping Center, to build additional stores on, and to build additional stores and buildings adjacent to the Premises; (ii) build other buildings or improvements in or about the Shopping Center; (iii) construct decked, subterranean or elevated parking facilities in or about the Shopping Center or the Common Area; (iv) change or consent to a change in the shape, size, location, number, height or extent of all or any of the buildings or other improvements in or about the Shopping Center, and (v) convey to others or withdraw portions of the Shopping Center.

[**NOTE**: One way to interpret this clause: if you're street-visible today, you might not be tomorrow. The location of The Pot & Bead was street visible, and it was great when we were brand new. Over five years, as the landscaping started to set in, trees started to obscure the view and there was nothing I could do about it.]

(c) In the event that Landlord renovates or remodels the front exterior of the Premises or the Shopping Center, Tenant agrees at its sole risk and expense to: (i) upon request of Landlord, remove its then existing signage to facilitate the remodeling work; (ii) upon direction of Landlord, re-install such signage (or if Landlord's signage criteria for the Premises has changes, install such signage as is appropriate under the new criteria and consistent with such exterior remodeling); (iii) promptly remodel the interior of the Premises, as appropriate, to be consistent with and accommodate any change in location or design of the said exterior; (iv) if Landlord's renovation plan includes the installation of new storefronts, Tenant agrees to promptly replace its storefront in accordance with Landlord's plan; (v) pay to Landlord, commencing upon the first day of the first full calendar month after the date of notice from Landlord to Tenant that said improvement program has been substantially completed, and for the duration of the term of this Lease, an annual sum equal to Two Dollars ($2.00) multiplied by the number of square feet of floor area of the Premises and said sum shall be deemed a part of the Minimum Rent; and (vi) otherwise cooperate with Landlord to facilitate such renovation and remodeling. Tenant's interior remodeling shall be undertaken and performed, subject to Landlord's prior written approval, in accordance with the provisions of this Lease.

Tenant consents to the performance of all work deemed appropriate by Landlord to accomplish any of the foregoing, and to any inconvenience caused thereby.

(d) Landlord may, at Landlord's option, elect to relocate the Premises to other space within the Shopping Center designated by Landlord (the "New Premises") upon compliance with the following requirements:

(i) Landlord shall deliver to Tenant a notice (the "Relocation Notice") not less than thirty (30) days prior to the date specified by Landlord as the date for Tenant's occupancy of the New Premises of Landlord's election to relocate Tenant's Premises and stating the location of the New Premises designated by Landlord. Landlord shall make a commercially reasonable attempt to accommodate the needs of Tenant with regard to the arrangement and location of the New Premises. Landlord shall include with the Relocation Notice outline plans and specifications for the work to be performed by Landlord in the New Premises, and Landlord shall use commercially reasonable efforts to relocate Tenant to New Premises which are similar in size and utility to the Premises. In the event Tenant decides the New Premises is unsuitable for any reason whatsoever, it may terminate this Lease by notifying the Landlord of its election to do so, in writing, within fifteen (15) days after receipt of the Relocation Notice. If Tenant elects to terminate this Lease, then this Lease will terminate on the date (the "Termination Date") which is the last to occur of (x) the date specified in the Relocation Notice as the estimated date for the relocation of the Premises, or (y) the last day of the first full calendar month next following the date of Landlord's receipt of Tenant's written notice of termination under this paragraph 18 (d). All rent and other charges payable under this Lease shall be adjusted as of the Termination Date, and the parties shall have the same rights and responsibilities under this Lease as if the Termination Date were the date set forth in this Lease as the date for the expiration of the term.

(ii) If Tenant elects to relocate to the New Premises, Landlord shall construct within the New Premises, at Landlord's expense, improvements which are substantially similar in quality and utility to the improvements located in the Premises on the date Landlord gives Tenant the Relocation Notice. Landlord shall pay the reasonable cost of moving Tenant's property and relocating Tenant's business from the Premises to the New Premises, and Landlord shall use commercially reasonable efforts to relocate Tenant's property and business from the Premises to the New Premises in a manner which minimizes the interruption of Tenant's business. Tenant shall fully cooperate with Landlord in the relocation of Tenant's business into the New Premises, and Tenant shall relocate its business to the New Premises and vacate the original Premises within five (5) days after Landlord notifies Tenant that the New Premises are available to Tenant's use.

(iii) If Tenant elects to relocate to the New Premises, this Lease shall automatically be amended to provide that, from and after the date Landlord completes its work in the New Premises and relocates Tenant's business to the New Premises (the "Delivery Date"), the term "Premises" as used in this Lease shall refer to the New Premises and not to the premises originally leased to Tenant under this Lease and, except as modified in this paragraph 18 (d), all terms, covenants and conditions of this Lease shall apply with full force and effect to the New Premises throughout the remainder of the term of this Lease as if the New Premises had originally been leased to Tenant in this Lease. Tenant shall install a new sign on the New Premises in accordance with Landlord's sign specifications for the Shopping Center. If requested by either party, the other party shall execute and delivery an amendment to this Lease consistent with this paragraph 18 (d) confirming the location of the New Premises and such other matters related to the New Premises or this Lease as may reasonably be required by the requesting party.

## 19. PERSONAL PROPERTY TAXES.

Tenant shall be responsible for and shall pay before delinquency all municipal, county, or state taxes assessed during the term of this Lease against any leasehold interest or personal property of any kind, owned by or placed in, upon or about the Premises by the Tenant.

## 20. ALTERATIONS AND TENANT'S IMPROVEMENTS.

(a) Tenant shall make no alterations or changes, structural or otherwise, to any part of the Premises, either exterior or interior, without Landlord's written consent, except as otherwise provided herein. In the event of any such approved changes, Tenant shall have all work done at its own expense. Request for such consent shall be accompanied by plans stating in detail precisely what is to be done. Tenant shall comply with all building codes, regulations and laws now or hereafter to be made or enforced in the municipality, county and/or state in which said Premises are located and which pertain to such work. Any additions, improvements, alterations and/or installations made by Tenant to the Premises (except only movable office furniture and fixtures) shall become and remain a part of the Premises and shall, at Landlord's option, become Landlord's property upon the termination of Tenant's occupancy of said Premises; provided, however, that if Landlord gives written notice to Tenant at the expiration or other termination of this Lease to such effect, it may require Tenant to restore said Premises to the condition in which the Premises are required to be on the later of (i) the end of the Abatement Period, or (ii) the date Tenant opens for business, at Tenant's sole cost and expense. Tenant shall keep the

Premises and all other parts of the Shopping Center free from any and all liens arising out of or in connection with any work performed, materials furnished or obligations incurred by or on behalf of Tenant, and agrees to bond against or discharge any mechanics', materialmen's or other such liens within ten (1) days after written request therefore by Landlord. Tenant shall hold Landlord harmless from and against all expenses, liens claims or damages to either property or person which may or might arise by reason of the making of any such additions, improvements, alterations and/or installations.

(b) Subject to the provisions of the preceding paragraph 20(a), any improvements made by Tenant shall immediately become the property of landlord and shall remain upon the Premises in the absence of agreement to the contrary. Tenant further will not cut or drill into or secure any fixture, apparatus, or equipment of any kind to any part of the Premises without first obtaining Landlord's written consent. Tenant agrees to accept delivery of the Premises in an "as is" condition. Upon delivery of the Premises to Tenant, Tenant shall, and hereby agrees at its sole cost and expense, to remodel, refurbish and redecorate the interior thereof, including the making of all interior improvements, alterations and changes to the Premises including, but not limited to, new ceiling, new lighting, new flooring, new wall coverings and new storefront, necessary to place same in a first class, modern and attractive condition and to enable Tenant to properly use the Premises for the purposes set forth in this Lease.

(c) All work to be performed by Tenant hereunder shall be in accordance with detailed plans and specifications for same to be prepared by Tenant and submitted to Landlord, within fifteen (15) days of the mutual execution of this Lease, for Landlord's written approval. If Tenant fails to provide Landlord with detailed plans and specifications for its work within the period provided in the preceding sentence, then any Abatement Period provided for in Article 3 shall be reduced by two (2) days for each day Tenant is late in delivering its plans and specifications to Landlord. If no Abatement Period is provided for in Article 3, then Landlord shall be entitled to collect from Tenant, as liquidated damages with respect to such default of Tenant in addition to Minimum Rent and other amounts payable hereunder, as Additional Rent, an amount equal to one-fifteenth (1/15) of the monthly amount of Minimum Rent then payable under this Lease, for each day Tenant delays in submitting its plans and specifications to Landlord in accordance with this Article 20. It is expressly agreed that Tenant shall not commence any such work until said plans and specifications have been approved by Landlord. All work to be performed by Tenant shall be performed in good and workmanlike manner, in accordance with all rules, regulations, codes and ordinances of any local, municipal, state and/or Federal authorities having jurisdiction thereof. Permits, licenses or approvals required for said work from such authorities shall be obtained by Tenant at its sole cost and expense.

(d) Tenant agrees that it shall fully complete the remodeling of the Premises as above set forth before the expiration of the Abatement Period. Tenant expressly agrees to protect, indemnify and save Landlord harmless from any liability to any person or estate for damage to person or property occurring, during the work proposed hereunder, whether before or after the commencement of the term of this Lease. It is expressly understood and agreed that any such alterations, changes or improvements shall in no way harm the structure of the Premises or diminish the value of same or of the Shopping Center. At any time after the expiration of the fifth (5th) anniversary of the Lease Date, and at any time after the end of each succeeding five (5) year period thereafter (if any), Tenant shall, within thirty (30) days after receipt of a written request from Landlord, commence and thereafter diligently pursue, in accordance with the provisions of this Article 20 and the other provisions of this Lease, all work required to remodel, redecorate and refurbish the Premises to the same condition as described in paragraph (b) above for the work to be performed by Tenant at the time of initial delivery of the Premises to Tenant.

(e) Landlord's approval of Tenant's plans and specifications under this Article 20 or any other provisions of this Lease is solely for the purpose of ascertaining whether Tenant's proposed altera-tions will have an adverse impact on the structural components or Common Facilities of the Shopping Center and to insure the aesthetic and architectural harmony of the Tenant's proposed alterations with the remainder of the Shopping Center. No approval of plans by Landlord shall be deemed to be a repre-sentation or warranty by Landlord that such plans or the work provided for therein will comply with applicable codes, laws or regulations or be in conformance with any insurance or other requirements which affect the Premises or the Shopping Center, or that the Premises are structurally adequate to support the work shown on such plans, and Tenant shall have the sole responsi-bility of complying with all such requirements notwithstanding Landlord's approval of Tenant's plans.

## 21. NOTICE OF NON-LIABILITY.

Notice is hereby given that Landlord shall not be liable for any labor or materials furnished or to be furnished to Tenant upon credit, and that no mechanics' or other lien for any such labor or materials shall attach to or affect the estate or interest of Landlord in and to the premises or the Shopping Center. Whenever and as often as any lien arising out of or in connection with any work performed, materials furnished or obligations incurred by or on behalf of Tenant shall have been filed against the Premises or the Shopping Center, or if any conditional bill of sale shall have been filed for or affecting any materials, machinery or fixtures used in the construction, repair or operation thereof, or annexed thereto by Tenant, Tenant shall forthwith take such action by bonding, deposit or payment as will remove or satisfy the lien or conditional bill of sale within ten (1) days of Landlord's written request therefor.

## 22. PROPERTY AT TENANT'S RISK.

(a) It is understood and agreed that all personal property and all non-structural improvements in the Premises, of whatever nature, whether owned by Tenant or any other person, shall be and remain at Tenant's sole risk and Landlord shall not assume any liability or be liable for any damage to or loss of such personal property, arising from the bursting, overflowing, or leaking of the roof or of water, sewer or steam pipes, or from heating or plumbing fixtures or from the handling of electric wires of fixtures or from any other cause whatsoever.

(b) All trade fixtures hereafter installed by Tenant in the Premises shall be new and subject to the provisions of Section 29 (a) herein, shall remain the property of Tenant and shall be removable by Tenant at the expiration or earlier termination of the term of this Lease provided that (i) Tenant shall not at such a time be in default under this Lease, and (ii) in the event of the removal of any or all of such trade fixtures Tenant shall promptly restore the damage done to the Premises by the installation and/or removal thereof. Should Tenant fail to so remove Tenant's trade fixtures and/or to so restore the Premises, Landlord may do so, collecting, at Landlord's option, the cost and expenses thereof, as Additional Rent, upon demand. Any such trade fixtures which are not removed and those which by the terms of this Lease are not removable by tenant at or prior to any termination of this Lease including, but not limited to, a termination by Landlord pursuant to this Lease, shall, unless Landlord gives Tenant notice to remove any or all of such trade fixtures, be and become the property of Landlord (without any obligation by Landlord to pay compensation for such trade fixtures). In the event Landlord gives Tenant such notice to remove any or all of such trade fixtures, Tenant shall promptly remove such of the trade fixtures as may be specified by Landlord in such notice. Notwithstanding anything herein contained to the contrary or any decision of any court to the contrary, the term "trade fixtures" shall not include any air-conditioning, heating, lighting, electrical and plumbing equipment installed by Tenant in the Premises, nor any wiring or other apparatus related thereto.

(c) In addition to all other remedies provided for in this Lease, to secure the payment of all Minimum Rent, Additional Rent or any other monies owned by Tenant to Landlord, Landlord shall have, at Landlord's option and upon notice thereof to Tenant, a security interest in all tangible personal property of Tenant on or about the Premises including, but not limited to, inventory, furniture, trade fixtures, equipment, etc., and this Lease is intended to be and shall be a security agreement, as defined in the Uniform Commercial Code. Tenant hereby authorizes Landlord, by and through its attorney, officers or other agent designated by Landlord, to execute and/or record a U.C.C.-1 on Tenant's behalf to perfect any security interest created under this Article, and Tenant shall reimburse Landlord for all fees or other costs incurred in connection with recording a U.C.C.-1. Tenant agrees, upon the request of Landlord, if required by applicable law, to execute any and all documents which Landlord deems necessary or desirable in order to perfect such security interest, including but not limited to, a U.C.C.-1 financing statement (a "U.C.C.-1").

## 23. INSURANCE.

(a) Tenant agrees to indemnify and save Landlord and Landlord's partners, officers, directors, employees and agents harmless from any and all liabilities, damages, causes of action, suits, claims, judgments, costs and expenses of any kind (including attorneys fees): (i) relating to or arising from or in connection with the possession, use, occupancy, management, repair, maintenance or control of the Premises, or any portion thereof; (ii) arising from or in connection with any act of omission of Tenant or Tenant's agents, employees or invitees; or (iii) resulting from any default, violation or injury to person or property or loss of life sustained in or about the Premises. To assure such indemnity, Tenant shall carry and keep in full force and effect at all times during the term of this Lease for the protection of Landlord and Landlord's managing agent and Tenant herein, public liability and property damage insurance with combined single limits of not less than One Million Dollars ($1,000,000.00) per occurrence; with not less than a Two Million Dollar ($2,000,000.00) aggregate per location. If any act or omission of Tenant in violation of the provisions of this Lease alters the classification or increase the rate of insurance on the Building or the Property then Landlord's costs and expenses incurred with respect to curing any such default of Tenant, and any costs and expenses incurred by Landlord (including, without limitation, attorney fees) as a direct or indirect result of any default of Tenant (whether or not cured by Tenant) shall, upon demand, be paid for by Tenant as Additional Rent.

[**NOTE:** Don't let the amount of liability insurance worry you. This is fairly standard, too, and most brand name insurance companies have business policies and plans and are used to working with small business.]

(b) Tenant shall be and remain liable for the maintenance, repair and replacement of all plate glass in the Premises with glass of like kind and quality. If requested by Landlord, Tenant shall keep the same insured under a policy of plate glass insurance.

[**NOTE**: My insurance did cover the glass replacement when we were burglarized six months after opening.]

(c) Tenant shall obtain and at all times during the term hereof maintain, at its sole cost and expense, policies of insurance covering the Premises and any permanent alterations to the Premises made by tenant or landlord in accordance with this Lease (excluding only structural improvements and components required to be insured and maintained by Landlord) including, without limitation, decorative finishes, special lighting or fixtures unique to Tenant's use of the Premises and any trade fixtures or other fixtures or property (including improvements which may not be removed by Tenant under the terms of this Lease), and all of Tenant's fixtures, equipment and inventory installed and/or located in the Premises, with the classification "All Risk Coverage" together with insurance against vandalism, malicious mischief, and sprinkler leakage or other sprinkler damage, boiler and pressure vessel insurance, and any proceeds of such insurance so long as this Lease shall remain in effect, shall be used only to repair or replace the items so insured.

(d) Said public liability and property damage insurance policies and any other insurance policies carried by Tenant with respect to the Premises shall: (i) be issued in form acceptable to Landlord by good and solvent insurance companies qualified to do business in the state in which the Premises is located and reasonably satisfactory to Landlord; (ii) be endorsed to name Landlord, Landlord's managing agent, Tenant and any other parties in interest from time to time designated in writing by notice from Landlord to Tenant as Additional Insureds; (iii) be written as primary policy coverage and not contributing either to or in excess of any coverage which Landlord may carry; (iv) provide for 30 days prior written notice to Landlord and Landlord's managing agent. Such insurance policies shall be obtained from an approved insurance company and Tenant takes occupancy of the Premises, showing the same to be in full force and effect. Neither the issuance of any insurance policy required hereunder, nor the minimum limits specified herein with respect to Tenant's insurance coverage shall be deemed to limit or restrict in any way Tenant's liability arising under or out of this Lease.

(e) In addition to the indemnity and insurance provision stipulated in this Article 23, the Tenant shall also obtain and at all times during the term of this Lease maintain the following additional insurance of the type marked below with an "X":

___ Gradual Pollution and/or Contamination Liability
___ Umbrella Liability in limits of not less than Two Million Dollars ($2,000,000.00)
___ Products Liability
___ Liquor Liability

## 24. DAMAGE.

If the Premises are damaged by fire or other cause covered by Landlord's policy of fire insurance with extended coverage or other property damage insurance carried by Landlord, all damage to the structural portions of the building required to be maintained by Landlord pursuant to this Lease shall be repaired by and at the expense of Landlord and the rent until such repairs shall have been made shall abate pro-rata according to the part of the Premises which is unusable by Tenant. However, if such damage was caused by the negligence of Tenant, its employees, agents, contractors, visitors or licensees, then all rentals shall be payable by Tenant during such period. Due allowance shall be made for reasonable delay which may arise by reason of adjustment of fire insurance on the part of landlord and/or Tenant, and for delay on account of "labor troubles" or any other cause beyond Landlord's control. If, however, the Premises are rendered wholly untenantable by fire or other cause, or Landlord shall decide not to rebuild the same, Landlord may, at its option, cancel and terminate this Lease by giving Tenant, within sixty (60) days from the date of such damage, notice in writing of its intention to cancel this Lease, whereupon the term of this Lease shall cease and terminate upon the third day after such notice is given, and Tenant shall vacate the Premises and surrender the same to Landlord, but in neither of the certain contingencies in this Article mentioned shall there be any liability on the part of Landlord to Tenant covering or in respect of any period during which the occupation of said Premises by Tenant may not be possible because of the matters hereinabove stated. If Landlord does not elect to terminate this Lease as provided above, Landlord shall proceed in a commercially reasonable manner to repair the portions of the Premises which Landlord is required to restore in accordance with this Article 24 and, upon the completion of such repairs, Tenant shall use diligent and commercially reasonable efforts to repair the portions of the Premises which are the responsibility of Tenant to insure under this Lease.

## 25. CONDEMNATION.

(a) If the Premises or any part thereof shall be taken by any governmental or quasi-governmental authority pursuant to the power of eminent domain, or by deed in lieu thereof, Tenant agrees to make no claim for compensation in the proceedings, and hereby assigns to Landlord any rights which it may have to any portion of any award made as a result of such taking. In the event of any such taking, this Lease shall terminate as to the portion of the Premises taken by the condemning authority and rental shall be reduced in proportion to the portion of the Premises so taken as of the date of such taking; provided, however, that in the event more than twenty percent (20%) of the floor area contained within the Premises is taken, Tenant shall have the option of terminating this Lease, which option shall be exercised by a notice delivered to Landlord within thirty (30) days of the date of such taking, whereupon the term of this Lease shall cease and terminate on the date of title vesting in the condemning authority. The foregoing notwithstanding, Tenant shall be entitled to claim, prove and receive in the condemnation proceedings such awards as may be allowed for relocation expenses and for fixtures and other equipment installed by it which shall not, under the terms of this Lease, be or become the property of Landlord at the termination hereof, but only if such awards shall be made by the condemnation court in addition to and stated separately from the award made by it for the land and the building or part thereof so taken.

(b) If any part of the parking area in the Shopping Center shall be acquired or condemned as aforesaid, and if, as a result thereof the ratio of parking spaces to building area does not meet the requirements of applicable codes, then the term of this Lease shall cease and terminate upon the vesting of title in such condemning authority unless the Landlord shall take immediate steps toward restoring the parking ratio to a ratio in excess of three or more spaces to each one thousand square feet of GLA, in which event this Lease shall be unaffected and remain in full force and effect without any reduction or abatement of rent. In the event of any termination of this Lease as provided in this Article 25, Tenant shall have no claim against Landlord nor the condemning authority for the value of any unexpired term of this Lease and rental shall be adjusted to the date of said termination.

(c) If the nature, location or extent of any proposed condemnation affecting the Shopping Center is such that Landlord elects in good faith to demolish or abandon the use of the Shopping Center, then Landlord may terminate this Lease by giving at least sixty (60) days written notice to Tenant at any time after such condemnation and this Lease shall terminate on the date specified in such notice.

## 26. RULES AND REGULATIONS.

Tenant shall at all times comply with the rules and regulations set forth on Exhibit B attached hereto, and with any additions thereto and modifications thereof adopted from time to time by Landlord, and each such rule or regulation shall be deemed to be a covenant of this Lease to be performed and observed by Tenant.

## 27. PARKING AREAS AN OTHER FACILITIES.

All parking areas and facilities furnished by Landlord in or near the Shopping Center, including employee parking areas, parking decks, the driveways, pedestrian sidewalks and ramps, landscaped areas, exterior stairways, and other areas and improvements provided by Landlord for the general use, in common, of tenants and other occupants of the Shopping Center, their officers, agents, employees and customers, shall at all times be subject to the exclusive control and management of Landlord and Landlord shall have the right from time to time to establish, modify and enforce reasonable rules and regulations therefore. Landlord grants to Tenant, during the term hereof, the non-exclusive right to use, in common with others, all automobile parking areas within the Shopping Center for the accommodation and parking of passenger automobiles of Tenant, its officers, agents, employees and customers. Tenant agrees that it will cause its officers, agents, and employees to park their automobiles only in such areas as Landlord may from time to time designate as employee parking areas.

[**NOTE**: I didn't think to ask at the time, but I should have inquired about having two or three spots dedicated for customers of The Pot & Bead. While most of the time we had plenty of parking, at least once a week the real estate agency in the space next to us held meetings and took every spot in our lot. We always received complaints from customers about this but the real estate agency refused to help us and we had no recourse with the Landlord.]

## 28. PERFORMANCE BY TENANT.

Tenant covenants and agrees that it will perform all agreements herein expressed on its part to be performed, and that it will, upon receipt of written notice specifying action desired by Landlord in connection with any such covenant (including the payment of money other than the rent reserved hereunder), promptly comply with such notice; and further that if Tenant shall not promptly comply with such notice to the satisfaction of Landlord, then Landlord may, at its option, make any payments so specified on behalf of Tenant or enter upon the Premises and do the things specified in said notice, and Landlord shall have no liability to Tenant for any loss or damage resulting in any way from such action by Landlord, and Tenant agrees to pay promptly upon demand any expense incurred by Landlord in taking such action. Any and all such costs or expenses shall constitute Additional Rent hereunder.

## 29. LANDLORD'S REMEDIES UPON DEFAULT.

Tenant shall be in default under this Lease if Tenant (i) fails to pay any installment of Minimum Rent, Additional Rent or other changes or money obligation to be paid by Tenant hereunder within five (5) days after the same shall become du e(all of which monetary obligations of Tenant shall bear interest at the highest rate allowable by law, not to exceed 18% annum from the date due until paid); or (ii) defaults in the performance of any of the covenants, terms or provisions of this Leas e(other than the payment, when due, of any of Tenant's monetary obligations hereunder) or any of the Rules and Regulations now or hereafter established by Landlord to govern the operation of the Shopping Center and fails to cure such default within twenty (20) days after written notice thereof from Landlord; or (iii) abandons the Premises or fails to keep the Premises continuously and uninterruptedly open for business; or (iv) files a voluntary petition in bankruptcy, or any similar petition seeking relief under any present or future federal, state or other bankruptcy or insolvency statute or law; or if a proceeding under any present or future federal, state or other bankruptcy or insolvency statute or law shall be filed against Tenant or any asset of Tenant, and such proceeding shall not have been dismissed or vacated within thirty (30) days of the date of such filing; or (v) makes an assignment for the benefit of its creditors. Upon the occurrence of any of the above events, Landlord, at its option, may pursue any one or more of the following remedies without any notice or demand whatsoever:

(a) Landlord, at its option, may at once, or at any time thereafter, terminate this Lease by written notice to Tenant, whereupon this Lease shall end. Upon such termination by Landlord, Tenant will at once surrender possession of the Premises to Landlord and remove all of Tenant's effects therefrom, and Landlord may forthwith re-enter the Premises and repossess itself thereof, and remove all persons and effects therefrom, using such force as may be necessary, without being guilty of trespass, forcible entry, detainer or other tort.

(b) Landlord may, without terminating this Lease, enter upon and take possession of the Premises and expel or remove Tenant and any other person who may be occupying the Premises or any part thereof, without being liable for prosecution or any claim for damages therefore, and, if Landlord so elects, make such alterations and repairs as, in Landlord's judgment, may be necessary to relet the Premises, and relet the Premises or any part thereof for such rent and for such period of time and subject to such terms and conditions as Landlord may deem advisable and receive the rent therefore. Upon each such reletting, the rent received by Landlord in respect of such reletting shall be applied first to the payment of any indebtedness other than rent due hereunder from Tenant to Landlord, including interest thereon; second, to the payment of any loss and expenses of such reletting, including brokerage fees, attorneys' fees and the cost of such alterations and repair; third, to the payment of rent due and unpaid hereunder, together with interest thereon as herein provided; and the residue, if any, shall be held by Landlord and applied in payment of future rent as the same may become due and payable hereunder. Tenant agrees to pay to Landlord, on demand, any deficiency that may arise by reason of such reletting. Notwithstanding any such reletting without termination, Landlord may at any time thereafter elect to terminate this Lease for such prior default.

(c) In the event Landlord shall re-enter the Premises and/or terminate this Lease in accordance with the provisions of this Article 29, Landlord may, in addition to any other remedy it may have, recover from Tenant all damages and expenses Landlord may suffer or incur by reason of Tenant's default hereunder, including without limitation, the cost of recovering the Premises and reasonable attorney fees. Tenant agrees that actual damages to Landlord resulting from Landlord's exercise of the remedies set forth in paragraphs (a) or (b) above, or from a failure of Tenant to operate in the Premises in accordance with the provisions of this Lease (including, without limitation, damages resulting from the adverse impact on the sales and percentage rental payable to Landlord by other tenants of the Shopping Center), will be difficult to ascertain, and therefore, after a default of Tenant hereunder, Tenant shall also pay to Landlord "Liquidated Damages" for the failure of Tenant to observe and perform the covenants of this Lease, which at the election of Landlord, shall be either: (a) (x) the sum of (i) the minimum monthly rent, plus (ii) the Additional Rent payable hereunder for the month immediately preceding such failure to operate, re-entry or termination, less (z) the net amount, if any, of the rents collected on account of the lease or leases of the Premises for each month of the period which would otherwise have constituted the balance of the term of this Lease, all of which sums shall become due and payable by Tenant to Landlord upon the first day of each calendar month during the otherwise unexpired portion of the term hereof; or (B) the whole of said Liquidated Damages calculated under clause (A) multiplied by the number of months then remaining in the lease term, discounted to present value at a rate of six percent (6%) per annum as of the date of termination or re-entry by Landlord; provided, however, that in the event Landlord shall relet the premises and the rent received by Landlord in respect of such reletting together with the discounted Liquidated Damages paid by Tenant, less the costs and expenses incurred by Landlord in such reletting, shall exceed the rent reserved hereunder for that period which would otherwise have constituted the remainder of the term hereof, then Landlord shall, upon the expiration of the period which would have constituted the term of this Lease, refund to Tenant the lesser of the amount of such excess or the discounted Liquidated Damages theretofore paid by Tenant.

(d) If the rent agreed to be paid, including all other sums of money which under the provisions hereto are declared to be rent, shall be in arrears in whole or in part for five (5) or more days, Landlord may at its option (if such arrearage remains unpaid after ten (10) days written notice to Tenant) declare the tenancy hereunder converted into a tenancy from month to month, and upon giving written notice to Tenant of the exercise of such option, Landlord shall forthwith be entitled to all provisions of law relating to the summary eviction of monthly tenants in default in rent.

(e) Anything in this Lease to the contrary notwithstanding, in order to cover the extra expense involved in handling delinquent payments, Tenant shall pay a "late charge" in an amount equal to the greater of (i) 5% of any delinquent payment, or (ii) $250.00, when any installment of Minimum rent (or any other amount as may be considered Additional Rental under this Lease) is paid more than five (5) days after the due date thereof. It is hereby understood that this charge is for extra expenses incurred by the Landlord in processing the delinquency.

(f) Tenant hereby appoints as its agent to receive service of all dispossessory or other proceedings and notices thereunder and under this Lease the person apparently in charge of the Premises at the time, and if no person then appears to be in charge of the Premises, then such service or notice may be made by attaching the same to the main entrance of the Premises, provided that, in such later event, a copy of any such proceedings or notice shall also be mailed to Tenant in the manner set forth in Article 36 hereof.

(g) Tenant shall be considered in "Habitual Default" of this Lease upon (i) Tenant's failure, on two (2) or more occasions during any Lease Year, to pay, when due, any installment of Minimum Rent, Additional Rent, or any other sum required by the terms of this Lease, or (ii) Tenant's repeated violation of, or failure to comply with, any term covenant or condition of this Lease after written notice of such violation or failure to comply has been given by Landlord to Tenant. Upon the occurrence of an event of Habitual Default on the part of Tenant, Tenant shall immediately be deemed to have released any and all options or rights granted, or to be granted, to Tenant under the terms of this Lease (including, without limitation, rights of renewal, rights to terminate, or rights of first refusal), and Landlord may, in addition to its other remedies under this Lease, by notice to Tenant, increase the security deposit required hereunder to an amount equal six (6) months Minimum Rent (or, at Landlord's option, a lesser period) such amount to be due and payable within ten (10) days after the date of such notice.

(h) Pursuit of any of the foregoing remedies shall not preclude Landlord from pursuing any other remedies therein or at law or in equity provided, nor shall pursuit of any remedy by Landlord constitute a forfeiture or waiver of any rent due to Landlord hereunder or of any damages accruing to Landlord by reason of Tenant's violation of any of the covenants and provisions of this Lease. Tenant hereby waives any right to assert or maintain any counterclaims against Landlord in any action brought by Landlord to obtain possession of the Premises. No act of Landlord (including, without limitation, acts of maintenance, efforts to relet the Premises, or any other actions taken by Landlord or its agents to protect Landlord's interests under this Lease) other than a written notice of termination, shall terminate this Lease. The acceptance of keys to the Premises by Landlord, its agents, employees, contractors or other persons on Landlord's behalf shall not be deemed or constitute to effect a termination of this Lease unless such early termination is evidenced by a written instrument signed by Landlord. The receipt or acceptance of payments of Minimum Rent or Additional Rent by Landlord, its agents, employees, contractors or other persons on Landlord's behalf after Landlord has elected to terminate this Lease or reenter as provided in this Article 29 shall not be deemed or constitute to effect a cure by Tenant to any default, but shall be deemed to be payment on account with respect to Tenant's underlying obligations, and Landlord may accept such check without prejudice to any other rights or remedies which it may have against the Tenant.

## 30. LAWS AND ORDINANCES.

Tenant will, at its own cost, promptly comply with and carry out all orders, requirements or conditions now or hereafter imposed upon it by the ordinances, laws and/or regulations of the municipality, county and/or state in which the Premises is located, whether required of Landlord or otherwise, in the conduct of Tenant's business, except that Landlord shall comply with any orders affecting the roof, structural walls and columns unless such compliance is due to Tenant's particular business or use of the Premises. Tenant will indemnify and save Landlord harmless from all penalties, claims and demands resulting from Tenant's failure or negligence in this respect.

## 31. ROOF RIGHTS.

Landlord shall have the exclusive right to use all or any portion of the roof of the Premises for any purpose, and shall have the right to erect additional stories or other structures over all or any part of said Premises.

## 32. SIGNS.

(a) Tenant shall not place or permit to be placed on the exterior of the Premises, on the door, window or roof thereof, in any display window space, or within five (5) feet behind the storefront of the Premises if visible from the Common Areas, any sign, placard, decoration, lettering, advertising matter or descriptive material without Landlord's prior written approval.

Tenant may, however, utilize such material within the Premises on a temporary basis to advertise special sales or promotions without Landlord's consent, provided that the material is professionally made, is in good taste, and is not taped or attached to any window of the Premises.

[**NOTE**: This was the clause about painting my windows. I could try to claim that I didn't need consent because it was temporary, but then again it was most definitely attached to the windows.]

(b) Additionally, any sign, advertising matter, or any other thing of any kind placed upon the exterior of the Premises shall be approved in writing by Landlord and shall conform to (i) any and all applicable laws, ordinances or regulations of any governmental authorities, and sign criteria adopted by Landlord, (ii) any insurance requirements, and (iii) the Sign Criteria attached to this Lease as Exhibit D. any such approved signs shall be maintained by Tenant in good condition and repair and in accordance with the standards of the Shopping Center, and Landlord shall have the right to require Tenant to upgrade or replace any such signs. Tenant shall obtain and pay for all permits and licenses required in connection with any such approved sign(s), and shall be responsible for the proper installation thereof. In no event shall Tenant place or maintain any sign, decoration, letter or advertising matter of any kind on the glass of any windows or doors of the Premises.

(c) Landlord shall have the right, without notice to Tenant and at Tenant's sole risk and expense, to remove any items displayed or affixed in or to the Premises which Landlord in good faith determines to be in violation of the provisions of this Article 32. All signs installed by Tenant shall be insured, and shall be maintained by Tenant at all times in first class condition, operating order and repair. Tenant shall commence to repair any of Tenant's signs which have been damaged within five (5) days after such damage occurs. Tenant shall perform such other maintenance to its signs and canopies as Landlord shall reasonably request. In the event Tenant fails to repair any of its signs as specified above, Landlord shall have the right to make such reasonable repairs as Landlord deems necessary at Tenant's sole cost and expense.

## 33. SUBORDINATION.

(a) This Lease is subject and subordinate to the lien of any ground leases and to all mortgages, deeds of trust to secure debt which may now or hereafter affect or encumber the Shopping Center or the real property of which the Premises form any part, and to all renewals, modifications, consolidations, replacements or extensions thereof. This Article shall be self-operative and no further instrument of subordination shall be required. In confirmation of any such subordination, Tenant shall execute within five (5) days after receipt, any certificate that Landlord may reasonably so request. No foreclosing lender nor any purchaser at foreclosure shall be liable for any defaults (including defaults of a continuing nature) by any prior landlord, or for the return of any security deposit. Tenant covenants and agrees to attorn to Landlord or to any successor to Landlord's interest in the Premises, whether by sale, foreclosure or otherwise.

(b) Notwithstanding the foregoing, in the event any ground lessor, mortgagee or the holder of any deed of trust or deed to secure debt shall elect to make the lien of this Lease prior to the lien of its ground lease or mortgage, then, upon such party giving written notice to such effect at any time prior to the commencement of foreclosure (which notice may be by the filing of a notice thereof for record among the land records), this Lease shall be deemed to be prior in lien to the lien of such ground lease or mortgage, whether dated prior or subsequent thereto.

313

## 34. ESTOPPEL CERTIFICATES.

Tenant agrees, at any time and from time to time, within five (5) days after written notice by Landlord, to execute, acknowledge and deliver to Landlord or to such person(s) as may be designated by Landlord, a statement in writing (i) certifying that Tenant is in possession of the Premises, has unconditionally accepted the same and is currently paying the rents reserved hereunder, (ii) certifying that this Lease is unmodified and in full force and effect (or if there have been modifications, that this Lease is in full force and effect as modified and stating the modifications), (iii) stating the dates to which the rent and other charges hereunder have been paid by Tenant and (iv) stating whether or not to the best knowledge of Tenant, Landlord is in default in the performance of any covenant, agreement or condition contained in this Lease, and, if so, specifying each such default of which notice to Landlord should be sent. Any such statement delivered pursuant hereto may be relied upon by any owner, prospective purchaser, mortgagee or prospective mortgagee of the Shopping Center or of Landlord's interest therein, or any prospective assignee of any such mortgagee. Tenant further agrees, at any time and from time to time, within five (5) days after written notice by Landlord, to deliver to Landlord its most recent financial statement, which shall not, in any event, be more than ninety (90) days old. If Tenant files quarterly and annual statements with the Securities and Exchange Commission, then Tenant's most recent "10-Q" (or, if applicable, "10-K") statement shall be supplied to Landlord. If Tenant has its financial statements audited on an annual basis, then Tenant shall supply Landlord with its most recent audited statement and with its most recent unaudited financial statement, certified to be true and correct by Tenant's chief financial officer. If Tenant does not regularly have its financial statements audited, then Tenant shall supply Landlord with its most recent unaudited financial information, certified to be true and correct by Tenant's chief financial officer, which information shall not, in any event, be more than ninety (90) days old. If Tenant does not regularly have financial statements prepared, then Tenant shall supply Landlord with such financial information respecting the financial condition of Tenant as Landlord may reasonable require including, without limitation, copies of Tenant's state and federal quarterly and annual income tax reports and statements, certified to be true and correct by Tenant or Tenant's chief financial officer. If Tenant fails to deliver to landlord any of the information described above, then Landlord may, at its option, elect (to the extent such documents or information is available from governmental or other sources) to obtain any such items or information which Tenant has failed to deliver, in which event Tenant shall reimburse Landlord for all costs and expenses incurred in obtaining such items plus an additional processing fee of three times the Landlord's actual cost of obtaining such items to compensate Landlord for the administrative work in performing Tenant's obligations under this Article.

[**NOTE**: Given we were a simple LLC, we only ever needed to provide gross sales numbers on a monthly basis. One of the ways this information is used is to attract new tenants to the shopping center. Often, the commercial real estate literature about a shopping center will include total sales of all the tenants for some period of time. It gives potential new tenants an idea of the activity in the shopping center.]

## 35. HOLD-OVER.

If Tenant shall not immediately surrender the Premises the day after the end of the term hereby created, then Tenant shall, by virtue of this agreement, become, at Landlord's option, either (a) a tenant at sufferance, or (b) a tenant from month-to-month. In either of such events, rent shall be payable at a monthly or daily rate, as the case may be, of triple the Minimum Rent and Additional Rental payable by

Tenant immediately prior to the expiration or termination of the term, with said tenancy to commence on the first day after the end of the term above demised; and said tenancy shall be subject to all of the conditions and covenants of this Lease insofar as such covenants and conditions are applicable thereto. Nothing contained in this Lease shall be construed as a consent by Landlord to the occupancy or possession of the Premises after the expirations of the term of this Lease. If Landlord fails to make an election under clause (a) or (b) within ten (10) days after the expiration or termination of the term, the hold-over tenancy shall be deemed to be a tenancy from month-to-month. If Tenant holds over as a month-to-month tenant, each party hereto shall give to the other at least thirty (30) days written notice to quit the Premises (any right to a longer notice period being hereby expressly waived), except in the event of non-payment of rent in advance or of the other Additional Rents provided for herein when due, or of the breach of any other covenant by the said Tenant, in which event Tenant shall not be entitled to any notice to quit, the usual thirty (30) days notice to quit being expressly waived; provided, however, that in the event Tenant shall hold over after expiration of the term hereby created, and if Landlord shall desire to regain possession of said Premises promptly at the expiration of the term aforesaid, then at any time prior to the date Landlord makes (or is deemed to have made) its election under clause (b) of this Article 35, Landlord at its option, may re-enter and take possession of the Premises forthwith, without process, or by any legal action or process in force in the state in which the Premises is located; provided, however, that if Landlord has accepted rent for any period beyond the expiration of the term and Tenant is not then in default under any of the provisions of this Lease, Landlord shall promptly refund to Tenant an amount equal to any excess rental received by Landlord with respect to any period after Landlord exercises its right to re-enter the Premises under this Article 35.

## 36. NOTICES.

All notices, rent or other payments required or desired to be given hereunder by either party to the other shall be sent by first class mail, postage prepaid, or by a reputable commercial messenger service, except that notices of default and notices related to the exercise of options or other rights under this Lease shall be sent by certified mail, return receipt requested or by a receipted overnight commercial messenger service (such as Federal Express or Airborne Express) for delivery on the next following business day. Notices sent by mail shall be deemed to be received on the date of actual receipt by the recipient or on the date delivery is refused. Notices sent by a receipted overnight commercial messenger service shall be deemed received on the next business day after depositing with such delivery service. Notices to the respective parties, and any amounts required to be paid hereunder, shall be addressed and sent as follows:

If to Landlord: [address deleted]

If to Tenant: [address deleted]

Either party may designate a substitute address, from time to time, by notice in writing sent in accordance with the provisions of this Article 36.

## 37. LANDLORD'S LIABILITY.

Any agreement, obligation or liability made, entered into or incurred by or on behalf of Landlord's binds only its property and no shareholder, partner, officer, agent or employee of the

Landlord assumes or shall be held to any liability therefore. Tenant agrees that Landlord shall have no personal liability with respect to any of the provisions of this Lease and Tenant shall look solely to the estate and property of Landlord in the land and buildings comprising the Shopping Center of which the Premises forms a part for the satisfaction of Tenant's remedies, including, without limitation, the collection of any judgment or the enforcement of any other judicial process requiring the payment or expenditure of money by Landlord, subject, however, to the prior rights of any holder of any mortgage or deed of trust covering all or part of the Shopping Center, and no other assets of Landlord shall be subject to levy, execution or other judicial process for the satisfaction of Tenant's claim and, in the event Tenant obtains a judgment against Landlord, the judgment docket shall be so noted. This Section shall inure to the benefit of Landlord's successors and assigns and their respective principals. Notwithstanding any provision herein or in any future law or judicial holding to the contrary, and in consideration of the Landlord's agreement to the provisions set forth in the Guaranty of this Lease which may limit the Guarantor's liability to an amount less than that for which Tenant would be liable in the event of a default, the maximum liability of the Landlord under this Lease is limited to and shall in no event ever exceed the maximum amount for which the Guarantor(s) would be then liable under the provisions of the Guaranty, and any judgment against Landlord shall be expressly limited to the foregoing amount.

## 38. DELAY.

In the event Landlord, for any reason is unable to deliver possession of the Premises to Tenant on or before the Rent Commencement Date, this Lease shall remain in full force and effect and Tenant shall not claim against Landlord by reason of any such delay but no rent shall be payable during the pendency of any such delay.

The expiration date of the term of this Lease shall be extended for a period equal to the period of such delay. If Landlord shall fail to deliver possession of the said Premises to Tenant within ninety (90) days after the latter to occur of (i) the Lease Date, or (ii) the date specified in this Lease for delivery of possession of the Premises to Tenant, then either party may, as its sole and exclusive remedy, terminate its Lease upon thirty (30) days prior written notice.

## 39. QUIET ENJOYMENT.

Landlord warrants that it has the right to make this Lease. Landlord covenants that if Tenant pays the rent and all other arrearages provided for herein, performs all of its obligations provided for hereunder and observes all of the other provisions, Tenant shall at all times during the term hereof peaceably and quietly have, hold and enjoy the Premises, without any interruption or disturbance from Landlord, or anyone claiming through or under Landlord, subject to the terms hereof.

## 40. APPLICABLE LAW.

This Lease shall be construed under the laws of the state in which the Premises is located.

## 41. WAIVERS.

Landlord and Tenant each hereby waivers (to the extent legally permissible) all the right to trial by jury in any claim, action, proceeding or counterclaim by either party against the other on any matters arising out of or in any way connected with this Lease, the relationship of Landlord and Tenant and/or Tenant's use or occupancy of the Premises. The parties hereby acknowledge and agree that the interpretation of this Lease will involve the interpretations of a complex commercial legal document, and that it is their intention and agreement that all matters relating to the interpretation of the provisions of this Lease be submitted to and determined by a judge trained in the law, and not by a jury. Tenant hereby expressly waives (to the extent legally permissible) for itself and all persons claiming by, through or under it, any right of redemption or right for the restoration of the operation of this Lease under any present or future law in case Tenant shall be dispossessed for any cause, or in case Landlord shall obtain possession of the Premises as provided in this Lease. Tenant understands that the Premises are leased exclusively for business, commercial and mercantile purposes and therefore shall not be redeemable under any provision of law.

## 42. NO RECORDING OF LEASE.

Tenant shall not record this Lease without first obtaining the prior written consent of Landlord, which Landlord may withhold in its sole and absolute discretion. If Landlord consents to the recording of this Lease or a memorandum of this Lease, Tenant shall, at Tenant's sole cost and expense, record a termination of such recorded document among the land records of the jurisdiction in which the Premises is located within thirty (30) days after the expiration or termination of this Lease.

## 43. REMEDIES CUMULATIVE; NO WAIVER.

All rights and remedies given hereby and/or by law or in equity to Landlord are separate, distinct and cumulative, and no one of them, whether exercised by Landlord or not, shall be deemed to be in exclusion of any of the others. No failure of Landlord to exercise any power given Landlord hereunder, or to insist upon strict compliance by Tenant with its obligations hereunder; and to custom or practice of the parties at variance with the terms hereof, shall constitute a waiver of Landlord's right to demand exact compliance with the terms hereof.

## 44. NO OPTIONS.

The submission of this Lease for examination does not constitute a reservation of or option for the Premises, and this Lease becomes effective only upon execution and delivery thereof by Landlord. Neither party shall have any legal obligation to the other in the event that the lease contemplated herein is not consummated for any reason. Discussions between the parties respecting the proposed lease described herein, shall not serve as a basis for a claim against either party or any officer, directory or agent of either party.

## 45. HEADINGS AND INTERPRETATION.

Captions and heading are for convenience and reference only and shall not in any way define, limit or describe the scope or content of any provision of this Lease. Whenever in this Lease any printed portion, or any part thereof, has been stricken out, whether or not any replacement provision has been added, this Lease shall be read and construed as if the material so stricken out were never included herein, and no implication shall be drawn from the text of the material so stricken out which would be inconsistent in any way with the construction or interpretation which would be appropriate if such material had never been contained herein. The Exhibits referred to in this Lease and attached hereto are a substantive part of this Lease and are incorporated herein by reference. Unless and to the extent otherwise expressly provided to the contrary in this Lease, time shall be of the essence with respect to all of the obligations of the parties under this Lease.

## 46. PARTIES; ASSIGNS AND SUCCESSORS.

Feminine or neuter pronouns may be substituted for those of the masculine form, and the plural may be substituted for the singular number, in any place or places herein in which the context may require such substitution or substitutions. The term "Landlord" as used in this Lease, means only the owner for the time being of the Landlord's interest in this Lease; and, in the event of this sale, assignment or transfer by such owner of the Landlord's interest in this Lease, such owner shall thereupon be released and discharged of all covenants and obligations of landlord hereunder thereafter accruing. Except as provided in the preceding sentence, all of the covenants, agreements, terms, conditions, provisions and undertakings in this Lease shall inure to the benefit of, and shall extend to and be binding upon, the parties hereto and their respective heirs, executors, legal representatives, successors and assigns, to the same extent as if they were in every case named and expressed. If two or more individuals, corporations, partnerships, or other business associations (or any combination of two or more thereof) shall sign this Lease as Tenant, the liability of each such individual, corporation, partnership or other business association to pay rent and perform all other obligations hereunder shall be deemed to be joint and several and any notice required or permitted by the terms of this Lease may be given by or to any one thereof, and shall have the same force and effect as if given by or to all thereof. In like manner, if the Tenant named in this Lease shall be a partnership or other business association, the members of which are, by virtue of statute or general law, subject to personal liability, the liability of each such member shall be joint and several.

## 47. MODIFICATION.

This writing is intended by the parties as the final expression of their agreement and as a complete and exclusive statement of the terms thereof. All negotiations, considerations and representations, and all prior and/or contemporaneous agreements between the parties have been fully incorporated herein. No course of prior dealings between the parties or their affiliates shall be relevant or admissible to supplement, explain or vary any of the terms of this Lease. No acceptance of, or acquiescence in, a course of performance rendered under this or any prior agreement between the parties or their affiliates shall be relevant or admissible to determine the meaning of any of the terms of this Lease. No representations, understandings or agreements have been made or relied upon in the making of this Lease other than those specifically set forth herein. This Lease can only be modified by a writing signed by all of the parties hereto or their duly authorized agents. It is understood that any bills, statements of account or rent statements presented by Landlord, or its agent, to Tenant are supplied for convenience only and shall not constitute a waiver of Landlord's right to collect additional amounts provided for herein in respect of any period(s) covered by such bill or statement.

## 48. SEVERABILITY.

If any term, covenant or condition of this Lease or the application thereof to any person or circumstance shall, to any extent be held invalid or unenforceable, the remainder of this Lease or the application of such term, covenant or condition to persons or circumstances other than those as to which it is held invalid or unenforceable, shall not be affected thereby and each term, covenant and condition of this Lease shall be valid and enforced to the fullest extent permitted by law.

## 49. NEGOTIATED AGREEMENT.

Tenant acknowledges that it has engaged counsel in connection with the negotiation of this Lease, or that Tenant has freely decided to enter into this Lease without engaging the services of counsel. In any legal proceeding respecting this Lease, this Lease will be construed with equal weight for the rights of both parties, the terms hereof having been determined by free and fair negotiation, with due consideration for the rights and requirements of both parties. Both parties agree that they have had equal input into the wording and phraseology of the provisions of this Lease, and that, therefore, no provision will be construed as drafted by one party or the other, without respect to whose draft of this Lease the wording or phraseology arises.

## 50. MORTAGEE PROTECTION CLAUSE.

Tenant agrees to give any mortgagees and/or trust deed holders, by Certified Mail, a copy of any notice of default served upon the Landlord, provided that prior to such notice Tenant has been notified, in writing, (by way of Notice of assignment of rents and leases, or otherwise) of the address of such mortgagees and/or trust deed holders. Tenant further agrees that if Landlord shall have failed to cure such default within the term provided for in this Lease, then the mortgagees and/or trust deed holders shall have an additional thirty (30) days within which to cure such default or if such default cannot be cured within that time, then such additional time as may be necessary if within such thirty (30) days, any mortgagee and/or trust deed holder has commenced and is diligently pursuing the remedies necessary to cure such default (including but not limited to commencement of foreclosure proceedings, if necessary to effect such cure), in which event this Lease shall not be terminated while such remedies are being so diligently pursued.

## 51. ENTITY TENANTS.

If Tenant is a corporation, partnership or limited liability company, the persons executing this Lease on behalf of Tenant hereby covenant and warrant that: Tenant is duly constituted as such entity and is qualified to do business in the state where the Premises are located; all Tenant's franchise and corporate taxes have been paid to date; all future forms, reports, fees and other documents necessary for Tenant to comply with applicable laws will be filed by Tenant when due; and such persons are duly authorized by the board of directors, partnership agreement or other applicable authority of such entity to execute and deliver this Lease on behalf of the Tenant. Attached hereto and made a part hereof is (a) a certificate of good standing, dated within sixty (60) days prior to the Lease Date, issued by the jurisdiction in which Tenant is organized, and (b) one or more of the following confirming the authorization and due execution of this Lease by Tenant: (i) a certificate of Tenant's Secretary if Tenant is a corporation; or (ii) a consent of the general partners if Tenant is a partnership, or (iii) a certified copy of the Articles of Organization, operating agreement or other evidence satisfactory to Landlord evidencing the authority of the members of a limited liability company executing this Lease on behalf thereof. If Tenant fails to deliver to Landlord any of the items described in clauses (a) or (b) above on or before the date submits this Lease to Landlord for execution, then Landlord may, at its option, elect (to the extent such documents or information is available from governmental or other sources) obtain any such items which Tenant has failed to deliver, in which event Tenant shall reimburse Landlord for all costs and expenses incurred in obtaining such items plus an additional processing fee of three times the Landlord's actual cost of obtaining such items to compensate Landlord for the administrative work in performing Tenant's obligations under this Article.

## 52. SURRENDER OF PREMISES.

At the expiration of or earlier termination of the term of this Lease, Tenant shall peacefully surrender the Premises to Landlord, in the same condition as the Premises were required to be in upon the expiration of the Abatement Period, ordinary wear and tear excepted to the extent the Premises is not required to be repaired and/or maintained by Tenant. Tenant shall surrender all keys for the Premises to Landlord and shall notify Landlord in writing of all combinations of locks, safes, and vaults, if any in the Premises. If the Premises are not surrendered as and when aforesaid, Tenant shall indemnify and hold Landlord harmless from and against all claims, loss or liability (direct, indirect, foreseeable or unforeseeable) resulting from the delay by Tenant in surrendering the Premises including, without limitation, any claims made by any succeeding occupant based upon Landlord's inability to deliver the Premises to any such succeeding occupant. Tenant shall comply with the provisions of Article 22 hereof respecting the removal of trade fixtures. Tenant's obligations to observe and perform the covenants set forth in this Article 52 shall survive the expiration or earlier termination of this Lease.

## 53. SURVIVAL.

Notwithstanding anything to the contrary contained in this Lease, the expiration of the Term of this Lease, whether by lapse of time or otherwise, shall not relieve Tenant from Tenant's obligations accruing prior to the expiration of the Term.

## 54. LANDLORD'S RIGHTS.

In addition to Landlord's rights of self-help set forth elsewhere in this Lease or as provided by law or by equity, if Tenant at any time fails to perform any of its obligations under this Lease in a manner satisfactory to Landlord, Landlord shall have the right but not the obligation, to perform or cause to be performed such obligations on behalf and at the expense of Tenant and to take all such action Landlord deems appropriate to perform or cause to be performed such obligations.

Landlord's costs and expenses incurred with respect to curing any default of Tenant (whether or not cured by Tenant) shall, upon demand, be paid for by Tenant as Additional Rent. In performing or causing the performance of any such obligations of Tenant, Landlord shall incur no liability for any loss or damage that may accrue to Tenant, the Premises or Tenant's Property by reason thereof. The performance by Landlord of any such obligation shall not constitute a release or waiver of any of Tenant's obligations under this Lease. Tenant shall reimburse Landlord upon demand for any costs or expenses, including attorney fees, incurred by Landlord in connection with the enforcement of Tenant's obligations under this Lease or otherwise incurred by Landlord in connection with any judicial proceedings regarding the rights and obligations of Tenant under this Lease. Any and all costs or expenses incurred by Landlord pursuant to the provisions hereof shall be considered as Additional Rent hereunder.

## 55. SHOWING OF PREMISES AND LANDLORD ACCESS.

Landlord shall have the right to enter upon the Premises for purposes of showing the Premises to prospective tenants during the last six (6) months of the Term. During such period, Landlord shall have the right to post the Premises with "For Rent" or other offering signs, as Landlord may deem appropriate. Landlord may enter the Premises at reasonable hours to exhibit the same to prospective purchasers, mortgagees, or tenants, to inspect the Premises to see that Tenant is complying with all its obligations hereunder, or to make required repairs.

## 56. SPECIAL STIPULATIONS.

The terms, covenants and conditions set forth in any Articles of this Lease numbered higher than this Article 56 ("Special

Stipulations") are intended to supplement and, in certain events, modify or vary, the other provisions set forth in the foregoing provisions of this Lease. If any of the Special Stipulations conflict with any of the foregoing provisions of this Lease, the provisions set forth in the Special Stipulations shall control; provided, however, that to the extent the preceding portions of this Lease may be read in a manner which will not conflict with the provisions of the Special Stipulations, then such interpretation shall be deemed to be the correct interpretation of the provisions of this Lease and the Special Stipulations.

# APPENDIX E

# The Reading List

You'll notice that most of the books on this list were published prior to 2010. They were the best business books, or at least my favorite business books, that I had found when I originally published my own books. In this new edition, I went searching for newer, better books . . . and didn't find many! If anyone came to me today and asked me what they should read if they're thinking about a startup, I'd still recommend every book on this list. I've only added three here at the beginning. Enjoy!

*The Startup Owner's Manual: The Step-by-Step Guide for Building a Great Company* by Steve Blank and Bob Dorf. K & S Ranch: 2012

Adeena's Tidbit: The authors of this book nailed it when they wrote: "A startup is not a smaller version of a large company. A startup is a temporary organization in search of a scalable, repeatable, profitable business model." While on the surface this book doesn't seem to apply to a small retail store, I gained a lot of insight I wish I had before I opened my doors to the public. This book, combined with the E-myth series mentioned below, is a must-read for anyone seriously contemplating starting a business.

*Likeable Business: Why Today's Consumers Demand More and How Leaders Can Deliver* by Dave Kerpen. McGraw-Hill: 2012
and

*Likeable Social Media: How to Delight Your Customers, Create an Irresistible Brand, and Be Generally Amazing on Faecbook (And Other Social Networks)* by Dave Kerpen. McGraw-Hill: 2012

Adeena's Tidbit: I reviewed many, many books looking for the best advice to pass on to others when it came to social media, especially since my retail store predated current trends. Dave Kerpen's books were the best of the best, giving both tangible advice and a lot to think about as you build your online, social media presence. While much of the advice overlaps, I highly recommend reading both.

*Pour Your Heart Into It: How STARBUCKS Built a Company One Cup at a Time* by Howard Schultz and Dori Jones Yang. Hyperion: 1997.

Adeena's Tidbit: A very inspiring book. If a guy from the Brooklyn projects can become this successful, so can anyone.

*The E-Myth Revisited: Why Most Small Businesses Don't Work and What to Do About It* by Michael E. Gerber. Collins: 1995.

Adeena's Tidbit: I'm amazed how many people who think about or start their own business don't know about this book.

*Don't Worry, Make Money: Spiritual and Practical Ways to Create Abundance and More Fun in Your Life* by Richard Carlson. Hyperion: 1997.

Adeena's Tidbit: If you're obsessed with making money, if all you can think about is what you're not making and why you're not making more, this book is for you.

*The Small Business Owner's Guide to a Good Night's Sleep: Preventing and Solving Chronic and Costly Problems* by Debra Koontz Traverso. Bloomberg Press: 2001.

Adeena's Tidbit: I've referred to this book quite a bit. Suffice to say, it's a must-have on the small business owner's bookshelf.

*The Retail Life: A Store Manager's Companion* by Tierney Alexander. Writer's Club Press: 2002.

Adeena's Tidbit: The small business owner often acts as the manager too, particularly in a Cute Little Store. I swear I could have written some of the chapters in this book—especially the one on employees.

*The Profitable Retailer: 56 surprisingly simple and effective lesions to boost your sales and profits* by Doug Fleener. Acanthus Publishing: 2005.

Adeena's Tidbit: Doug Fleener is a retail consultant who I've hired to help me with my business at times. Anything Doug writes or says is worth reading and listening to.

*How To Buy a Business* by Richard A. Joseph, Anna M. Nekoranec and Carl H. Steffens. Kaplan Publishing: 1992.

Adeena's Tidbit: There's a whole chapter on the concept of "due diligence."

*Retail Business Kit for Dummies* by Rick Segel. For Dummies: 2001.

Adeena's Tidbit: If you are truly starting from scratch when it comes to understanding the financials of a business, start here. This book also contains a "S.W.O.T." exercise.

*Legal Guide for Starting & Running a Small Business* by Fred S. Steingold and Ilona M. Bray. NOLO: 2005, 8th edition.

Adeena's Tidbit: I consider this book a must-have for any small business owner. It doesn't replace using a lawyer, but gives a good explanation so you know when to spend your money on one. This book also has a good chapter on understanding commercial leases.

*Business Plans for Dummies* by Paul Tiffany and Steven D. Peterson. For Dummies: 2004, 2nd edition.

Adeena's Tidbit: If you haven't thought about writing a business plan before, start here.

*Start Run & Grow a Successful Small Business* by CCH Incorporated. CCH Incorporated: 2005, 5th edition.

Adeena's Tidbit: While not focused solely on retail business, this book has an excellent chapter on business plans and more detail on understanding the financials of a business than *Retail Business Kit for Dummies*.

*The Small Business Bible: Everything You Need To Know To Succeed In Your Small Business* by Steven D. Strauss. John Wiley & Sons: 2004.

Adeena's Tidbit: This book has a good chapter on "your web presence."

*Rules for Renegades: how to make more money, rock your career, and revel in your individuality* by Christine Comaford-Lynch. McGraw Hill: 2007.

Adeena's Tidbit: This book is an inspiration. Christine Comaford-Lynch has seen both extraordinary highs and frightening lows in her career and life. In her book, she passes on some worthwhile advice, but the example she sets, as someone who came from no real education and no means, proves that anyone willing to work hard and take chances can succeed.

*Thinking Inside The Box: the 12 timeless rules for managing a successful business* by Kirk Cheyfitz. Free Press: 2003.

Adeena's Tidbit: If nothing else, read the table of contents. If fact, print out both pages and hang them up so you can see them every day. That list, which includes such fantastic advice from "If you don't manage your cash, you won't be managing anything for long" to "Give customers what they want, not what you want to give them" is worth the price of the book.

*Marketing Your Retail Store in the Internet age* by Bob & Susan Negen. Wiley: 2007.

Adeena's Tidbit: When I was struggling to come up with ideas to market my business on a budget, this book was there for me. Each tactic has an associated cost scale (inexpensive to very expensive) and associated time estimate. I was able to implement some of the ideas right away.

While a lot of books with the word "Internet" in the title tend to age quickly, this book is still relevant and should be so for a few years more at least.

*The Small Business Survival Guide: how to manage your cash, profits & taxes, 3rd Edition* by Robert E. Fleury. Sourcebooks: 1995.

Adeena's Tidbit: Feeling a little overwhelmed managing your finances? Get this book. It has a workbook feel to it and can help you learn to organize and get a handle on cash management (you did read how lousy I was at that in this book, right?) and money priorities. This should be a part of the small business owner's book collection from day one.

*The Complete Guide to Selling a Business, 2nd edition* by Fred S. Steingold. Nolo: 2005.

Adeena's Tidbit: When I decided to sell my business without a broker, this was the book that I kept referring to over and over, through each step of the way. This is amust-have for anyone selling their business.

*The Business Sale System: Insider Secrets to Selling Any Small Business* by James Laabs. First American Publishing: 2007.

Adeena's Tidbit: This was a very interesting read and I wish I had read it early on when I first started to think about selling and not at the end of 2007. I particularly loved the last chapter "Summary of Key Guidelines." Two of those guidelines I "starred" and highlighted and underlined:

"Buyers are concerned about the future of your company more than the past."

"As the seller, it's your job to keep deal momentum going strong."

That last one was key—and key to why I think the broker situation didn't work out. It was my responsibility the whole time. Broker or no.

The only downside to this book: throughout, it is very optimistic and assumes that the seller has several buyers to negotiate with at once. That never happened when I was working with the broker. When I was on my own, I had lots of inquiries, but never was on the verge or working with two or more serious offers at the same time.

*What No One Ever Tells You About Starting Your Own Business, 2nd edition* by Jan Norman. Dearborn: 2004.

Adeena's Tidbit: This book is perfect for the reading attention-span challenged. It's 101 one- to two-page anecdotes and advice on different questions and topics regarding starting and running a business. There is a little bit of advice on money troubles, but nothing on selling a business or exit strategies. A nice reference book.

*How to Succeed as a Small Business Owner... and Still Have a Life* by Bill Collier. Porchester: 2006.

Adeena's Tidbit: The title of Section 3 sums up this book and its point very nicely: "If you put in long hours, have trouble getting away from work for more than a day or two at a time, and don't make any more money than you did when you worked for someone else, you haven't created a business. You've created a job." Folks seem to expect to work themselves to death when they start a business and while that might be true in the earliest stage of a new business, it shouldn't always be that way. Mr. Collier understands that.

*Buying Your Own Business* by Russell Robb. Adams: 1995.

Adeena's Tidbit: This is the book I referenced in Chapter 2 that has a decent section on understanding how businesses for sale are priced. Caveat is that this book was written to apply to companies with sales between $2million and $50 million. A lot of Cute Little Stores, like The Pot & Bead, don't come close to that $2 million mark.

*Streetwise Small Business Turnaround: Revitalizing Your Struggling or Stagnant Enterprise* by Marc Kramer. Adams Media: 1999.

Adeena's Tidbit: A must-read, even if your business is doing well. There were a lot of examples that showed where the business went wrong. The parts on managing spending and debt can also be useful for people who aren't in real trouble, but still need to manage these things.

# INDEX

80/20 rule, 61

Accountant, 6, 90, 91, 95, 103, 122, 142, 235, 238

Advertising, 62, 241
 cost per click, 76
 costs, 93
 internet strategy, 248
 money spent on, 143, 144, 253
 on premises, 311
 promotional strategy, 247
 print, 158
 word of mouth, 80

Bankruptcy, 184

Borrowing money, 94, 249

Burglary, 31, 98, 110, 226

Business
 broker, 171, 176, 186, 192, 201, 205
 buying, 54, 58,
 for sale, 173
 selling, 7, 55, 119, 171, 175, 181, 186, 194, 200, 203, 208, 333

Business Plan, 15, 69, 90, 100, 119, 133, 139, 146, 165, 222, 229

Chamber of Commerce, 22, 73, 90, 102, 144, 239

Closing, 119, 158, 178, 183, 184, 196, 211
 due to natural disaster, 35, 123

Competition, 66, 69, 79, 181, 186, 231, 244

Consulting, 12, 14, 39, 84, 101, 133, 149, 220, 235

Contingency Plan, 119, 250

Credit Cards, 93, 132, 138, 236, 252

Customer Service, 20, 42, 60, 63, 66, 148, 155

Customers

appreciation, 61, 72
 behavior, 56, 62
 compliments, 104
 finding, 26, 74
 helping out, 52
 perception, 20, 34, 42, 67, 164, 199
 understanding, 20, 84
 unhappy, 40, 61, 63, 80

Debt, 7, 93, 104, 125, 127, 173, 183, 184, 211, 215, 249

Due diligence, 58, 206, 331

Elevator speech, 15

Email, 55, 61, 73, 80, 154, 164, 168, 187, 191, 193

Employees
 applying, 154
 appreciation, 41, 46
 bonus, 51
 feedback, 43, 151
 firing, 47, 152
 interview, 44, 155, 209
 pay, 39, 43, 47, 50, 91, 118, 125, 144
 quitting, 43, 126, 206
 store manager, 20, 33, 42, 54, 111, 115, 117, 330

Entrepreneurship, 3, 12, 16, 19, 119

Exit strategy, 112, 147, 171, 213, 256

Facebook, 70, 75, 76, 78–86

Financing
 bank loan, 88, 90, 92, 126, 128, 129, 178, 181
 collateral, 55, 88, 184
 finding a bank, 88, 90
 friends and family, 94
 refinancing, 90, 129, 184
 SBA loan, 87–88

working capital, 90, 126, 133, 232, 249
Google, 50, 76, 165, 166–167, 196
Grand Opening, 31, 72, 244, 253
Human Resources, 149, 150
HVAC, 182, 287–288
Insurance, 34-36, 92, 299
    after disaster, 36
    opting out, 35
    proof of, 28
Laws, 45, 183, 311
Lawyer, 17, 30, 38, 55, 56, 93, 103, 172, 177, 183, 190, 205–207, 208
Lease
    breaking, 182
    Common Area Maintenance (CAM), 27, 144, 226, 272
    negotiations, 26, 27, 29, 135, 178–179, 198, 323
    rent vs. own, 29
    requirements, 27, 36, 156
    responsibilities, 97, 182, 286
Legal
    operating agreement, 17, 119
Letter of Intent (LOI), 191, 204–205
Loans, see "Financing, bank loan"
Marketing, 20, 71–75, 164, 200
    costs, 57, 83, 144
    targeted, 62, 64, 168
NFIB, 35, 67
Operating agreement, 17, 119
Organization, 101–102
P&L, see "Profit & Loss Statements"
Paint Your Own Pottery, 14–16, 66, 179, 234, 242
Partnership, 17, 119, 204, 212
Paying Yourself, 21, 91

Payroll, 144
Personal finances, 90, 104, 126
Planning, 98, 100, 120, 131
Procedures, 49, 53, 63, 99, 117, 150
Profit & Loss Statements, 93, 174, 202
Quickbooks, 91, 93, 135, 236
Refinancing, see "Bank, refinancing"
Rent, 263–267
    additional rent, 272, 278
Retail, 19
    multiple locations, 54, 142, 220
    myths, 74, 329
Risks, 18, 27, 38, 59, 94, 105, 150, 215
Salary, viii, 6, 20, 57, 144, 251
Sales, 61, 134–136, 138–140, 146, 177
Sales Agreement, 56, 201, 208
Schedule of Assets, 208, 227
Security
    deposit, 253, 266
    for loan, 56
    system, 31–34, 252
Sexual Harassment, 149–150
Small Business Administration (SBA), 87
Small Business Development Center (SBDC), 23, 222,
Startup Expenses, 232–233
Taxes, 92
    940 form, 129
    941 form, 122, 124, 129
    federal, 92, 122–124
    payroll, 122–125
    real estate, 144, 274
The Painted Pot, 37
Twitter, 70, 77–79, 81–86
US Department of Labor, 45, 91
Water problems, 96, 182
Website, 75–76, 163–165